CHARTING

A

BOLD

COURSE

CHARTING
A
BOLD
COURSE

Training Leaders for
21st Century Ministry

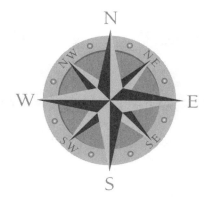

ANDREW SEIDEL

MOODY PUBLISHERS
CHICAGO

All Scripture quotations, unless otherwise indicated, are taken from the *New American Standard Bible®*, © Copyright The Lockman Foundation 1960, 1962, 1963, 1968, 1971, 1972, 1973, 1975, 1977, 1995. Used by permission.

Scripture quotations marked NIV are taken from the *Holy Bible, New International Version®*. NIV®. Copyright © 1973, 1978, 1984 by International Bible Society. Used by permission of Zondervan Publishing House. All rights reserved.

Library of Congress Cataloging-in-Publication Data

Seidel, Andrew.
  Charting a bold course: training leaders for 21st century ministry / Andrew Seidel.
    p. cm.
Includes biographical references.
  ISBN 0-8024-3422-3
  1. Christian leadership. I. Title.
  BV652.1.S45 2003
  253—dc21
                                                                2003012110

1 3 5 7 9 10 8 6 4 2

Printed in the United States of America

For all the support and encouragement
through thirty-seven years of marriage,
this book is
lovingly dedicated to Gail,
a leader herself,
who has personally influenced hundreds of women
in their relationship with Jesus Christ

CONTENTS

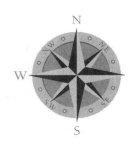

FOREWORD

CHRISTIAN LEADERSHIP HAS ACQUIRED a bad odor in recent years as media spotlights have uncovered pockets of noxious self-proclaimed pacesetters of moral teaching. Our society's penchant for creating celebrities has diluted the true worth of leadership with a facade of fame, so that many sincere believers cannot recognize healthy and reliable influencers.

Consequently, a critical need exists for a plain-spoken, definitive explanation of what makes an effective Christian leader. We have had glimpses of greatness in our public political life and in our military prowess. Portraits of acclaimed battlefield strategists like Generals Dwight Eisenhower and George Patton walk the pages of our history books and line the halls of the Pentagon. Possibly the twentieth century's most effective leader for positive political change, Ronald Reagan, defined his won statesmanship: "To have a vision to dream of a better, safer world, and the courage, persistence and patience to turn that dream into a reality."

Former President Reagan fleshed out his belief of vision, action, and courage by his singular voice that demanded a response from the global community, and in so doing dismantled the oppressive gears of communism. Our present-day call for an army of clear-eyed leaders to model truly wholesome Christian living—and to be able to motivate others as well—in our complex international neighborhood demands a word from a leader of leaders, one who has been seen and who knows what it takes to attack and win against the forces of human suffering and injustice.

Emerging from his apprenticeship in the upper ranks of the United States military, from a significant urban pastorate of more than a decade, from a demanding stint of overseas missionary service to impoverished nations, and from the common angst of academia, Dr. Andrew Seidel steps into his literary classroom like a seasoned coach to tell it like it is. To his readers who are running the race of life, his quiet, confident voice speaks without a hint of condescension. His uncanny ability to instill resolve in his followers confirms instinctively that they will not fail if they engage his game plan. This study is not about winning medals, but the classic race, for the ultimate prize, described by the apostle Paul: "Run in such a way as to get the prize. . . . We do it to get a crown that will last forever" (1 Corinthians 9:24–25 NIV).

Charting a Bold Course stands upon four pillars: character, vision, relationships, and skills. Without any one of these components, the reach for success is hobbled. The strategy is biblical, workable, and road-tested in real life.

It has been my great delight to instruct Dr. Seidel in the classroom and to serve with him as a colleague. I have witnessed firsthand how he fleshes out the framework of his teaching. His passion has been ignited by Jesus Christ, the Leader of all leaders, and his goal is now to develop durable, effective, and godly leaders for his generation. Every life which has been touched by the grandeur of Christ's power yearns to communicate to others the indescribable peace and joy of knowing Him personally, and to recommend Him to others. But our world is no friend of grace, even though the need is critical. Therefore, the platform to win a hearing and to lead others toward eternal life requires a daunting and well-informed regimen.

Here is a blueprint, the way to accomplish what seems impossible. Here is the unvarnished reality of what it takes to craft a life worthy of divine commendation. These robust and demanding imperatives require rigorous self-appraisal and severe self-discipline.

My own decades of experience in Christian ministry echo this need for exhaustive training with a growing urgency; there is no greater need today than credible leadership. Men and women of character will win the ultimate reward if they are properly trained. This premier course-in-print belongs not only on the ready-reference shelf, but in the backpack of every student who wants to lead his generation into spiritual achievements—a book for regular, purposeful discussion and for private review. Like workout sessions in the gym, it yields the fruit of lasting excellence in the Christian arena.

HOWARD G. HENDRICKS
Distinguished Professor and Chairman
Center for Christian Leadership
Dallas Theological Seminary

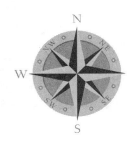

INTRODUCTION

Leadership development is more than a course or a workbook—it is a lifelong process. God shapes and molds a man or a woman over the years to form the leader that He desires that person to be. The shaping curriculum is intense and varied. It is founded in the early experiences of family life, fleshed out in the learning experiences of education and relationships, and fulfilled in the many experiences of actual leadership.

LESSONS IN LEADERSHIP

Some of the lessons in leadership are simple; others are more complex. Some are satisfying and fulfilling; others are painful and puzzling. But through them all, God takes the raw material of the man or woman, adds unique gifts and abilities, and then builds the person into a leader through the experiences of life that mold the character, nurture the relationships, build the vision, and sharpen the skills. You can follow the process in the lives of many biblical characters, such as Moses, David, Jeremiah, Nehemiah, and the apostles.

The process of leadership building is never easy, for it demands the development of our trust in God and the breaking of our dependence upon our own resources. Neither of these comes easily or quickly. But the end result is a man or woman whom God can use in a significant way to extend His kingdom.

Earlier views of leadership described leadership in heroic terms. Somehow the leader was always adequate for the situation. In the most difficult of circumstances, the leader would reach deep within himself and summon reserves of energy, skill, or shrewdness to somehow win the day. The reality, however, is that none of us is always adequate for every situation. God has not intended us to be. Rather, God has equipped each of us in unique ways to serve Him. But He has done so in ways that require us to trust Him and rely on His adequacy. In addition, He has structured His church in such a way that we need each other. To our independence-prone views, He has added some painful reality: He alone is always adequate. In the same breath, He offers to make us adequate as we trust in Him (2 Corinthians 3:4–6).

This course—one designed to be taken with other present and potential leaders—can help you see more clearly how God has been about this process in your life, how He has gifted you, developed you, trained you. In the pages that follow, our goal is to stimulate your thinking, increase your awareness, develop your confidence in God, and encourage your growth in leadership. The church of Jesus Christ in this generation is in desperate need of leaders who lead from a position of trust!

THE LEADERSHIP DEVELOPMENT PROCESS

Leadership development occurs best in the context of active ministry leadership. A class or course may be helpful, but it is not optimal. The most effective growth in leadership occurs as you reflect upon your leadership experiences and seek to learn both from your mistakes and from input in leadership understanding and skills. In Chapter 2, you will see a clear example of Jesus' use of developmental experiences to grow His disciples in leadership. You, too, will grow best if you reflect, discuss, and learn in a small group setting. We are all very skillful at denial and seeing things as we want them to be. It helps to have the clarity of perspective which comes from a group of colleagues who are committed to growing together.

Therefore, in order to get the maximum benefit from *Charting a Bold Course*, study this book with others in a small group setting. The assignments and responses will be more effective when you participate with others, hearing their responses and struggles as well. As you complete this book, commit to being faithful to do the following things:

1. *Spend at least two hours per week in preparation for the group sessions.* During the week before the group sessions, be sure to *study* the material, including reading any Bible references; *write* your answers to the questions and do the projects specified in each lesson; and *reflect* on how the content of each lesson applies personally in your life.

2. *Participate in group discussions or projects.* During the group sessions, take active part. Listen to your colleagues and reflect your thoughts and responses back to them.

3. *Continue to refine leadership skills during all other times.* You can do this as you practice spiritual disciplines, incorporating selected spiritual disciplines into your normal devotional life on a regular basis; interact with an elder mentor; and continue to engage in ministry, particularly in your local church.

A word about elder mentors. Your mentor could be an elder of the church or some other respected leader in the church or ministry organization. Such leaders, whether from your church or organization, should become familiar with the course and be made available to participants. Whoever leads the course should recruit these leaders to be mentors. If participants are working with elder mentors, they may even choose to work with the elder in his church ministry as a way of meeting the "engage in ministry" responsibility. The next section gives extended suggestions for effective mentoring and can be given to new and potential mentors.

QUALIFICATIONS FOR PARTICIPANTS

This book is not intended to be a discipleship course, though there are certainly elements of discipleship included. It is intended to focus on the key areas of leadership in order to help you grow in your leadership. Therefore, those participating in the *Charting a Bold Course* group should have the following qualifications which provide the foundation for development in leadership:

1. The person knows Jesus Christ as personal Savior, and this relationship is clearly evident.
2. The person has demonstrated a high level of spiritual maturity characterized by a consistent growth in his relationship to Christ and stability in his or her life.
3. The person has a working knowledge of the Scriptures and of basic Christian doctrine.
4. The person has been faithfully involved in ministry through the church.
5. In a church situation, the person's potential for future leadership is recognized by the elders and staff of the church.

A final suggestion about the discussion itself: Because of the personal nature of some of the exercises, it may be more appropriate at times for mixed groups of both men and women to split up into gender groupings for discussion.

SUGGESTIONS FOR MENTORS

If you are thinking about or have accepted the role of being an elder mentor, this section is for you. If you are a participant, show this section to your (potential) mentor and discuss it.

Taking on the responsibility of mentoring another person can be one of the most significant and fulfilling experiences of your ministry in the church. Your role will be that of a friend, a coach, a fellow servant who is further along in the process of growing in Christ and serving Him through ministry in your church. You do not have to be an authority on every leadership issue, but you do need to be willing to do what Paul described in 1 Thessalonians 2:8, ". . . well-pleased to impart to you not only the gospel of God but also our own lives, because you had become very dear to us."

A mentoring relationship is a very powerful relationship. By your position as an elder (or leader in an organization), you have earned the respect of people in the church (the organization). The one you mentor will benefit greatly from your personal involvement in his life. Begin preparing by reviewing the book so you will know what subjects your protégé will be confronting. Once you begin meeting, ask him about the most recent *Charting a Bold Course* session and what he found most challenging. Ask what he is going to do to grow in this area.

During your meetings with your protégé, be sure to do the following:

+ Ask your protégé to share his or her Life Story presentation with you (chapter 3); then discuss it together. You will find it helpful to do the Life Story exercise yourself and share your own story with your protégé.

+ Have your protégé discuss what he has learned about his gifts and temperament and how these relate to leadership situations.

+ Be willing to help your protégé deal with personal character flaws. Provide encouragement and accountability for him or her in the process.

+ Share your own pertinent leadership experiences in the church or in your profession. Be willing to share your leadership struggles and failures and what you learned from them. None of us is a successful leader in every situation. The best, and most respected, leaders are those who learn from their mistakes.

+ Talk about those leaders you have respected and tell what you learned from them.

+ Talk about the church (or ministry organization), the vision and values of the church ministry, how they have impacted you, and where you hope to see the church/organization go in the future. Help him understand the culture of your church/organization.

+ Find out your protégé's life goals and think about how you can encourage or help him or her achieve them.

+ Be available and open for questions, ready to provide direction or give help.

When the protégé and you meet together, set a regular schedule. It may be every other week. Probably neither of you have time for a weekly meeting. The key is consistency rather than frequency. Make use of normal opportunities to meet together. You could have lunch at a coffee shop after church or meet for breakfast before work.

If you are an elder, arrange to include your protégé in an elder meeting when appropriate. Ask the person you are mentoring to join you in your church ministry as an observer/participant. Working together will give many opportunities for interaction subjects for discussion. At some point, try to have your protégé and family in your home for an evening. The opportunity to observe your family life makes a great impact on others by demonstrating the reality of your character and leadership in the relationships that are most important to you.

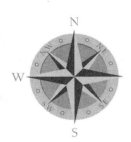

A LEADERSHIP MODEL

A POSSIBLE COURSE SCHEDULE

WHETHER YOUR SMALL GROUP CHOOSES to meet weekly, monthly, or at a different interval, here is a possible course schedule that will help participants prepare for the discussion and move at a consistent pace. Note: Consider having a weekend retreat during the spring semester.

FALL

WEEK	SUBJECT	SPECIFIC TOPIC	SCRIPTURE
1	INTRODUCTION	Philosophy of Leadership	Luke 22; Philippians 2:5–8; 1 Thessalonians 1; Ephesians 4
2	PILGRIMAGE	Overview: Leadership as pilgrimage	Mark
3		Life Story Presentations	Psalm 139; 1 Samuel; 2 Samuel
4	• Identity	Overview: Divine design; identity in Christ	Acts 8, 9; Philippians 3
5		Divine design; Temperament/style	
6		Divine design; Spiritual gift/strengths	1 Corinthians 12–14; Ephesians 4:11–16
7	• Integrity	Overview: The role of integrity; personal values/goals	Genesis 39; Daniel 6:3–23; Acts 5:1–11
8	• Intimacy	Appropriate openness/vulnerability	Mark 3:14 and others
9	CHARACTER	Overview: The qualifications of character	1 Timothy 3; Titus 1
10		Flaws, Strategies, and Character Development	Mark

SPRING

WEEK	SUBJECT	SPECIFIC TOPIC	SCRIPTURE
11	RELATIONSHIP	Overview: Relationships in the leader's family	John 13; Ephesians 5
12		Role relationships in the church	Philippians 2:3–8; Romans 12:3–21
13	VISION	Personal life vision	Nehemiah 1:1–2:20
14		Ministry vision	Various
15		Communicating vision	Nehemiah 2:11–20; Luke 19:10; John 3:17
16	SKILLS	Understanding the church: Purpose, organization, culture	Various Acts 2:42–47
17		Planning	Proverbs 16:9; 19:21; 16:3; 21:5
18		Communicating effectively	
19		Handling conflict	Acts 6:1–6; 11:1–18; 15:1–35; 36–41
20		Time management and delegating	

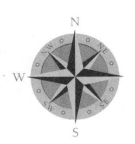

A LEADERSHIP MODEL

A LEADERSHIP MODEL PROVIDES AN INTEGRATED framework for thinking about leadership. There are as many ideas about leadership as there are writers on the subject. The role of a leadership model is to bring coherence to the discussion and show how the various parts fit together. The model we will use in this course is seen below. Look over the various parts of this "Leadership Compass" and then read the description that follows.

THE LEADERSHIP COMPASS

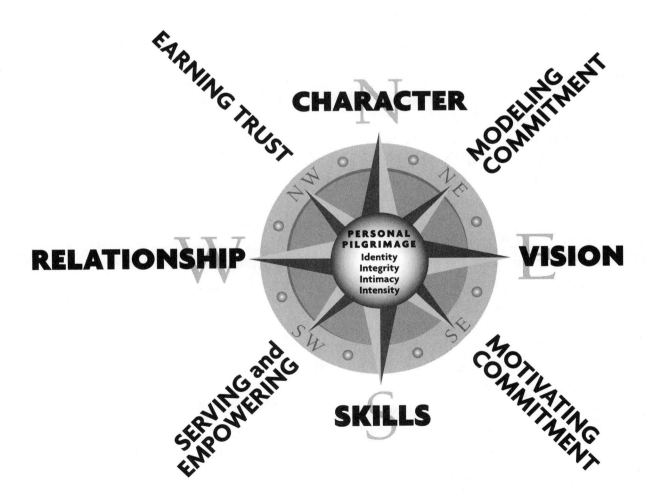

PERSONAL PILGRIMAGE: THE CORE OF LEADERSHIP

At its heart, Christian leadership has a spiritual core. The *personal pilgrimage* through which God takes His leaders forms the basis of all they do in exercising leadership. Because all lead as an expression of who they are, God brings into every Christian leader's life those experiences needed to mold and shape him or her into the person He wants. The process is often difficult, sometimes painful, but always done with the faithful support of the One upon whom we are invited to "cast all [our] anxiety" (1 Peter 5:7).

God orchestrates the pilgrimage process to work on four major areas of the leader's inner life. The ultimate goal of our spiritual development is, of course, to conform us to the image of Jesus Christ (2 Corinthians 3:18). From a leadership perspective, this means that we should progressively lead more as Christ led. Certainly it means that we lead from a perspective of trust in God rather than trusting in our own resources and skills. And it means we lead to accomplish His purposes, not our own.

First, the pilgrimage process impacts our sense of *identity*, that concept of who we are as God created us. Our identity includes our personality type or temperament, our gifts, strengths, and weaknesses. Our relationship with God provides a secure personal identity based on His faithful love and unqualified acceptance. This sense of security sets us free to lead others by serving them for Christ's sake. Our God-given gifts and strengths focus our leadership, while our limitations and weaknesses cause us to need the gifts of others.

Second, in the course of our pilgrimage, our personal *integrity* is challenged and strengthened. Our experiences expose inconsistencies between who we are inside and what we present ourselves to be in our interactions with others. The result of this exposure is a growing consistency between our inner life and our public presentation. In this way we develop greater integrity.

Third, we learn to develop an appropriate level of *intimacy* with those whom we lead. We invite those we lead into real relationship with us, knowing that they will trust us more and grow more themselves when we are open enough for them to see our constant seeking to walk with God.

Finally, through the course of our life experiences, God builds into us a passion for what He has equipped us. This passion is expressed in a godly *intensity* about the issues, needs, or roles that God desires us to focus our attention on in serving Him by giving leadership to His people. It is by focusing in these areas that you find your greatest sense of fulfillment and through which you make your greatest impact.

The core of leadership is spiritual. It is the quality of the leader's ongoing relationship with God Himself which gives life and direction to all the elements of his leadership. God is the One who will ultimately give the wisdom and strength needed to lead well.

THE FOUR MAJOR ASPECTS OF LEADERSHIP

1. Character

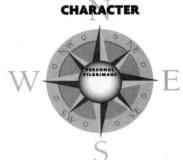

Christian leadership has a moral pole. In our Leadership Compass, *character* is the "true north" of leadership. It is character that gives a sense of dependability to our leadership and insures that we lead in ways that are productive rather than destructive. Elements of character are the foundation for a biblical qualification for leadership (1 Timothy 3:1–7 and Titus 1:5–9).

Character is always in process. We learn more about ourselves each day and we find our character continuously tested in new ways. Too often, flaws in our character are exposed, and we must deal with them. If we choose to remain ignorant of our character flaws, or work only to hide them, at some point our leadership will be destroyed.

As you work through this course, you will notice how significantly character impacts all of the other elements of leadership.

2. Vision

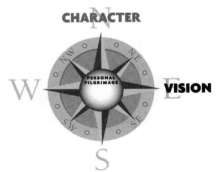

Leadership always involves setting a direction for change. It is about influencing people toward the accomplishment of a purpose, toward some new reality. *Vision* is the mental picture of a desirable future for the ministry. It is a way of communicating to people where your leadership is taking them.

Without vision there is no leadership. Vision is one important element that distinguishes leaders from managers. Leaders ask, "Where does God want us to go in serving Him?" Managers ask, "How does God want us to serve Him more effectively where we are?" Both are necessary in any ministry, and all effective leaders have some managerial skills or make sure that others with such skills are able to function in their ministries.

21

3. Relationship

All leaders must be able to build the *network of relationships* necessary for the vision to be realized. No matter how greatly gifted he or she may be, the leader cannot fulfill the vision alone. This is the way God has designed the church to function (Ephesians 4:11–16).

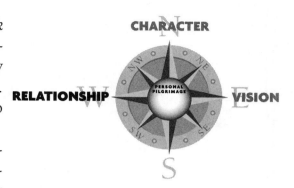

In ministry, a leader typically deals with volunteers. This presents special leadership challenges. The ministry leader does not have many of the leadership tools available to other leaders—he lacks the command authority of an army officer or the salary control of a business leader, for instance. The ministry leader's primary influence tool is the relationships he builds with those he leads. No matter how sterling the character or exciting the vision, he will not lead for long if he is not able to build and maintain the relationships necessary to fulfill the vision.

4. Skills

Many *skills* are needed to bring leadership into concrete actions that bring about fulfillment of the vision. One of the most important skills for church leadership is the *skill of understanding the church culture*. Leadership that does not consider the unique culture of its own local church is doomed to a succession of problems and probably failure.

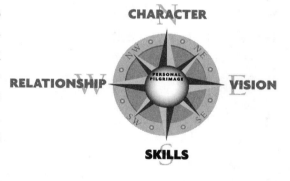

Another significant skill is *planning*, which deals with the practical steps necessary to turn a vision into concrete reality. Determining key objectives, setting goals, and developing strategies are necessary elements in planning in any leadership situation.

All leaders must develop the *skill of communicating effectively*. Since leadership involves mobilizing the efforts of many people, communication is a critical skill. But communication is a more complicated process than most of us realize. Good leaders are those who continually improve their communication skills.

Related to communication is the *skill of handling conflict* in a constructive manner. That there will be conflict should be understood as a "given" in every leadership situation. When you combine fallen human nature and the desire for stability with the inevitable changes produced by leadership, you have an explosive mix. Some level of conflict is inevitable; the key is to learn how to deal with conflict constructively.

Time management, which includes the *skill of delegating*, is critical to the leader's own personal management of his life, for leadership makes many demands on the leader. Delegating is a means of involving others in the fulfillment of the vision, giving them the opportunity to exercise their gifts and make their unique contribution to the team's success.

There are many other skills which could be discussed, but those listed above form the basis for leadership action.

INTERACTION AMONG THE FOUR MAJOR ASPECTS OF LEADERSHIP

The four major aspects of leadership interact to produce some of the essential elements of leadership (see complete Leadership Compass below).

Character and *vision* interact to make the leader *model commitment* to the vision. Because of his character, the leader will not ask of his followers that which he is unwilling to give himself. Therefore, by his actions he demonstrates his own commitment to fulfilling the vision. He is in his own life willing to make the sacrifices required by the vision. Only then can he ask others to give of themselves to fulfill the vision.

It is through the leader's *character* expressed in *relationship* with others that he *earns trust* from them. As they see his character demonstrated in the way he relates to them, they learn that they can depend upon him. They see that he is not pursuing his own interests, that he is reliable, honest, and not selfishly manipulative.

The leader uses his *skills* in *relationship* to those he leads to *serve and empower* them. The function of the leader's skills is to facilitate the involvement of all his followers so that they may exercise their gifts and provide the results of their strengths to the fulfillment of the group's vision. Whether it is skill in planning, communicating, delegating, or dealing with conflict, the leader's goal is to enable others to make their contribution to the fulfillment of the vision. In this way he serves and empowers them.

As followers see the compelling nature of the *vision*, they are attracted to join the team to see the vision realized. However, a critical question they deal with is the leader's competence to guide them to the fulfillment of the vision. Therefore, the leader's *skills*, in conjunction with his *vision*, are a strong factor in *motivating commitment* on the part of the followers whose voluntary involvement is essential to success.

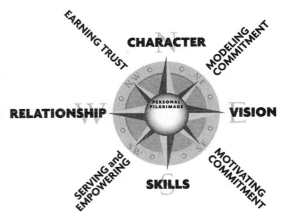

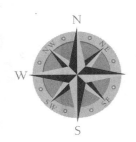

A BIBLICAL PHILOSOPHY OF LEADERSHIP

GOD HAS ALWAYS PLACED A HIGH PREMIUM on leadership. The Scriptures chronicle the impact on the people of God of a continuous line of human leaders—Abraham, Jacob, Joseph, Moses, Joshua, Samuel, David, Nehemiah, Peter, John, and Paul, just to name a few. Most of the leaders highlighted in the Scriptures were part of the nation of Israel in the Old Testament or the church of the New Testament era. But secular leaders also receive attention because they were part of the historical context in which the spiritual leaders lived and led. The whole of biblical history can be viewed as a record of God's raising up and developing human leaders to lead His people in accomplishing His will.

Some of God's leaders led well; some led poorly. But the one constant is that God has almost always used human leaders to accomplish His purposes on the earth. In Old Testament history, the leaders of God's people tended to be singular personalities, unique men and women who stood out as individual heroes. They were kings, prophets, priests, or judges. The leaders included lower-level citizens, such as those appointed by Moses to act as judges (see Exodus 18:25–26); but, for the most part, Old Testament leaders were highly individualistic, heroic leaders.

> *Just about everything we have been taught about traditional management prevents us from being effective leaders. And just about every popular notion about leadership is a myth.*
>
> James M. Kouzes
> and Barry Z. Posner
> *The Leadership Challenge*

With the establishment of the church, a major shift in leadership took place. The church has neither kings nor judges, but all believers are priests. Furthermore, all believers are given spiritual gifts with which they are enabled to render significant service for the kingdom of God. Some are specially gifted in the area of leadership; but leadership has become much less of a solitary, heroic occupation. Leadership during the church age is much less individual, much more collegial; it is much less directing or ruling, much more serving and enabling. Church leadership is marked by a plurality of elders and deacons and no singular human head of the church.

This shift in leadership style from Old Testament to New anticipates by almost two thousand years the shift that is today taking place in modern secular leadership thinking. As James Kouzes and Barry Posner suggest, some major changes are taking place in our understanding and practice of leadership. Not everyone readily understands the magnitude of the changes. Old approaches and methods die slowly. Perhaps we can better understand why the apostles had such a difficult time understanding Jesus' approach to leadership in His church. It was so different from what they were used to.

LEADERSHIP THAT IS UNLIKE SECULAR LEADERSHIP

Christian leadership is not like the world's leadership. Jesus Christ made this point clearly and emphatically. The key New Testament text on leadership is Luke 22:24–27. Study this passage in its context, and then answer the questions below:

1. *How would you describe the "Gentile" way of leadership? What are some of the characteristics of people who lead this way?*

_____

_____

_____

2. *What current examples of this kind of leadership can you think of? Which government, political, business, or church leaders today lead like "the kings of the Gentiles"? What specific actions, attitudes, or approaches put them in this category?*

_____

_____

_____

LEADERSHIP THAT IS MARKED BY SERVANTHOOD

Even though this was not the first time the disciples heard Jesus connect servanthood with leadership (see Mark 9:35 for example), it was still a hard concept for them to grasp.

3. *Why do you think they had such a difficult time?*

_____
_____
_____

4. *Do the two terms "servanthood" and "leader" seem antithetical? Why or why not?*

_____
_____
_____

5. *How would you describe "servanthood" on the part of a leader?*

_____
_____
_____

Most of us are uncomfortable with the idea of being a servant, and we often have wrong ideas of what Jesus means when He says that a leader must be a servant. We think of servants as passive; therefore servant leadership is considered by some to be a passive style of leadership in which the leader simply does what others want him to do. But is that what Jesus meant? We should be able to look at Jesus' own leadership, since He calls our attention to it (Luke 22:27), to help clarify our understanding of servant leadership.

6. *How would you summarize Jesus' example as described in Philippians 2:5–11?*

_____
_____
_____

7. *Does this mean that Jesus was a passive leader? What do the following passages reveal about Jesus' leadership style?*

Matthew 6:33 _____
Matthew 16:24–28 _____
Matthew 28:19 _____
Mark 8:14–21 _____

John 2:13–22 _____

John 13:13–17 _____

John 15:12–17 _____

One could hardly read the above passages and think that Jesus was a passive leader. Quite the contrary, He gave clear direction and exercised great authority in the lives of His followers. He also directly and powerfully challenged those who were against Him. When He gave commands, He expected to be obeyed. But, in many ways, the kings of the Gentiles acted similarly.

8. *So what is the difference between Jesus and the rulers of the Gentiles?*

_____

_____

_____

_____

One major difference is that Jesus never exercised authority for His own personal benefit. His motivation was always to fulfill His Father's plan and serve His followers. Therefore, even when He exercised authority or required compliance, His leadership was always described by service. Servanthood is not defined by the actions themselves but by the motive and goal that generate the actions.

9. *Contrast Jesus' leadership with that of Diotrephes, described in 3 John 9. What was the characteristic attitude of Diotrephes as a leader? What were his motives and goals?*

_____

_____

_____

_____

_____

PAUL AS A SERVANT LEADER

A difficult concept is always clarified by a good example. To better understand servant leadership, consider Paul's example of his leadership in the lives of the believers in Thessalonica (1 Thessalonians 2:1–12).

10. *What parallels do you notice between Luke 22:24–27 and 1 Thessalonians 2:1–12? Mark up the two Bible passages on the next page to note the parallels.*

Luke 22:24–27

24 And there arose also a dispute among them as to which one of them was regarded to be greatest.

25 And He said to them, "The kings of the Gentiles lord it over them; and those who have authority over them are called 'Benefactors.'

26 "But it is not this way with you, but the one who is the greatest among you must become like the youngest, and the leader like the servant.

27 "For who is greater, the one who reclines at the table or the one who serves? Is it not the one who reclines at the table? But I am among you as the one who serves."

1 Thessalonians 2:1–12

1 For you yourselves know, brethren, that our coming to you was not in vain,

2 but after we had already suffered and been mistreated in Philippi, as you know, we had the boldness in our God to speak to you the gospel of God amid much opposition.

3 For our exhortation does not come from error or impurity or by way of deceit;

4 but just as we have been approved by God to be entrusted with the gospel, so we speak, not as pleasing men, but God who examines our hearts.

5 For we never came with flattering speech, as you know, nor with a pretext for greed—God is witness—

6 nor did we seek glory from men, either from you or from others, even though as apostles of Christ we might have asserted our authority.

7 But we proved to be gentle among you, as a nursing mother tenderly cares for her own children.

8 Having so fond an affection for you, we were well-pleased to impart to you not only the gospel of God but also our own lives, because you had become very dear to us.

9 For you recall, brethren, our labor and hardship, how working night and day so as not to be a burden to any of you, we proclaimed to you the gospel of God.

10 You are witnesses, and so is God, how devoutly and uprightly and blamelessly we behaved toward you believers;

11 just as you know how we were exhorting and encouraging and imploring each one of you as a father would his own children,

12 so that you may walk in a manner worthy of the God who calls you into His own kingdom and glory.

11. *In the 1 Thessalonians 2:1–12 passage Paul uses three images to describe his leadership. What are the three images, and what does each contribute to our understanding of servant leadership? Are you surprised at the images Paul uses? Complete the chart below to determine the emphasis of each image.*

Text	Image (What is the image used?)	Emphasis of the Image (What point was Paul trying to make?)
2:7–8		
2:9–10		
2:11–12		

LEADERSHIP THAT IS FOCUSED ON EQUIPPING OTHERS

Any philosophy of Christian leadership must consider carefully the passage in Ephesians 4:7–16. The importance of this "gifts" passage comes from the fact that it describes the function of gifted leaders in the church. God gave these gifted leaders to the church primarily to equip others for service.

12. *Read Ephesians 4:7–16 carefully. The following three statements are conclusions drawn from the passage:*

✦ Both leaders and followers are equal members (parts) of the body of Christ. Only Christ is the Head.

What are some leadership implications of this statement?

_____

_____

_____

_____

✦ Individual believers fulfill different functions in the body. Some are leaders; some are followers, but no one individual has all the gifts. Therefore there is an interdependence of all in the body of Christ; the growth of the body requires the contribution of all.

What are some leadership implications of this statement?

_____

_____

_____

_____

✦ All believers, both leaders and followers, are gifted by God for service. There is a healthy diversity of gifts.

What are some leadership implications of this statement?

_____

_____

_____

CHARTING A BOLD COURSE

A DEFINITION AND SUMMARY

Look back over the preceding pages, giving particular attention to the key passages you studied. Now try to summarize your discoveries in a definition of servant leadership and a set of corresponding leadership principles. (Once you finish preparing your summary, compare it with the listing on the final page of this chapter.)

My Definition of Servant Leadership:

_____
_____
_____
_____
_____
_____

Summary Principles of Servant Leadership:

_____
_____
_____
_____
_____
_____
_____
_____
_____
_____
_____
_____
_____
_____
_____
_____
_____
_____
_____
_____

REFLECT

1. *Can you think of people who exemplify the characteristics of servant leadership as you have defined and
summarized them? Who would they be? What specific
characteristics identify them as servant leaders?*

_____

_____

_____

_____

_____

_____

> *If you wish to be a leader
> you will be frustrated, for
> very few people wish to be
> led. If you aim to be a
> servant you will never be
> frustrated.*
>
> *Frank F. Warren*

2. *To what extent do these summary principles fit your life? In what areas do you see a need
to develop?*

_____

_____

_____

_____

_____

3. *In what two areas or characteristics of your life do you need to grow in order to be more
of a servant leader?*

_____

_____

_____

_____

_____

4. *What specific action(s) can you take during the next week to grow in these areas?*

_____

_____

_____

_____

SUMMARY PRINCIPLES OF SERVANT LEADERSHIP

From the study of key passages in Luke 22, Ephesians 4, and 1 Thessalonians 2, the Center for Christian Leadership has spotted the following principles for effective servant leadership and leaders:

+ Servant leaders are self-sacrificing rather than self-seeking (Luke 22:24–27).
+ Servant leaders lead by relationship and example rather than from position and pressure (1 Thessalonians 2:7–12).
+ Servant leadership is active rather than passive (1 Thessalonians 2:11–12; Ephesians 4:11–12).
+ Servant leadership gives direction rather than allowing drifting (1 Thessalonians 2:11–12).
+ Servant leaders exercise appropriate authority, always for the fulfillment of their mission rather than for personal gain or advantage (1 Thessalonians 2:11–12).
+ Servant leadership functions best by equipping and empowering others to work together rather than by functioning solo (Ephesians 4:11–16).
+ Servant leaders lead by personal involvement in caring for people and their needs rather than demanding their own needs be met (1 Thessalonians 2:7–8).
+ Servant leadership is a matter of character and gift rather than position and connections (Luke 22:24–27; Ephesians 4:7, 11–12).

T W O

THE LEADER'S PILGRIMAGE

LEADERSHIP DEVELOPMENT IS A LIFELONG JOURNEY in which our sovereign God orchestrates the experiences, crises, and tests of life to develop in a man or woman those qualities essential to godly leadership. Beyond developing leadership skills, it is more the progressive development of those inner qualities that enables a skilled person to be a godly servant leader. Who you *are* as a leader determines what you *do* in leading.

THE MEANING OF "PILGRIMAGE"

We use the term *pilgrimage* for the core reality of leadership: refining inner qualities to become a godly servant leader. You can track this process through the lives of the great leaders of the Scriptures. Joseph's years of mistreatment and imprisonment weaned him away from being his father's pampered favorite son and tested his dependence upon God. The powerful temptation of Potiphar's wife sharpened the edges of his integrity. All of this prepared Joseph to be a leader of character and faithfulness when he became Pharaoh's second in power, responsible for the physical and economic survival of Egypt.

> *It was a method worthy of God to select the most aggressive and influential enemy of the Church, and its bitterest persecutor, and to transform him into the greatest apostle, the profoundest theologian, the most persuasive apologist and the most tireless missionary of the Church he once aimed to destroy.*
>
> *J. Oswald Sanders*
> *Robust in Faith*

It has been said that in achieving His world-purpose, God's method has always been a man. Not necessarily a noble man, or a brilliant man, but always a man with capacity for a growing faith. Granted this, there appears to be no limit to the pains God is willing to take in his training.

J. Oswald Sanders
Robust in Faith

The brash, overly confident young Jew who persecuted the church later became the apostle Paul. His first attempts at ministry, accomplished with the same aggressive personal confidence, ended in dismal failure. After a narrow escape, Paul, like Moses before him, spent some years in isolation while God built qualities of humility and dependence into his life. He never forgot his persecution of the church, and this kept him focused on the greatness of God's grace in choosing him to be His servant. With considerable feeling, Paul never hesitated to call himself "a bond-servant of Christ" (Romans 1:1; Galatians 1:10; Philippians 1:1, etc.).

The examples could be multiplied: Moses, David, Elijah, Hezekiah, Jeremiah, Nehemiah, Peter, John, and many others. Central to all their stories is a process through which God molds and prepares them and then uses them to provide leadership for His people.

THE GOAL OF PILGRIMAGE

The goal of the pilgrimage process has two primary elements. The first is the more basic: to make each of us become more like Jesus Christ. Paul states this clearly in several passages. He tells the Corinthian believers that "we all, with unveiled face, beholding as in a mirror the glory of the Lord, are being transformed into the same image from glory to glory, just as from the Lord, the Spirit" (2 Corinthians 3:18).

God has made this process part of His preordained plan for each believer (Romans 8:29). He will bring, or allow, into our lives whatever experiences are necessary to mold us to become more Christlike.

The second element of the goal is related to the first. God wants us to learn that we are dependent upon Him. The Son of God Himself, whom we are to grow to be like, was dependent upon His Father in heaven (John 5:30). Our continuous temptation is to rely on our own resources of thought, skill, energy, or connections. We are so committed to our own adequacy that the process of learning not to depend upon our own resources is often slow and painful. The world can give many examples of successful leaders who were successful because of their own skills and resources. But no one can be the leader that God wants him or her to be, or accomplish all that God desires, without learning to depend entirely upon God and the resources that He provides (John 15:5).

PILGRIMAGE AND LEADERSHIP DEVELOPMENT

God also uses the pilgrimage process as a broader leadership development experience. The Center for Creative Leadership has studied the leadership development process carefully. They summarize their conclusions by saying that three developmental experiences are essential if a person is to develop in leadership: assessment, challenge, and support.[1]

Assessment gives a person an understanding of his or her current leadership skills, gifts, abilities, and temperament. It also helps the person identify areas for growth and improvement. Mentors, leaders, and supervisors can give assessment personally. Assessment instruments can also be used (see chapters 5 and 6, where assessment instruments will be used to identify your spiritual gifts and temperament).

Challenge causes people to be moved out of their comfort zone and into situations in which they must grow and adapt because their existing abilities and resources are inadequate. This is a healthy place to be, where our faith is stretched and our dependence upon God is increased. Challenge can come from a multitude of sources:

+ Novelty. New experiences, things we have not done before, stretch us and make us think and work in new ways.

+ Difficult goals or assignments. New experiences that require us to do more than just work harder in ways we are familiar cause us to grow by pushing us into doing things with which we are not familiar.

+ Conflict situations. Conflict experiences require us to reexamine the way we think about things. They tend to broaden our perspective and enable us to do things differently.

+ Hardships. Difficult, painful situations cause us to confront our own inadequacies; they help us learn to depend upon God and others. They teach us patience and perseverance; they help sharpen our personal priorities and give us empathy for others.

Support is needed to help us make it successfully through challenging experiences. Development requires change, and significant personal change is often daunting and uncomfortable. The support of loved ones, colleagues, and friends is vital in keeping us developing rather than opting for staying in our comfort zones.

LEADERSHIP DEVELOPMENT EXPERIENCES FOR JESUS' DISCIPLES

To gain insight into the dimensions of the leader's pilgrimage, look closely at the way Jesus Christ led His disciples through the process. Make a quick overview of the experiences in the apostles' pilgrimage as recorded primarily in the gospel of Mark. Use the chart that begins on the next page, "The Disciples' Pilgrimage," to record your observations on the incidents selected. In each event or experience notice the role the disciples played. Were they simply observers of something Jesus accomplished alone, or did Jesus involve them as participants? What did Jesus intend to teach them in each experience; what lessons should they have learned? Make notes in the spaces provided.

In this process note also where you see Jesus giving His disciples experiences of *assessment, challenge,* and *support.* Then reflect on your observations by answering the questions that follow. Be prepared to discuss your insights together.

The Major Lessons

Look back over your chart of observations and then focus on the key incidents listed below.

1. The Twelve Sent Out (Mark 6:7–13)

a. *After observing Jesus manifest His power for some time, the Twelve are given authority by Jesus and sent out in pairs to preach, teach, heal, and cast out demons. Why do you think Jesus told them to take nothing for their journey?*

_____

_____

_____

_____

b. *How do you think they felt and acted when they returned and reported their experiences to Jesus? (6:30–32)*

_____

_____

_____

_____

THE DISCIPLES' PILGRIMAGE

Text of Mark	Event/Experience	Disciples' Roles in the Event/Experience	Jesus' Teaching Point: "What they should have learned"
5:1–20	Healing Gerasene demoniac	*Observers*	*Jesus has the power of God*
5:21–43	Healing Jairus's daughter	*Observers (in the room with Him)*	*Jesus is God . . . He raised the dead*
5:25–34	Healing woman with hemorrhage	*Observers*	*Jesus' power is experience through faith*
6:1–6	Teaching in Nazareth; Unbelief—few miracles	*Observers*	*Unbelief destroys the experience of God's power*
6:7–13	The Twelve sent out		
6:30–32	Apostles report; Rest and refreshment		
6:33–44	Feeding five thousand people		
6:45–52	Storm on the sea; Walking on water		
7:1–23	Jesus challenged by the Pharisees and Scribes		
7:24–30	Healing Syrophoenician woman's daughter		
7:31–37	Healing deaf man		

Text of Mark	Event/Experience	Disciples' Roles in the Event/Experience	Jesus' Teaching Point: "What they should have learned"
8:14–21	Hungry in the boat		
8:27–38	Peter's confession of Christ		
9:30–37	Jesus foretells His death and resurrection		
10:32–45	Jesus foretells His sufferings, death, and resurrection		
14:27–31	Peter and others asserting their faithfulness and loyalty		
16:14–20	Jesus reproaches the disciples; Jesus commissions the disciples		

c. *What did they learn from this experience?*

_____

_____

_____

_____

2. The Feeding of the Five Thousand (Mark 6:33–44)

a. *Why do you think Jesus intentionally put them on the spot with the command, "You give them something to eat"? (See also John 6:5–6.)*

_____

_____

_____

_____

b. *This was a critical experience in the lives of the apostles, and Jesus expected them to learn something from it that they could apply to other experiences. Notice that Mark indicates this in Mark 6:52. What should they have learned?*

_____

_____

_____

3. The Storm at Sea (Mark 6:45–52)

    a. *Mark omits a major part of the experience of the storm. What is missing (see Matthew 14:28–32)?*

_____

    b. *Notice how Jesus responded to Peter (Matthew 14:31). Why do you think He spoke this way to Peter?*

_____

_____

_____

_____

    c. *What implications would this have for us in leadership in the church?*

_____

_____

_____

_____

    d. *Summarize the lessons the apostles should have learned through the experiences of Mark 6.*

_____

_____

_____

_____

4. Peter's Confession of Christ (Mark 8:27–38)

    a. *Compare the parallel passage in Matthew 16:13–19. What did Matthew include in his expanded account?*

_____

_____

_____

CHARTING A BOLD COURSE

b. How do you think Peter felt after this interchange?

_____

_____

_____

How might this relate to what happened next (Mark 8:32ff)?

_____

_____

_____

c. What was Peter doing that would call forth such a powerful reaction from Christ?

_____

_____

_____

_____

d. What does it mean to "set your mind on man's interests rather than God's" (see Matthew 16:23)?

_____

_____

_____

_____

In what ways do you do this in your own life or ministry?

_____

_____

_____

_____

Summary Lessons

1. At least four times in Mark 6–8 Jesus comments on the disciples' lack of understanding (6:52; 7:18; 8:17,21). Why do you think they had such a hard time "getting it" after all they had observed and experienced?

_____

_____

_____

2. The Pharisees observed many of the same miracles as the apostles. What was it that grieved Jesus so deeply about the Pharisees in Mark 3:1–5?

_____

_____

_____

3. Compare the apostles' experiences in Mark 6:45–52; 8:14–21; 16:14. What is the common description of the apostles in all of these passages?

_____

_____

_____

How does a believer get this way?

_____

_____

_____

In what ways do you see the same characteristic in your life and ministry?

_____

_____

_____

4. Compare the following passages: Mark 9:30–34; 10:33–45; 14:27–31; and Luke 22:14–24. What two elements do all of these passages have in common?

   a. _____
   b. _____

How do you account for this?

_____

_____

_____

In what ways does the struggle found here show up in your life and ministry?

_____

_____

_____

How can you gain freedom from this struggle?

_____

_____

_____

_____

To think more concretely about your own personal pilgrimage, we will use the Life Story exercise in the next chapter. As you go through the process of reviewing and objectifying the process of God's working in your life, keep in mind the major lessons Jesus taught the apostles in the passages we have just studied.

5. *How would you summarize those lessons?*

_____

_____

_____

_____

_____

Think for a moment of a church leadership situation—someone leading an elder board, deacon board, a home group, or a special ministry, such as women's ministry, or teaching an adult class. Look at the lessons you've listed in response to question 4 and then answer the following question.

6. *If the leader had not learned the above lessons, how would that likely show up in his ministry and relationships?*

_____

_____

_____

_____

_____

HOW TO RECOGNIZE A SERVANT LEADER

A summary list follows of characteristics of a servant leader, based on chapters 1 and 2. Read through the list, then write your comments or additions in the space provided.

+ A servant leader's primary commitment is to Jesus Christ and His purposes in both the life of the leader and in the lives of followers. (See Colossians 1:28 for the primary commitment: "that we may present every man complete . . .")

+ A servant leader is personally committed to a worthwhile vision, one in which those led can also find fulfillment.

+ A servant leader is motivated by a Christlike love for those led; he seeks neither acclaim, nor status, nor special privileges for himself.

+ A servant leader's major concern is always for what is best for those led in the fulfillment of the larger vision or purpose.

+ A servant leader's greatest sense of fulfillment is found in the personal development and maturing of those he leads. Thus John found "no greater joy than this, to hear of my children walking in the truth" (3 John 4).

+ A servant leader has a strong sense of duty and a willingness to accept responsibility. Thus Paul declared, "I am obligated both to Greeks and non-Greeks" (Romans 1:14 NIV).

+ A servant leader is willing to be vulnerable and make himself accountable.

+ A servant leader takes care to listen to others and communicate his value of them.

+ A servant leader has a humble spirit, which recognizes the gifts, strengths, weaknesses, and flaws in himself and others.

+ A servant leader is willing to share power, responsibility, acclaim, and attention with others.

Comments or Additions:

_____
_____
_____
_____
_____

Note

1. *The Center for Creative Leadership Handbook of Leadership Development,* Cynthia D. McCauley, Russ S. Moxley, and Ellen Van Velsor, eds. (San Francisco: Jossey-Bass, 1998), 8–16.

T H R E E

THE LEADER'S LIFE STORY

THERE IS NOTHING LIKE A GOOD STORY to make us drop everything and focus our attention on the unfolding drama in the lives of the characters. Images and emotions seem to come alive in our minds as we hear the story, and the story elements become personal to us. The best stories deal with common human experiences of joy and sorrow, of suffering and vindication, of obstacles and accomplishment, of success and failure. These are among the key elements of life as we experience it, and God uses all of them to develop each of us as persons and as leaders.

Through stories, the emotional connection with the characters makes a greater impact upon us. Perhaps this is why so much of the Bible comes to us in stories. We resonate personally with the people, whether they are heroes of faith and accomplishment, like Moses or David; or common people, like Ruth, the centurion with a sick servant (Luke 7:1–10), or the man born blind (John 9)—or even the stories that Jesus told: the father with a wayward son (Luke 15:11–32), the unforgiving servant (Matthew 18:21–35), or the good Samaritan (Luke 10:30–37).

> *Leadership is autobiographical. If I don't know your life story, I don't know a thing about you as a leader.*
> *Noel Tichy*
> *Harvard Business Review*

One of the most difficult things for any of us to do is to maintain perspective when we are enmeshed in the challenges, stresses, and pains of ordinary life and ministry. The stories of others can help give us perspective. And knowing and understanding our own stories helps give us needed perspective on what God is doing in our lives and how He wants to use us in His service.

GOD'S AUTHORSHIP

It is often a new perspective to think of your life as a story, with you as the main character and God as the Author of *your* story. This chapter is intended to help you clearly and thoughtfully think through the question, How has God authored my story up to this point in my life? The Life Story process is designed to bring perspective by helping us to see that nothing in our lives has happened apart from God's personal involvement.

To say that God is the Author of our story is not to say that we are just actors reading lines that someone else has written and over which we have no control. Nor is it to suggest that we are in an improvisational theater where we devise our own lines independently in reaction to circumstances. The dynamic of our relationship with God, the Author of our story, is much more personal. Just as any actor brings his or her own personality and views into the interpretation of the lines that have been written, so God has incorporated both His sovereign design and our personal responsibility into the creation of our stories.

> *It will emerge clearly that God's methods, though infinite in variety, are constant and eternal. Unnoticed, He invades the affairs of men, weaving into His perfect plan the tangled strands of human experience. Man is always left free to act, but never so as to frustrate His ultimate plan.*
>
> J. Oswald Sanders
> *Robust In Faith*

As the ultimate Author of our life stories, God works with us through many different means. He uses His Word and the presence and power of His Spirit in us. He uses the unique way He has created us, our personal design of gifts and natural abilities, as well as using other people and the circumstances in which we live. God also incorporates our responses to these influences into the story He is creating.

God has given us the freedom to choose how we'll respond to Him at all times; Adam and Eve proved that through their failure in the garden. But even the far-reaching effects of their sin didn't destroy God's plan for the world. And neither will our sins or failures stop Him from writing our story.

A clear understanding of your Life Story can bring encouragement, insight, perspective, hope, and life change to you and others as we recognize the pen of the Author of heaven on the pages of our lives.

LIFE STORY AND LIFE ISSUES

God's authorship is most clearly seen through the *formative* relationships and experiences He has brought into our lives. These relationships and experiences are the tools that God uses to mold and shape us to who and where we are today, the point at which the remainder of our story is being written.

While we sometimes think that God's authorship of our lives did not begin until we became believers in Christ, the reality is that it started long before. As God told David, He, the Author, was intentionally involved with each of us from the time of conception (Psalm 139:13–16). And Paul explains that God was involved even before that (Ephesians 1:4). Even before we were aware of His presence, God was choosing us, forming us, and introducing people and events into our lives to draw us to Himself.

So God is the Author, and somehow He allows us to influence our story with the choices we make. A common struggle we all face is the temptation to live independently of God. Making sense of this inner struggle can be very challenging. When we pursue life on our own terms, we impede the process of spiritual growth God intended. God certainly does not condone our sinful behavior. But He ultimately uses everything, even our sins and failures, to accomplish His purposes. God wastes nothing. Paul explained to the Athenians, "The God who made the world and all things in it . . . He Himself gives to all people life and breath and all things. . . . For in Him we live and move and exist"(Acts 17:24–25, 28).

David recognized God's authorship in his life. His psalms are clearly the living expressions of a man who saw his life—his story—in light of a bigger story written by God. He writes, "Where can I go from your Spirit? Where can I flee from your presence? If I go up to the heavens, you are there; if I make my bed in the depths, you are there" (Psalm 139:7–8 NIV). David concludes, "All the days ordained for me were written in your book before one of them came to be" (v. 16 NIV). Like David, we need to see the experiences of our lives as coming from God's hand.

Jacob and David's Stories

In every person's life, one's story is also God's story—the story of how the Creator is active in an individual's life. For example, Jacob's deceit in stealing his brother's birthright seems to be a story of a man ignoring God's plans and suffering the threat of death from a first heartbroken and then bitter, vengeful brother (see Genesis 27–34). Was Jacob a failure? Not ultimately, as God uses the event to reshape him and fulfill God's own plans.

As J. Oswald Sanders wrote, "The supreme lesson of Jacob's story is that *no failure need be final.* There is hope with the God of Jacob for any temperament, any disposition.

No past failure puts the possibility out of reach. When God has saved and apprehended a man, He pursues him with undiscourageable perseverance with the sole purpose of blessing him." Sanders added: "God will turn the tables on the devil by lifting us from the scrap heap and creating a wider and more fruitful ministry out of our very defeats. He always honours faith, however feeble and trembling."[1]

The exciting story of David and Goliath (1 Samuel 17) has been told so many times that it has become an archetype: the defeat of a seemingly overpowering enemy by the apparently weaker person who has an unrecognized source of strength. But the story occurs within the framework of a larger story. God was about a process in David's life, and his story includes all that God was doing. When Saul questioned why David, an untrained youth, thought he could take on Goliath successfully when all of his trained soldiers—not to mention himself, the tallest man in all of Israel—were too afraid to do so, David told him more of his story. David recognized that God had already given him some lesser yet formative experiences of faith to prepare him for this greater challenge. David told Saul, "Your servant was tending his father's sheep. When a lion or a bear came and took a sheep from the flock, I went after him and attacked him, and rescued it from his mouth. . . . Your servant has killed both the lion and the bear" (1 Samuel 17:34–36).

David had learned from those experiences and applied the lesson he learned about trusting God to the greater challenge facing him in the giant, so far undefeated, Philistine. One of the key elements of growth through reflection on our life story is gaining the ability to learn from our experiences.

There were also formative relationships in David's life that had a significant level of pain but which God used to build David's faith. When Samuel asked David's father, Jesse, to assemble his sons so that the one God had selected to replace King Saul could be anointed, Jesse did not think David was significant enough to be included (1 Samuel 16:11). And later, when David brought food to his brothers in the army and, hearing Goliath's challenge, expressed courage and faith to face him, Eliab, David's oldest brother, ridiculed him severely and questioned his motives and value (17:28). He was still the youngest son, the little brother who was not to be taken seriously.

A recurring part of David's story was time in the wilderness. In his younger years he spent many hours alone, bearing the responsibility of watching over his family's sheep. During those solitary times, David devoted himself to music and poetry that expressed and deepened his relationship with God. God, the Author, also used this time to develop David's physical gifts and skills and test his courage. From these pages of David's Life Story came some of the most intimate and heartfelt expressions in all of Scripture, the Psalms. Later, David spent many more years in the wilderness, on the run from Saul's selfish anger, before he was ultimately crowned king. During these years God developed him as a leader, tested his integrity, built his endurance, and deepened his faith. He would become the greatest king in Israel's history.

Throughout his years, there were low points—fool-ish decisions, painful relationships, strong temptations, and terrible deceit and sinfulness. In all of these things, God was still involved with David, teaching him, mold-ing him, breaking him. David learned that sin has con-sequences, that even God's leaders are accountable, and because of their positions even more accountable than everyone else. But he also learned that God is merciful and faithful and forgiving.

> *God knows no unfinished task. . . .[The] Christian experience . . . is replete with evidence of the tenacity and tireless patience of God's love.*
> *J. Oswald Sanders*
> *Robust in Faith*

If David was writing his Life Story, he would say that all of these experiences were formative. The relation-ships and experiences formed his character and changed his life. As God wrote each new chapter in David's Life Story, the elements of the unfolding story made David who he was.

Like David, our lives tell great tales. That's because the Author of heaven is about His business, writing on our hearts through relationships and experiences His master-pieces of re-creation.

An Issue of Faith

We encourage you to work through the Life Story process as an exercise of faith.[2] The time invested in prayer and reflection is well worth it. It is a process through which we are called to trust God's sovereign work in our lives and to believe He's good even in the midst of our pain. We learn to trust that the events of our lives have a larger mean-ing. Marshall Shelly, editor of *Leadership*, had this to say about God's authorship in his life after having lost two children:

> Even as a child, I loved to read, and I quickly learned that I would most likely be confused during the opening chapters of a novel. New characters were introduced. Disparate, seemingly random events took place. Subplots were complicated and didn't seem to make any sense in relation to the main plot. But I learned to keep reading. Why? Because you know that the author, if he or she is good, will weave them all together by the end of the book. Eventually each element will be mean-ingful.[3]

Author Eugene Peterson reflected, "I'm living in a plot with characters, and all the stuff connects in some way or another. What happens today—even though I don't understand it and it doesn't make any sense—is going to make sense thirty chapters down the road."[4]

Why Complete the Life Story Process?

In addition to extending our trust in God, completing and sharing a Life Story have several other compelling benefits, including

- ✦ getting a clearer perspective on the experiences of your life. You will often be able to see how God has used difficult events to mold your character or equip you in some way.

- ✦ becoming more focused in your life and ministry. Often your special gifts and abilities, which God has developed in you through experiences, are best discerned through seeing your Life Story. You may notice recurring themes of effectiveness that will lead you to focus your efforts on similar challenges in the future.

- ✦ being able to better deal with problem issues in your life by surfacing areas that you deal with in an unhealthy way. As you look at your Life Story, you may notice recurring strategies you have used in painful situations, strategies that have damaged your relationships and caused you and others difficulty.

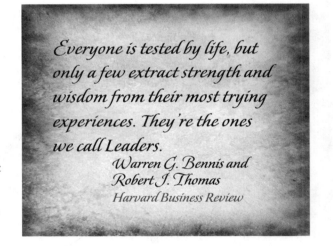

Everyone is tested by life, but only a few extract strength and wisdom from their most trying experiences. They're the ones we call Leaders.
Warren G. Bennis and
Robert J. Thomas
Harvard Business Review

- ✦ building closer, more meaningful relationships. The more personally you know someone, the stronger the bond between you.[5]

- ✦ being able to see the grace and faithfulness of God in your life. Seeing the events of your life depicted together will enable you to better see God's grace, even in the most painful events.

PUTTING TOGETHER YOUR STORY: A PROCESS OF DISCOVERY

Now it is time to begin your process of discovery. As Eugene Peterson commented, your life is a plot full of characters. As you reflect on your past, you will recall a string of memories, moments of joy and moments of sorrow. Some of them you may not understand, but keep in mind that God uses the best and the worst to accomplish His purposes. Completing your Life Story is a challenge, but when you have finished you will have a better perspective of how the events of your life fit together.

You will find the following four-step process helpful in putting together your Life Story:

Step 1: Laying out the details of your Life Story

Step 2: Arranging the chapters of your Life Story

Step 3: Distilling the lessons from your Life Story

Step 4: Preparing to tell your Life Story

Take your time as you work through the steps. The results will be well worth the effort.

Step 1: Lay Out the Details of Your Life Story

The first step is to lay out the details. This is the most time-consuming of the four steps. It requires significant time in observation, so it is vital that you give yourself plenty of time to pray and reflect.

To do this, use the Life Story Chart located on page 57. Divide your life into logical time sequences from birth to present (i.e., where you lived, where you went to school/worked, etc.). You might think of these divisions as "chapters." Record those divisions along the horizontal line extending to the right from the zero. The vertical line represents the range of positive (+) and negative (-) experiences.

Start the observation process by writing brief notes about positive and negative relationships, places, successes, and failures that come to mind under the different life divisions. If you need more space to write, you could make your own Life Story Chart on a piece of 11x17 paper. (See the appendix for a sample completed chart.)

Several questions follow to stimulate your observation time. Do not hesitate to use your own questions in this process too. Remember, this is your Life Story and God has used many different means to bring you to where you are today.

In light of your relationships and experiences:

1. When you think of your parents (or those who had the role of parents) what memories come to mind?

2. What have been the greatest influences in your life?

3. Who are the most memorable people from your past?

4. What do you remember about where you grew up?

5. What have been the most difficult or painful experiences in your life?

6. What did you think about God during various chapters of your life?

7. What portions of the Bible have been most meaningful to you? Why?

8. What have been the major decision points of your life?

9. What dreams have you had over your lifetime?

Step 2: Arrange the Chapters of Your Life Story

The next step is to create a Life Story Worksheet, by transferring the same life divisions from the Life Story Chart to the Life Story Worksheet. (Blank worksheets are included at the end of this chapter.)

1. Clarify your story by going back and highlighting those relationships and experiences on your chart that are the *most formative*. To do this, identify those relationships and experiences that have had lasting impact; these are the most formative. Record your formative events on the Life Story Worksheet in the appropriate life division columns, under "Brainstorming." (See the sample worksheet in the appendix as a model.)

2. Focus on determining how God has authored your story. As you pray and reflect on each formative event, ask two questions: "What has God revealed about *Himself*—His attributes, character, and works?" and "What has God revealed about *me*?" As you answer this second question, note your (1) gifts (God-given, Spirit-driven abilities), (2) flaws, (3) strengths, and (4) weaknesses.

Record your thoughts under the "God's Authorship" section of the Life Story Worksheet found at the bottom of each life division.

Step 3: Distilling the Lessons from Your Life Story

Now it's time to complete the Life Story Worksheet. Here's how:

1. Reflect on the formative experiences and identify any recurring themes in your life that seem to stand out. For example, perhaps you notice a recurring life theme of accomplishing goals. You now see it in light of your natural temperament coupled with a family environment that encouraged success. Or maybe you discover that a painful experience combined with a natural or spiritual gift has led you to particular acts of service. Identifying themes will help you effec-

tively evaluate and articulate your story.

Pay special attention to the hardships and painful experiences of your life. Remember, God uses such difficult experiences in major ways, perhaps because He has our attention more fully at those times or because we more openly confront our own inadequacies in those circumstances.

2. Based on what you have identified, go back and create titles for each of your life divisions. What title characterizes each chapter of your Life Story? Record each title on the Life Story Worksheet.

3. Take a separate piece of paper, entitle it "Who I am Today," set up headings of *strengths, weaknesses, limitations,* and *flaws,* and write a brief description of yourself. Note: As defined further in chapter 10, strengths are those special capabilities you have as spiritual or natural gifts. Weaknesses are unrealized or undeveloped abilities that you can develop. Limitations refer to capabilities that we do not possess and could not develop to a significant level even with much effort. Flaws are character deficiencies that must be dealt with.

4. Entitle a second sheet of paper "What I Need to Do to Develop Christlike Character." Based upon your work in point 3 above, prayerfully design an action plan for developing Christlike character in these areas of your life.

   + Identify two areas of strength or gifts that you would like to develop further.
   + Also choose one weakness and one flaw that you need to address.
   + Develop a plan which includes practical steps toward life change in these areas. Your plan will help you submit to and cooperate with God as He writes the next chapters of your life.

5. Entitle a second sheet of paper "How God Has Prepared Me for Leadership." On the sheet identify ways God has equipped you to lead. What experiences were important in this process? How do your strengths and gifts fit into your leadership abilities? How do your flaws and weaknesses impact your ability to provide leadership?

Step 4: Preparing to Tell Your Life Story

Finally, prepare to communicate your story by selecting a method of presentation. Many people have found a little creativity goes a long way. Think through how you can use different expressions to communicate your story.

Be creative! Here are some innovative ways to tell your story:

+ Use drawings, personal photographs, magazine cutouts, computer graphics, even old video clips or family movies to animate your *Life Story*.

+ You may want to use a map or a time line. (A time line of *my* life is included in the appendix as a sample "Life Story Diagram.")

+ You might even include music or poetry to make your story more memorable.

+ Remember, you will be telling your own story as God has written it, so tell it honestly and tell it well.

> *The leaders of the future, whether they are executives, politicians, or educators, are going to have to do two things really, really well. They are going to have to learn to talk in pictures, and they are going to have to be storytellers.*
> Jim Crupi
> *American Way magazine*

Among the creative approaches I remember are one man's trifold brochure; the six panels corresponded to the title and five chapters of his Life Story. Another was one woman's four playbills, broadway-like posters that depicted the major chapters of her Life Story.

Before presenting your Life Story, consider these questions:

+ Can you present your story within thirty to forty-five minutes?

+ Do your chapter titles reflect the content of each life division? Can you explain why you chose the titles you did?

+ Can you make a clear connection from chapter to chapter? Is there flow?

+ How do the materials you use support and enhance your message?

With your story completed, you may see some things in better focus. Refer back to "Step 3: Distilling the Lessons from Your Life Story." Are there any lessons you would change or add?

Once the preparation work is done, share your Life Story with others. Since your story is personal, you may want to start by sharing it with a small group that has demonstrated openness, acceptance, and trust. Here are a few good reasons to share your story with others:

+ You reveal the grace of God.
+ Others can relate to and learn from your experiences.
+ You will deepen relationships.
+ You will establish accountability.
+ You will have greater self-understanding.

LISTENING TO A LIFE STORY

Equally important to presenting your Life Story is to listen to others presenting their own. As you listen to someone else, your basic approach should be to respond to the other's story with attention and affirmation.

1. Give the storyteller the support he or she needs.

One of the greatest gifts you can give another person is your undivided attention. After a person has taken the risk to share his or her life story with a group, that individual has a great need for affirmation. The more open and honest the person has been, the more vulnerable he or she feels. When people in the group respond with acceptance and encouragement, a powerful sense of community results. God's incredible power for life change is released when we experience through others the grace of acceptance in the face of genuine vulnerability. Where you see evidence of God's work in the person's life, tell him so. It will encourage him, and it may open a door that he has not seen before.

> *Indeed, our recent research has led us to conclude that one of the most reliable indicators of true leadership is an individual's ability to find meaning in negative events and to learn from even the most trying circumstances. Put another way, the skills required to conquer adversity and emerge stronger and more committed than ever are the same ones that make for extraordinary leaders.*
>
> *Warren G. Bennis and Robert J. Thomas*
> *"Crucibles of Leadership"*
> *Harvard Business Review*

2. Enter into the storyteller's heart.

In listening to a person's Life Story, your main question for yourself needs to be, *Am I entering into this person's heart—am I feeling his pain [fears and angers] and his passion [hopes and dreams]?* How close are you to shedding a tear when they cry, or to genuinely laughing with them? Have you sensed their feeling of liberation because of grace? Do you feel they have felt the impact of grace? of being accepted unconditionally by God? Do you care about their welfare (apart from their benefit to you)? These are questions to test your own heart.

This does not require a weak emotionalism, but an intentional engagement of your heart. We need to prayerfully seek God's enablement to love people in ways that touch their lives for good. One of the worst experiences a storyteller could have is to share difficult personal experiences and receive little or no response from those listening.

Notes

1. J. Oswald Sanders, *Robust in Faith* (Chicago: Moody, 1965), 36.

2. The Life Story process used in this chapter is adapted from the process developed by the Center for Christian Leadership of Dallas Theological Seminary.

3. Marshall Shelly, "My New View of God," *Leadership,* Fall 1996, 89.

4. From an interview with Eugene Peterson: Sandra Glahn, "Part II: "What's your Story?" *The Threshing Floor,* March 1997, a newsletter of the Dallas Theological Seminary, Dallas, Texas.

5. For example, Lou Holtz, successful college football coach at Notre Dame and now South Carolina, once explained how he aimed to turn around his winless South Carolina team. He realized his players did not know one another, so he required they tell their life stories at team meetings. "Everybody's got a story. And when our guys look at a teammate, I don't want them to see just a name and a face. I want them to know the story." Quoted in Tony Barhart, "Familiarity Breeds Success," *Atlanta Journal-Constitution,* 23 September 2000, 07.

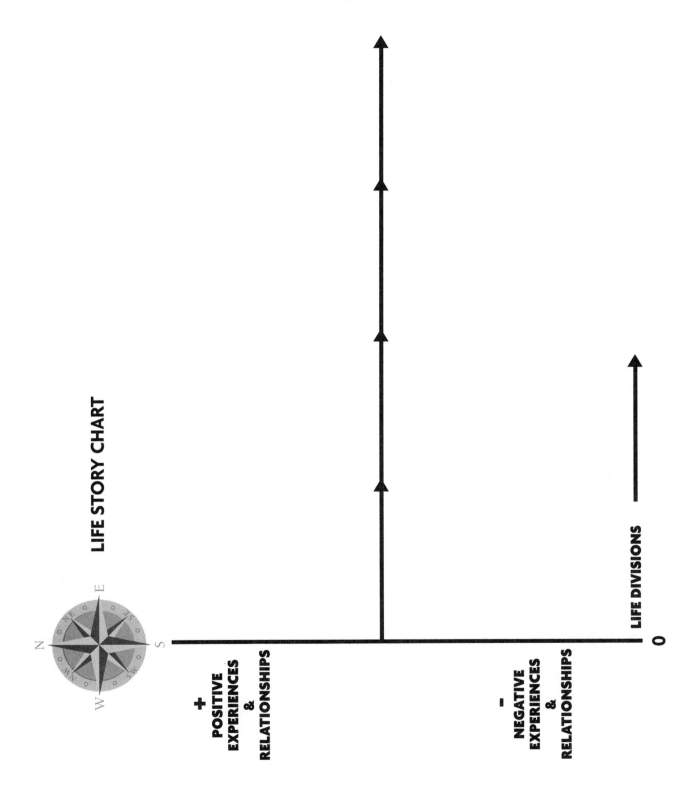

LIFE STORY CHART

+

POSITIVE
EXPERIENCES
&
RELATIONSHIPS

−

NEGATIVE
EXPERIENCES
&
RELATIONSHIPS

LIFE DIVISIONS

0

LIFE STORY WORKSHEET

LIFE DIVISIONS				
CHAPTER TITLES				
BRAIN-STORMING *Formative Events, Hard Times, Good Times, Impacting Family Experiences, etc.*				
GOD'S AUTHORSHIP *What was God doing in these situations? How did He use them in your life?*				

LIFE STORY WORKSHEET

LIFE DIVISIONS				
CHAPTER TITLES				
BRAIN- STORMING *Formative Events, Hard Times, Good Times, Impacting Family Experiences, etc.*				
GOD'S AUTHORSHIP *What was God doing in these situations? How did He use them in your life?*				

F O U R

THE LEADER'S IDENTITY IN CHRIST

A PERSON'S IDENTITY HAS TO DO WITH WHO he perceives himself to be. Identity is like an inner map of his being, and all he does is in harmony with this inner map. The boundaries on the map form a set of governing principles that determine how he expresses himself. The boundaries on our inner maps circumscribe things like our personal sense of worth or value, our evaluation of our capabilities, strengths, and weaknesses, and our view of where we fit in the society around us.

For the most part, people stay within the lines—we function within the boundaries of our developed personal identity. Sometimes we try to deceive others by camouflaging our identity and presenting ourselves in ways that, deep inside, we know are out of synch with who we think we are. These are not conscious attempts to take the healthy risk of expanding the borders of our inner maps. They are rather cheap imitations that take the place of true growth and development.

A positive and accurate sense of personal identity is critical to a healthy, productive life. Without a positive sense of personal identity, a Christian (like all other persons) will likely tend toward two extremes. Either he will withdraw from fully engaging life out of fear that he will not be adequate, or he will feel driven to aggressively assert himself to prove his adequacy. If his sense of personal identity is not accurate, he will likely overvalue his own worth or abilities, usually to the depreciation of the value or contribution of others. Paul warns us of such a common tendency (Romans 12:3–8). If he underrates his own worth or abilities, he will probably miss out on the joy of fulfilling the role God has equipped him to play in this life.

> *No leader sets out to be a leader per se, but rather to express himself freely and fully. That is, leaders have no interest in proving themselves, but an abiding interest in expressing themselves. The difference is crucial, for it's the difference between being driven, as too many people are today, and leading, as too few people do.*
> *Warren Bennis*
> *On Becoming a Leader*

If this is true for people in general, it is particularly true for leaders, for a Christian leader's major contribution is to influence other people toward the fulfillment of God's purposes for them and for the church or ministry to which they belong. If Warren Bennis is correct, the best leaders have "an abiding interest in expressing themselves." That means that their sense of personal identity forms the core reality of their leadership, for good or for ill. Leaders imprint their own sense of personal identity upon those they lead. Often they do so without conscious thought, but they all do so.

For that reason alone, it is essential that godly leaders understand their own identity accurately and know how it impacts those they lead. Among the most dangerous of leaders is the one who does not know himself, and thereby unwittingly affects those he leads in ways he does not understand.

UNDERSTANDING OUR PERCEPTIONS, ACTIONS, AND RESPONSES

One component of our identity is our sense of personal worth or significance. Because we live in a fallen, imperfect world, our sense of significance is hardly ever as great as we would wish it to be. Painfully feeling this lack, we embark on a search for greater significance to enhance our identity. This search, which we all pursue to some degree, impacts three major areas: (1) how we see reality, (2) what we do, and (3) how we relate to others.

Let's look at each of these areas—our perceptions, actions, and responses—individually.

1. How we see reality

We can see situations, events, and people as threats to our significance or as opportunities. We can view them from a perspective of fear or of confidence. Life can be perceived as a closed system in which the approval, acceptance, or praise that other people receive is unavailable to us. Or, we can perceive life as an open system in which things like praise and acceptance and value can always grow to the level deserved.

Whichever view of reality we take, our evaluation of specific events and experiences will be strongly affected. Our view of reality causes us to exercise "selective perception." We see what we expect to see in people and events. As a result, our view of "reality" may be very different from that of someone else in the same situation.

2. What we do

We choose to do things that we think will give us the sense of identity and significance we desire. For example, many people, perhaps even most people, get their sense of identity and significance from what they do, what they accomplish. Something more is at work here than simply justifiable satisfaction from a worthy job done well. What is involved is a desperate search for identity, meaning, and value. So we tend to get our identity from our work, or our ministry. In order to accomplish this, we feel a need to be:

+ successful
+ in control
+ in power
+ needed
+ respected

Life can become a joyless experience this way, for who ever feels successful enough, fully in control, or adequately respected?

3. How we relate to others

The personal deficit we feel becomes a motivator of our actions toward others. We tend to try to use others to get what we think we need to establish our identity on a satisfactory foundation. We want their approval, love, respect, praise, presence, and friendship. Somehow there is never enough, so we try harder to get them to give us what we think we need. Somewhere we cross the line that separates a legitimate desire to please from an illegitimate, manipulative attempt to get them to give us what we so deeply want.

All of us act and respond to others accord-

> *When leaders operate with a deep, unexamined insecurity about their own identity, they create institutional settings that deprive other people of their identity as a way of dealing with the unexamined fears in the leaders themselves.*
>
> *Parker J. Palmer*
> *"Leading from Within"*
> *Insights on Leadership*

ing to our perceptions. A classic example comes in the life of Saul of Tarsus.

1. *Read the following passages and make a note of the strong words that describe Saul, the Jewish leader, and his actions and attitudes toward the followers of Jesus before he encountered the risen Christ.*

Acts 8:1–3

_____

_____

_____

_____

Acts 9:1–2

_____

_____

_____

_____

Galatians 1:13–14

_____

_____

_____

_____

1 Timothy 1:13

_____

_____

_____

_____

2. *Look back over the list you have just made of attitudes and actions. Why do you think Saul was so intense in his persecution of Christians? What he did goes beyond opposition to a rival group. Why was he so violent and murderous?*

_____

_____

_____

_____

3. *What clues to Saul's motivation do you find in the following passages?*

Galatians 1:10 (Note especially in this verse the terms "now" and "still.")

_____

_____

_____

_____

Galatians 1:14

_____

_____

_____

_____

Philippians 3:3–7

_____

_____

_____

_____

4. *Summarize what was happening in these three situations. What were Saul's core issues?*

_____

_____

_____

_____

_____

_____

But Saul met Jesus Christ on the road to Damascus and was forever changed. It appears that the change took time to develop, for Paul's first evangelistic efforts did little but stir up trouble. He simply turned his natural aggressiveness to a new purpose. The results were conflict and threats from the unbelieving leaders, and he barely escaped from Damascus with his life (Acts 9:18–25).

> *Self-preservation, self-esteem and self-worth are strong and legitimate drives for leaders. As in the case of Jesus, the extension of these drives into self-love, self-conceit and self-glory can also be the most insidious temptations for those who lead.*
> *David L. McKenna*
> *Power to Follow, Grace to Lead*

67

When he went to Jerusalem, the same thing happened. The believers were skeptical and afraid of him. The Jews tried to put him to death, which seemed to be their preferred solution for everything unpleasant to them. It was not until, and perhaps because, Paul was sent away to Tarsus that the church in Jerusalem enjoyed any peace (Acts 9:26–31).

But the more Paul walked with God, the more he changed, and the more his sense of personal identity and self-concept changed. Look at the following passages to see how Paul's sense of identity changed.

Philippians 3:3–21

5. *What has changed in Paul's thinking?*

_____
_____
_____
_____

6. *What is most important to him?*

_____
_____
_____
_____

7. *What are the elements of his personal identity now?*

_____
_____
_____
_____

2 Corinthians 12:5–11

8. *Where does Paul's contentment come from?*

_____
_____
_____
_____

9. *Look back over the core issues in Paul's life, which you identified in question 4. What has happened to those issues? How would you summarize Paul's sense of identity now?*

_____

_____

_____

_____

10. *What does his sense of identity depend upon now?*

_____

_____

_____

_____

Do you pick up that sense of freedom in Paul's words? Getting his identity from the right source seems to set him free from the things that drove him before. He has a new perspective on the circumstances of life; he has a sense of confidence in God's sovereignty; and he has a sense of peace about other people. He is no longer seeking their approval; he is not dependent upon their response to him; he is no longer competing with them.

As a result, they have lost their power over him, and he is free. He has the confidence to do what he believes God is calling him to do, no matter what the opposition to him might bring. The one Person he cares about pleasing is God Himself. This is where the leader finds his positive and true identity—in God, his creator and sustainer, and in His Son, Christ the Redeemer.

> *The great spiritual gift that comes as one takes the inward journey is to know for certain that who I am does not depend on what I do. Identity does not depend upon titles, or degrees, or function. It depends only on the simple fact that I am a child of God, valued and treasured for what I am.*
>
> *Parker J. Palmer*
> *"Leading from Within"*
> *Insights on Leadership*

Identity is part of a larger package. It includes character issues as well as issues of strengths and weaknesses. In succeeding chapters we will spend time identifying our God-given temperaments, gifts, and strengths. These are part of our sense of identity. But the core issues of identity, as you saw in the life of the apostle Paul, are deeper. The core issues have more to do with:

✦ How do I measure my worth?

✦ Whose approval am I seeking? Who am I trying to please?

✦ In what or whom is my confidence placed?

✦ What am I depending on to give my life meaning?

✦ What is my "place" in life? How do I fit into the society around me?

The foundation of all of these issues is our relationship with God through Jesus Christ. The Scriptures show us how we can and should respond to these issues.

11. *Below are some important Scripture passages. Read each one and ask yourself, What does this passage say about me, about who I am? Then write a brief completion to the statement, "I am . . . ."*

• **Psalm 139:1**	I am	_____
• **Psalm 139:13**	I am	_____
• **Psalm 139:14**	I am	_____
• **Psalm 139:16**	I am	_____
• **Romans 5:1**	I am	_____
• **Romans 5:8**	I am	_____
• **Romans 6:6**	I am	_____
• **Romans 8:1**	I am	_____
• **Romans 8:15**	I am	_____
• **Romans 8:38–39**	I am	_____
• **Ephesians 1:3**	I am	_____
• **Ephesians 1:4**	I am	_____
• **Ephesians 1:11**	I am	_____
• **Ephesians 1:13**	I am	_____
• **Ephesians 2:5**	I am	_____
• **Ephesians 2:6**	I am	_____
• **Ephesians 2:10**	I am	_____
• **Ephesians 2:19**	I am	_____

Obviously, many more passages of Scripture could have been listed. However, these should suffice to demonstrate that we are greatly loved, by the one Person whose love will always be constant; we are justified, forgiven, and secure in His love and acceptance.

The purpose of this is not to make us either proud or complacent. It is to give us a secure foundation to become what God wants us to be and to lead the way God wants us to lead. Our identity in Christ is the mold in which our character is formed; it is the foundation upon which our leadership is constructed.

Being a servant leader requires a person to be willing to give of himself or herself unselfishly in leading others. It is only the leader who is secure in his own identity in Christ who has resources to give to others unselfishly. It is the leader who is secure in his identity who can stand up to criticism and personal attacks when he knows he is right but has to go against the prevailing thought.

Consider the example of Christ Himself in this area. In the Upper Room (John 13:1ff), Jesus humbled Himself and served the apostles by washing their feet. He washed the feet of men whom He knew would betray Him (John 13:21ff), deny Him (v. 38), and desert Him. John indicates that it is what Jesus knows about Himself that gives Him strength to serve these men.

> *Followers adamantly demand that a leader possess a high degree of integrity when it comes to self-perception. A combination of self-confidence and humility seems to me to be crucial, for this oxymoronic quality makes it possible for the group to be decisive.*
>
> *Max DePree*
> *Leadership Jazz*

12. *What elements of Jesus' own personal identity were critical to His deliberate decision to serve? Read John 13:1–3.*

_____

_____

_____

13. *In what areas do you struggle with your own sense of identity or adequacy?*

_____

_____

_____

14. *Can you trace the root of these feelings to any event or experience(s) that you depicted on your Life Story? If so, which one(s)?*

_____

_____

_____

15. *To what extent does a desire for approval or appreciation from others determine what you choose to do?*

_____

_____

_____

16. *Whose approval is an absolute "must have" for you? Why is this so?*

_____

_____

_____

Imagine you are the elder charged with overseeing the youth ministry. The youth minister, Jake, is a volunteer, a sharp young man who seems to relate very well to the kids in the youth ministry. But the other day an adult member of the youth committee came to you and complained about the way Jake runs the youth committee meetings.

"I get so frustrated in those meetings, I want to pound my fist on the table!" the committee member said. "We talk and talk and talk, but nothing ever gets done! Whatever the subject, there will be different views from various members of the committee. Getting Jake to make a decision is impossible! I don't know if I can do this anymore!"

17. *What might be going on here? How would you handle this situation?*

_____

_____

_____

_____

SOME QUESTIONS TO PROBE YOUR UNDERSTANDING OF YOURSELF

18. *When did you feel the greatest sense of accomplishment?*

_____

_____

_____

19. *When did you feel the greatest sense of failure?*

_____

_____

_____

20. How did you handle your feelings of failure?

_____

_____

_____

21. What are your three greatest fears?

_____

_____

_____

22. What is the most significant thing you have learned in the last six months?

_____

_____

_____

23. How did this learning influence your life?

_____

_____

_____

24. What is the most significant spiritual lesson you have learned in the last six months?

_____

_____

_____

25. How did this learning influence your life; what have you done differently since learning this lesson?

_____

_____

_____

26. If you could change one thing about your early life experiences, what would it be? How would you want it to be different?

_____

_____

_____

_____

27. Think of a situation or experience that you remember as one in which you took a significant risk.

    a. List the situation and describe how you felt beforehand. What seemed most risky about the situation?

_____

_____

_____

    b. What caused you to go ahead and take the risk?

_____

_____

_____

    c. What did you learn from the experience?

_____

_____

_____

28. In what situations do you feel most confident?

_____

_____

_____

29. In what situations do you feel most unsure? Indicate what you do to handle these feelings.

_____

_____

_____

_____

30. In what areas do you most clearly see God working in your life now?

_____

_____

_____

_____

_____

F I V E

THE LEADER'S TEMPERAMENT

THE CORE OF OUR PERSONAL IDENTITY IS FOUND in our relationship to God through Jesus Christ. When that relationship is consciously established and we are aware of the faithfulness of God's love and acceptance and the security of our position in Christ, we have the freedom and inner strength to serve others. No longer do we need to use others to attempt to fulfill our own needs. Because our true needs are met in relationship with Christ, we are free to give and serve and lead in a godly way.

THE ROLE OF OUR TEMPERAMENT

What is true of us inside is expressed to others through our temperament and our spiritual gifts as well as our strengths, weaknesses, limitations, and flaws. Our temperament is a unique, God-given part of our identity. It is the characteristic way in which we relate to people and events or tasks. There is no "best" temperament, no "spiritual" temperament. Each temperament has its own strengths and weaknesses. Much like spiritual gifts, God gave all of the temperaments because all of them are needed.

Whether you realize it or not, your temperament will determine how your leadership expresses itself to others. Some leaders are more personally dominant, directing the activities of those they lead. Others are more careful planners, who are more cautious and reserved in their leadership behavior. Still others are people-oriented leaders who personally involve those they lead in their plans and actions. Some leaders inspire others; some leaders are quietly competent so that others conclude they need to follow in order to accomplish a goal. God has utilized all types of temperaments in the leaders He has chosen to use.

IDENTIFYING YOUR TEMPERAMENT

To get a better idea of your temperament, we will use the "DISC Behavior Survey" and corresponding information from the book *Understanding How Others Misunderstand You*, by Ken Voges and Ron Braund. The DISC survey helps you determine which of four personality styles characterize you. DISC is an acronym for four styles: dominance, influencing, steadiness, and compliance. We will only be using a small amount of the very helpful information in the book. To pursue further information on the various temperament types and discover how the DISC assessment process can be helpful in other setting, including marriage and premarital relationships, please contact In His Grace, Inc.[1] The following "DISC Behavior Survey" is used by permission of In His Grace, Inc.

1. *Work through the "DISC Behavior Survey" section on the next page. Follow the instructions given to answer the questions and plot the results, using the "DISC Profile" graph. Then Complete the four "Understanding Your . . . Style" worksheets that follow the graph.*

2. *Now that you have identified your temperament type, basic style, and your leadership, relational, and negotiating styles, look back over the descriptions you wrote.*

   Do the descriptions seem to accurately describe you?

   _____ Yes _____ No. *Why? or why not?*

   _____

   _____

   _____

   What are the most accurate statements?

   _____

   _____

   _____

   Which statements seem to be the least descriptive of you?

   _____

   _____

DISC Behavior Survey

NATURAL BEHAVIOR: _____

NAME

Instructions: Focus on your *instinctive behavior* and not what you perceive is the best response. Be aware, there are no right or wrong answers. [2]

> **How to respond:** Rank each *horizontal* row of words on a scale of 4, 3, 2, 1 with 4 being the word that *best* describes you and 1 being the *least* like you. Use all rankings in each line only once. The first line below is an example (Do not count it in your totals):

2	Dominant	1	Influencing	4	Steadiness	3	Compliant
	Forceful		Lively		Modest		Tactful
	Aggressive		Emotional		Accommodating		Consistent
	Direct		Animated		Agreeable		Accurate
	Tough		People Oriented		Gentle		Perfectionist
	Daring		Impulsive		Kind		Cautious
	Competitive		Expressive		Supportive		Precise
	Risk Taker		Talkative		Gentle		Factual
	Argumentative		Fun-Loving		Patient		Logical
	Bold		Spontaneous		Stable		Organized
	Take Charge		Optimistic		Peaceful		Conscientious
	Candid		Cheerful		Loyal		Serious
	Independent		Enthusiastic		Good Listener		High Standards

____ Total   ____ Total   ____ Total   ____ Total

☐   ☐   ☐   ☐

*Note: If the sum of your totals does not add up to 120, you did not complete the survey correctly or you made a mistake in adding up the totals. Recheck your work.

This assessment survey is designed to determine your general DISC styles. For a more precise evaluation, the authors recommend instruments using a "Most/Least" selection process which provides an expanded profile analysis. [3]

TALLYING YOUR SCORE:

1. On the previous page, enter the letter "D" in the box under the first column (starting from the left); enter "I" in the second, "S" in the third, and "C" in the fourth.

   Transfer the DISC totals from the bottom of the previous page to the tally box below:

TALLY BOX

D	I	S	C

2. Using the totals from your tally box, plot your D-I-S-C dimensions on the graph to the right; then connect the four points.

3. After completing your graph, circle all plotting points above the midline. My High Style(s) are: _____

4. Below are the definitions of the four DISC styles. Circle the information that best describes you.

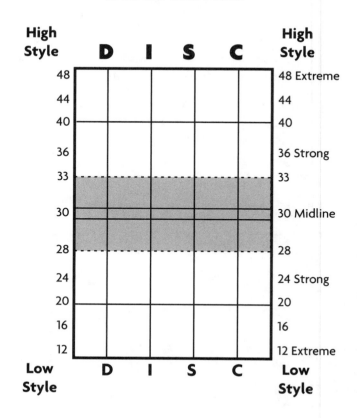

DISC PROFILE

DEFINITIONS OF DISC STYLES

Dominant Styles: Work toward *achieving goals* and *results;* they function best in an *active, challenging* environment.

Influencing Styles: Work toward *relating to people through verbal persuasion;* they function best in a *friendly, favorable* environment.

Steadiness Styles: Work toward *supporting and cooperating* with others; they function best in a *supportive, harmonious* environment.

Compliant Styles: Work toward *doing things right* and *focusing on details;* they function best in a *structured, orderly* environment.

Assignment: Based on the information above, write a personalized definition.

I tend to work toward . . . _____

And function best in an environment that is . . . _____

_____

UNDERSTANDING YOUR BASIC STYLE

Action Plan: Circle the four words under the High and Low Styles that correspond with High and Low Styles on your graph on the preceding page. For a better understanding of your Basic Style, take a few minutes to consider these basic style traits that you circled for *Act, Want, Fear,* and *Response* in each of the High or Low Styles in our basic style. Do the traits accurately describe you?

HIGH STYLE	D	I	S	C
Act	Assertive	Persuasive	Patient	Contemplative
Want	Control	Approval	Routine	Standards
Fear	Losing	Rejection	Change	Being Wrong
Response	Anger	Blame	Nonparticipation	Criticism

- midline -

	D	I	S	C
Act	Cooperative	Unemotional	Responsive	Free-Spirited
Want	Harmony	Logic	Variety	Nonstructured
Fear	Confrontation	Illogical Act	Status Quo	Conforming
Response	Indifference	Suspicion	Physical Action	Emotion

LOW STYLE	D	I	S	C

Use the words circled to complete the sentences at the bottom of this page, defining your basic style. (If a point on your graph is in the mid-zone, you should use words either above or below, whichever you feel most accurately describes you. Use the same approach on the following pages as you define your leadership, relational, and negotiating styles.)

DEFINING YOUR BASIC STYLE

As a/an _____ style blend, I naturally act _____

act

because I want _____

want

If I perceive that I may face _____

fear

I may respond with _____

response

UNDERSTANDING YOUR LEADERSHIP STYLE

Action Plan: Again, Circle the four words under the High and Low Styles that correspond with High and Low Styles on your graph on page 78. In understanding your Leadership Style, take a few minutes to consider the style traits that you circled for *Preferred Tasks, Leadership Style, Strength,* and *Limitation* in each of the High or Low types in your style. Do the traits accurately describe your leadership style?

HIGH STYLE

	D	I	S	C
Preferred Tasks	Challenging	People Related	Scheduled	Detailed
Leadership Style	Decisive	Interactive	Cooperative	Traditional
Strength	Problem Solver	Encourager	Supporter	Organizer
Limitation	Too direct	Too disorganized	Too indecisive	Too detailed

-------------------------------- midline --------------------------------

	D	I	S	C
Preferred Tasks	Routine	Technical	Diverse	Unorthodox
Leadership Style	Participative	Structured	Reactive	Instinctive
Strength	Team Player	Logical Thinker	Energy Source	Risk Taker
Limitation	Too indirect	Too impersonal	Too intense	Too nontraditional

LOW STYLE

	D	I	S	C

Using the chart above, define your leadership style by completing the statements below. As an example, consider the style blend of high S and C with a midline I and a low D. The sentence below is a description of the corresponding Leadership Style:

"I prefer tasks that are *scheduled, detailed,* and *routine.* My Leadership Style tends to be *cooperative, traditional, and participative.* My strengths are being *a supporter, organizer,* and *team player.* Regarding my limitations, I tend to be *too indecisive, detailed, and indirect;* therefore I need a High *D,* Low *S* on my team."

DEFINING YOUR BASIC STYLE

I prefer tasks that are _____ . My leadership style tends to be _____ .

My strengths are being a _____ . Regarding my limitations, I

tend to be too _____ ; therefore, I need a High _____ , Low

_____ on my team.

UNDERSTANDING YOUR RELATIONAL STYLE

Action Plan: Again, Circle the High and Low Styles below that correspond with High and Low Styles on your graph on page 78. In understanding your Relational Style, take a few minutes to consider the style traits that you circled for how to *Respond, Relate, Reinforce,* and *Help* you when under stress. Do the traits accurately describe how you relate?

HIGH STYLE	D	I	S	C
Respond	Be direct	Be friendly	Be nonthreatening	Be specific
Relate	Briefness	Freedom to express feelings	Friendly tones	Patient answers
Reinforce	The bottom line	Social recognition	Time to process	Freedom to validate
Help	Get out of the way	talk to me	Give assurances	Leave me alone
- midline -				
Respond	Allow time to process	Be logical	Focus on action	Focus on activities
Relate	Nonverbal assurances	Accurate data	Variety	Nonstructured
Reinforce	Time to react	Support	Control	Encouragement
Help	Give me a hug	Respect privacy	Are spontaneous	Are Flexible
LOW STYLE	D	I	S	C

Using the chart above, define your relational style by completing the statements below.

DEFINING YOUR RELATIONAL STYLE

As High_____ and Low _____ blend, my suggestion to others in responding

to me is _____

in relating to me with _____ .

In reinforcing me give me _____ .

When I'm under stress, you can be helpful to me if you _____ .

UNDERSTANDING YOUR NEGOTIATING STYLE IN RESOLVING CONFLICT

Action Plan: Again, (Circle) the High and Low Styles below that correspond with High and Low Styles on your graph on page 78. For understanding your Negotiating Style, take a few minutes to consider the style traits that you circled for *Comfortable, Fears, Tension,* and *Conflict* in each of the High or Low types in your style. Do the traits accurately describe how you handle conflict?

HIGH STYLE

	D	**I**	**S**	**C**
Comfortable	Decisive	Enthusiastic	Supportive	Structured
Fears	Losing	Rejection	Change	Being Wrong
Tension	Demands Action	Emotional Attacks	Complies	Avoids disagreeing
Conflict	Avoids contact	Complies	Stubbornly Attacks	Demands Details

-------------------------------------- midline --------------------------------------

Comfortable	A Team Player	Detached	Spontaneous	Unstructured
Fears	Confrontation	Illogical Actions	Status Quo	Conforming
Tension	Becomes Quiet	Remains calm	Challenges others	Becomes arbitrary
Conflict	Stuffs feelings	Reacts covertly	Assesses blame	Becomes sarcastic

LOW STYLE   D   I   S   C

Using the chart above, define your negotiating style by completing the statements below.

DEFINING YOUR NEGOTIATING STYLE IN RESOLVING CONFLICT

I am most comfortable being _____ .

When I feel fears of _____ it causes tension for me.

Under tension, I may _____ .

If this intensifies the conflict, I may _____ .

SOME STRENGTHS AND WEAKNESSES
OF THE TEMPERAMENT TYPES

D	I	S	C
STRENGTHS			
Dominant	Exciting	Steady, stable	Conscientious
Forceful	Enthusiastic	Can be counted on	Tries hard to "get it right"
Gets things done	Expressive	Concerned for others	Task oriented
Initiates action	Involved	Good team player	Tenacious
Makes quick decisions	Often inspiring	Easygoing	Grasp of the details
Competitive	Confident	Patient	
Risk taker	Very social	Calm in a crisis	
	Handling surprises	Good follow-through	
WEAKNESSES			
May be too dominant	Doesn't listen well	Tends to be too quiet	Too into the details
Insensitive to people	Doesn't want to disappoint anyone	Can be passive	Perfectionistic
Makes snap decisions	Misses the details	Resists change	Not expressive
Misses the details	Doesn't always follow-through	Avoids confrontation	Has difficulty with unclear situations or structures.
Hates routine tasks		Avoids risky decisions	

3. *Look over the strengths and weaknesses of your temperament type.*
    a. *Do the descriptions seem to apply to you?*
       _____ Yes _____ No.

    b. *Think through and list two or three things you could begin to do now to reinforce your strengths and minimize your weaknesses:*

    _____

    _____

    _____

    _____

    _____

Show your results to your spouse. Ask her or him if the results seem to fit you. Your spouse has probably observed these characteristics in your life and can reinforce the results of the profile. Her or his observations will help you see your temperament from the viewpoint of those to whom you relate.

4. *What were your spouse's comments? List them below.*

_____

_____

_____

_____

_____

_____

5. *With your temperament type and styles in mind, look back over your Life Story. In what events of your Life Story do you see your temperament and basic styles most clearly?*

_____

_____

_____

_____

_____

True understanding comes from reflecting on your experience.
Warren Bennis
On Becoming a Leader

In what events in your Life Story do you see your strengths or weaknesses operating most clearly?

_____

_____

_____

_____

Notes

1. You may write In His Grace, Inc., at 3006 Quincannon Lane, Houston, TX 77043-1201, or call (713) 934-8810. You may e-mail Ken Voges at kvoges@aol.com or contact In His Grace at http//www.inhisgraceinc.com. *Understanding How Others Misunderstand You* book is available at bookstores and is published by Moody Publishers. The *Understanding How Others Misunderstand You* workbook is available through In His Grace.

2. A PowerPoint presentation regarding the administering of the DISC Behavior Survey can be downloaded at "no charge" by going to www.inhisgraceinc.com. Click on DISC Surveys and then on DISC presentations.

3. A "most" and "least" DISC assessment can be taken at "no charge" by going to www.inhisgraceinc.com. Click on DISC on-line. Enter the access code #891461.

IDENTITY

S I X

THE LEADER'S GIFTS AND STRENGTHS

GOD BLESSES HIS PEOPLE WITH UNIQUE STRENGTHS that may be used to make a significant impact for the cause of Christ in the world. These abilities come in two primary ways: Some are spiritual gifts; others are special natural talents.

Our natural talents are those special abilities we are born with. They come by heredity and are ours from birth. Both believers and nonbelievers have natural talents, for God has built these into the human race because we are created in His image. Some people have special talents in the area of physical skills or coordination; others have musical or artistic talents; still others have special facility with mathematics or scientific studies. Our lives are enriched in many ways by the special talents that people possess.

THE MEANING OF SPIRITUAL GIFTS

Spiritual gifts, on the other hand, are given only to believers. The Scripture describes spiritual gifts as being sovereignly given by God the Holy Spirit (1 Corinthians 12:11). They are apparently bestowed at the time a person becomes a believer in Christ. Every biblical passage which deals with spiritual gifts emphasizes in some way that every believer receives at least one spiritual gift. (Note the "every" and "each" statements in Romans 12:3; 1 Corinthians 12:7; Ephesians 4:7; 1 Peter 4:10.)

The purpose of spiritual gifts is clearly to bring glory to God (1 Peter 4:11) and to build up the church, the body of Christ (1 Corinthians 12:7; Ephesians 4:11–16; 1 Peter 4:10). Spiritual gifts are not for our private use or for building us up. Rather, they are intended to be used to build up the church by adding to its number (cf. the gift of evangelism), bringing its people to maturity (cf. the gifts of teaching, leading, and exhorting), or ministering to the needs of its people (cf. the gifts of helps, hospitality, and showing mercy).

A spiritual gift is therefore simply a special, God-given ability to serve others for the benefit of the church of Jesus Christ.

THE DIFFERENT KINDS OF SPIRITUAL GIFTS

Several passages give lists of spiritual gifts, and not all of the lists are identical. You can find lists in these passages:

+ Romans 12:4–8
+ 1 Corinthians 12:4–10
+ 1 Corinthians 12:28–30
+ Ephesians 4:11
+ 1 Peter 4:11

The differences in the lists are partly accounted for by the different purposes and emphases of the individual biblical authors. Depending on their purpose, they highlighted some and ignored others. Or, as in 1 Peter 4:11, the author's purpose was to give a simple summary of all the gifts in two categories in order to emphasize that whatever is done should be done for the glory of God.

In order to determine your spiritual gift, we will use the instrument *DISCovering Your Spiritual Gift.* The "Introduction to Spiritual Gifts," "A Spiritual Gifts Inventory," and the "Glossary of Inventoried Spiritual Gifts" are all from *DISCovering Your Spiritual Gift,* ©1994, C. Gene Wilkes and used by permission of C. Gene Wilkes.

ABOUT *YOUR* GIFTS

Once you have completed the spiritual gifts questionnaire labeled "DISCovering Your Spiritual Gift" (including the "Gifts Inventory"), consider what you have learned about your gift(s) by answering the following questions.

1. *Indicate which gifts most intensely describe you. Then read the appropriate descriptions of your gifts in the "Glossary of Inventoried Spiritual Gifts." Do the gifts you identified as yours seem to fit? In what ways do they fit or not fit?*

_____

_____

_____

_____

_____

DISCOVERING YOUR SPIRITUAL GIFT

Introduction to Spiritual Gifts

Spiritual gifts are the key to understanding the church and how God intends the church to function. The church is the visible body of Christ, and Scripture describes it as a living organism, unified in purpose while diverse in its parts. Each member has its place of service in the body, and every part belongs to the body (1 Cor. 12:12–26). The church is many members gifted by God and united for service. Spiritual gifts are part of God's gift of grace (Rom. 12:3, 6; Eph. 4:7, 11). To receive God's grace for salvation is to receive God's gifts for service in Christ's body. . . .

A diversity of gifts means variety of ministries (1 Cor. 12:14), and different roles mean various ways to serve the body (Eph. 4:11). God gives the gifts for service to the church (1 Cor. 12:7). Spiritual giftedness, not tenure or expertise, is the basis for spiritual usefulness in the church. The church functions best when its members know how God has gifted them and when they are in a place of service motivated by that giftedness.

The goal of understanding spiritual gift(s) is to discover your place of service in the body. You may match your gift(s) with a place of service that already exists within your church; for example, you may match your gift of teaching with a need for Bible teachers. Or, you may match your gift(s) with a ministry that exists outside your local church. Your gift(s) may also motivate you to find places of ministry that do not yet exist in your church. God gifted you to serve His body. The adventure is discovering both the gift and place of service for the good of all (1 Cor. 12:7).

The number of gifts you will inventory have been limited to gifts listed in the three primary biblical lists. You also will not inventory the "sign" gifts of miracles, healings, tongues, and the interpretation of tongues.[1] The ultimate goal is to understand and incorporate those gifts directly related to service in your church.

A unique feature of this inventory is "corresponding body parts" for each gift. In 1 Cor. 12, Paul used the metaphor of a foot speaking to a hand, "because I am not a hand, I don't belong to the body" (v. 15). Paul did not equate a particular part with a corresponding gift, but the analogy is consistent with how he described the church's similarity to a human body. For example, someone with the gift of service or helps serves the body as a hand. Another example is that a member with the gift of apostleship serves the body as a foot that carries the body into missions.

The corresponding body parts to spiritual gifts in this inventory are only aids to memory and application. The questions take into account your personal perceptions of your giftedness as well as what others in the body have said about how you serve the church.

Please complete the inventory before you read the glossary of gifts at the end of this inventory.

A SPIRITUAL GIFTS INVENTORY

Please read each of the following statements. Decide the degree to which the statement describes you. **Then, check (✓) each statement as it relates to your spiritual life.**

[NOTE: When reference is made to "others in the body" or "members of the body" this pertains to Christians you have known throughout your Christian walk.]

Statement	Much (3)	Some (2)	Little (1)	None (0)
1. Believers have said that when you speak you strengthen their faith.				
2. Members of the body appreciate your willingness to wait on tables.				
3. You find great joy in teaching the Word of God.				
4. Others in the body have thanked you for your encouragement in times of need.				
5. In response to God's grace, you give joyfully to mission projects.				
6. Other members of the body have asked you to lead them.				
7. You often find yourself guiding others in the direction of how you perceive God leading.				
8. Others in the body consider you their heart that compassionately draws them to the needs and concern of others.				
9. You find joy in being sent out from the church to begin others churches.				
10. You find joy in sharing your faith with those who are lost.				
11. God has led you to care for the spiritual well-being of a group of believers.				
12. You see the differences between God's way and the world's ways of doing things.				
13. You know the Scriptures well and find joy in knowing more about them.				
14. You are able to look beyond human capability to the power of God in difficult times.				
15. You sometimes sense the difference between good and evil people just by talking to them.				
16. Believers often consider you the mouthpiece for the group in spiritual matters.				
17. You enjoy doing tasks that free others to lead.				
18. The church has set you aside as a teacher of God's Word.				

Check (✓) each statement as it relates to your spiritual life.

	Much (3)	Some (2)	Little (1)	None (0)
19. You sense your role in the body is to strengthen and encourage others to remain true to the faith.				
20. You find great joy by investing God's assets in people and projects in order to grow the church.				
21. You sense God has gifted you to stand before the body and direct their actions.				
22. God has gifted you to organize others to accomplish a task or goal.				
23. You are motivated by love to become involved in the needs of others.				
24. God has worked through you to lead others to Christ while you were on mission for Him.				
25. Others in the body may consider you a "foot" that carries them to lost people.				
26. Others in the body consider you their "knees" because you are willing to kneel down to care for others.				
27. The group often calls upon you to make decisions.				
28. You know the futility of worldly knowledge when compared to knowing God.				
29. Others have thanked you for your encouragement to trust God above all else.				
30. You sometimes feel others are masquerading as someone they are not.				
31. Lost people have commented that when you spoke, God convicted them of sin.				
32. Other Christians in the body consider you a "hand" that supports the work of others.				
33. Members of the body have commented on your fervor and accuracy in teaching the Bible.				
34. You know you are doing God's will for your life when you have built up another believer.				
35. God has convinced you that every believer should give according to his or her ability.				
36. Others in the body consider you an "eye" that sees beyond the present to what God wants the church to become or do.				
37. You are asked to manage ministries within the body.				
38. You feel the suffering of others and are drawn to join them in that suffering.				
39. Others have responded to your testimony and have been strengthened by it.				

Check (✓) each statement as it relates to your spiritual life.

	Much (3)	Some (2)	Little (1)	None (0)
40. You consider reaching lost people to be the church's primary task.				
41. You sometimes see your role in the church as a shepherd caring for the sheep.				
42. Others in the body consider you a "right brain" person who interprets the wisdom and ways of God.				
43. Others in the body consider you a "left brain" person who analyzes accurately the facts of God.				
44. You put your trust and hope in God before other people or your own capabilities.				
45. You believe in spiritual beings and sometimes can see their work in the lives of others.				
46. Believers have said that when you speak you build them up in the Lord by your words.				
47. You prefer serving to speaking or leading within the body.				
48. You have a thorough knowledge of Scripture.				
49. Others in the body consider you an "arm" which you put around others to encourage them.				
50. Your first response to need is to offer your hand to share what you have.				
51. You humbly accept roles of leadership within the body.				
52. You are comfortable solving problems by offering solutions that include others.				
53. You do not become depressed by the problems of others, but you sense how they are feeling.				
54. Others in the body consider you a "foot" that carries them to missions outside the church.				
55. You are hurt when others in the body do not have the concern for the lost like you.				
56. You are often the first one to respond to needs within the church.				
57. Others in the body have commented on your ability to apply God's principles to real life.				
58. You sometimes sense you get a glimpse of understanding the mysteries of God.				
59. Others in the body consider you their "temperament" who calls them to put their trust in God first.				
60. You listen carefully to those who claim to be speaking a message from God, to know their motives.				

Check (✓) each statement as it relates to your spiritual life.

	Much (3)	Some (2)	Little (1)	None (0)
61. You are willing to speak God's truth even in hostile settings.				
62. You find joy in serving the body by doing things to assist those who need help.				
63. Others have encouraged you by saying you seem to understand the "mind of Christ."				
64. You find joy in introducing others to the body.				
65. You consider it a privilege to give generously to the work of God.				
66. Others seek you to direct the affairs of the church.				
67. Others in the body consider you an "eye" that sees effective ways to reach its common goals.				
68. You sense the needs of those within the body when others may not.				
69. You gladly accept leadership in mission projects.				
70. God has used you to lead others to put their trust in Christ.				
71. Others have thanked you for how you cared for them in a time of spiritual need.				
72. You pray for God to reveal His deepest wisdom to you.				
73. You consider knowing the facts of Scripture as significant as knowing the principles from Scripture.				
74. You sometimes find yourself alone in believing what God could do if we would just let Him.				
75. Others in the body consider you their "ears" that discern distracting voices and causes.				

SCORING

When you have completed responding to the statements and recording your responses (✓), transfer your responses to the tally box on the next page. In the corresponding box, place a unit value of (3) for **much**, (2) for **some**, (1) for **little**, and (0) for **none**.

When you have completed transferring your responses from the statements, total the scores in the total column.

TALLY BOX						TOTALS	GIFTS/MINISTRIES
1	16	31	46	61	▶		**Prophecy**
2	17	32	47	62	▶		**Service**
3	18	33	48	63	▶		**Teaching**
4	19	34	49	64	▶		**Exhortation**
5	20	35	50	65	▶		**Giving**
6	21	36	51	66	▶		**Leadership**
7	22	37	52	67	▶		**Administration**
8	23	38	53	68	▶		**Mercy**
9	24	39	54	69	▶		**Apostle**
10	25	40	55	70	▶		**Evangelist**
11	26	41	56	71	▶		**Pastor**
12	27	42	57	72	▶		**Wisdom**
13	28	43	58	73	▶		**Knowledge**
14	29	44	59	74	▶		**Faith**
15	30	45	60	75	▶		**Discernment**

Circle your three highest totals. Note the corresponding gift/ministry and record below:

List the three gifts with the highest numbers:

1 _____   2 _____   3 _____

My DISC temperament is:

_____

GLOSSARY OF INVENTORIED SPIRITUAL GIFTS[2]

Prophecy (Mouth)

The gift of prophecy is proclaiming the Word of God boldly, leading to conviction of sin and building up the body. Prophecy manifests itself in preaching and teaching. (See 1 Cor. 12:10; Rom. 12:6.)

Service/Helps (A hand)

Those with the gift of service or helps recognize practical needs in the body and joyfully give assistance to meet those needs. Those with this gift do not mind working behind the scenes. (See 1 Cor. 12:28; Rom. 12:7.)

Teacher/Teaching (Mind)

Teaching is instructing members in the truths and doctrines of God's Word for the purposes of building up, unifying, and maturing the body. (See 1 Cor. 12:28; Rom. 12:7; Eph. 4:11.)

Exhortation (Arms)

Exhortation is encouraging members to be about the work of the Lord. Members with this gift are good counselors and motivate others to service. Exhortation exhibits itself in preaching, teaching, and ministry. (See Rom. 12:8.)

Giving (A hand)

Members with this gift give freely and joyfully to the work and mission of the body. Cheerfulness and liberality are characteristics of this gift. (See Rom. 12:8.)

Leadership (An eye)

Leadership aids the body by leading and directing others to accomplish the goals and purposes of the body. Leadership motivates people to work together in unity toward common goals. (See Rom. 12:8.)

Administration (An eye)

Those with this gift lead the body by steering others to stay on the intended direction of the body. Administration helps the body to organize for action according to long-term goals and purposes. (See 1 Cor. 12:28.)

Mercy (Heart)

Those with this gift aid the body by empathizing with hurting members in order to keep the body healthy and unified by keeping others aware of the needs within the body. Cheerful acts of compassion characterize this gift. (See Rom. 12:8.)

Apostle (A foot)

The church sends apostles from the body to plant churches or be missionaries. An apostle motivates the body to look beyond its walls in order to carry out the Great Commission. (See 1 Cor. 12:28; Eph. 4:11.)

Evangelism (A foot)

God gifts His church with evangelists to lead others to Christ effectively and enthusiastically. This gift builds up the body by adding new members to its fellowship. (See Eph. 4:11.)

Pastor (Knees)

This gift looks out for the spiritual welfare of those in its care. Shepherding is not limited to a pastor on staff. Pastors, like shepherds, care for members of the church. (See Eph. 4:11.)

Word of Wisdom (Right brain)

Wisdom is the gift that discerns the work of the Holy Spirit in the body and applies its teachings and actions to the needs of the body. (See 1 Cor. 12:28.)

Word of Knowledge (Left brain)

Knowledge is the God-given ability to learn, know, and explain the truths of God's Word. A word of knowledge is a Spirit-revealed truth. This gift manifests itself in teaching and discipleship training. (See 1 Cor. 12:28.)

Faith (Temperament)

Faith trusts God to work beyond the human capabilities of the people. Believers with this gift encourage others by trusting in the face of apparently insurmountable odds. (See 1 Cor. 12:9.)

Discernment (Ears)

This gift aids the body by recognizing the true intentions of those within or related to the body. Discernment tests the messages and actions of others for the protection and well-being of the body. (See 1 Cor. 12:10.)

2. *Look back over your Life Story (chapter 3). You may see instances in your Life Story in which you exercised those gifts you discovered in your questionnaire.*

   a. *If you are aware of times you used these gifts, what were the instances and what were the results?*

   _____

   _____

   _____

   _____

   b. *How did you feel in those instances in which you exercised your gifts?*

   _____

   _____

   _____

3. *To verify the possession of a particular spiritual gift, you should be able to identify times in your life when you exercised that gift. You should also have received feedback from others that confirms your possession of the gift.*

   a. *Show your spiritual gift results to your spouse and/or close friend and ask them whether the gifts you identified fit you. What are their comments?*

   _____

   _____

   _____

   b. *What comments have you received from others indicating your possession of a particular spiritual gift (or gifts)?*

   _____

   _____

   _____

If you have an agreement among the results of your "DISCovering Your Spiritual Gift," your own experiences in ministry, and the responses of others to you, you can feel confident that you possess the gifts involved. No spiritual gifts questionnaire is sufficient in itself to identify your gifts without substantiation from actual opportunities to exercise the gifts.

Your personality type influences how you exercise your spiritual gifts. Note again:

My DISC personality type is: _____

My top three spiritual gifts are:

1 _____

2 _____

3 _____

> *Leaders know themselves;*
> *they know their strengths*
> *and nurture them.*
> *Warren Bennis*
> *Training and Development*

4. *Considering the strengths and weaknesses of your temperament type, list some thoughts you have about how these two aspects of your identity would function together.*

_____

_____

_____

_____

Be prepared to discuss your spiritual gifts and temperament type in your group, with your mentor, and/or with your colleagues or close friends.

The other aspect of your strengths is your natural abilities. By this point in your life you should have a good idea about what your natural abilities are.

5. *Each individual has natural, God-given abilities.*
   a. List below five of your natural abilities which you have recognized.

_____

_____

_____

_____

   b. Describe two occasions in which you used your natural abilities in some form of ministry. What were the results in each case?
   (1) _____

_____

_____

   (2) _____

_____

_____

Often your natural abilities are used in the expression of your spiritual gifts. For example, a man with a natural ability dealing with mechanical things expresses his spiritual gift of helps by helping church widows with their automobile maintenance and repair. For him it is fun; it is something he does well and enjoys doing.

6. *What correlation have you found between your natural abilities and your spiritual gifts?*

_____
_____
_____

7. *What particular opportunities for ministry at your church seem to be in harmony with your spiritual gifts, natural abilities, and temperament?*

_____
_____
_____

8. *How can you use in your current ministry the knowledge you have gained of your temperament, gifts, and abilities?*

_____
_____
_____

9. *How can you use it in your marriage and family relationships?*

_____
_____
_____

Notes

1. Many conservative Christians believe these gifts ceased with the closing of the canon of Scripture. Others believe God still uses these gifts but not as prominently as in building the early church. Still others hold to the common use of these gifts within the life of the church today. Our emphasis is to inventory those gifts that relate directly to service within the body. [This note is by C. Gene Wilkes.]

2. For more information or additional copies of the glossary and/or the "DISCovering Your Spiritual Gift" introduction and inventory, contact:

    In His Grace, Inc.
    3006 Quincannon Lane
    Houston, TX 77043
    (713) 934-8810; (713) 462-2208 (fax)
    or write Dr. C. Gene Wilkes at Legacy Drive Baptist Church; 4501 Legacy Drive; Plano, TX 75024;
    (972) 618-4600 or (972) 618-9001 (fax).

INTEGRITY

S E V E N

THE LEADER'S VALUES AND GOALS

INTEGRITY IS THE BASIC ELEMENT OF CHARACTER. It is the first characteristic of those welcomed into God's presence (Psalm 15:2). And it is the first characteristic that distinguishes godly leadership: "So he shepherded them according to the integrity of his heart, and guided them with his skillful hands" (Psalm 78:72).

THE MEANING OF INTEGRITY

Integrity has to do with a sense of consistency between a person's inner values and his outward words and actions. In figure 1, there is a large area of consistency in the individual's values, words, and actions, and thus a large degree of integrity.

A good biblical example of integrity is Joseph as he served in Potiphar's house (Genesis 39). Potiphar's wife was attracted to Joseph and made improper advances toward

Figure 1

A LIFE OF INTEGRITY

INTEGRITY

VALUES

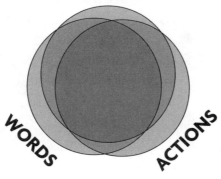

WORDS   ACTIONS

him. The way Joseph handled the situation revealed his integrity. Read the account in Genesis 39 and answer the questions below:

After analyzing the text, what would you identify as Joseph's primary values?

_____
_____
_____
_____

What were Joseph's words? Were they consistent with his values?

_____
_____
_____
_____

What were Joseph's actions? Were they consistent with his values?

_____
_____
_____
_____

> *Despite the mass of confusing data, the most conspicuous and proven fact is that effective leadership depends upon integrity, the leader's character as perceived by followers.*
> *James E. Means*
> *Leadership in Christian Ministry*

Similar examples of integrity are found in Daniel's response to the king's plan for training the young captives (Daniel 1) and in his response to Belshazzar (Daniel 5:13–17). In each case Daniel's values, words, and actions were thoroughly consistent.

Integrity helps us know what to expect from others. If we see a consistency between what a leader says and what he does, we feel more confident about how he will act in the future. One of the most disconcerting characteristics of some leaders is their unpredictability. This suggests that they are not making decisions on the basis of deeply held values but on how they may feel at the moment. It is hard to trust such leaders. People will trust those in whom they detect consistency—a sign of integrity.

HOW A LACK OF INTEGRITY SHOWS ITSELF

A lack of integrity may take one of four different forms. First, there is an inconsistency between a person's words and his actions.

Figure 2
VERBAL INCONSISTENCY
(Lack of Honesty)

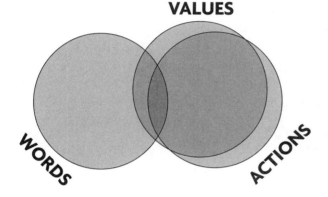

In virtually every survey we conducted [since we began our research in 1981], honesty was selected more often than any other leadership characteristic. Honesty is absolutely essential to leadership. If people are going to follow someone willingly, whether it be into battle or into the boardroom, they first want to assure themselves that the person is worthy of their trust.

James M. Kouzes and
Barry Z. Posner
Credibility

The Ananias and Sapphira Syndrome

Figure 2 represents the person who acts according to his true values though his words present a different picture. This was the case with both Ananias and Sapphira (Acts 5:1–10), who presented a gift of money as though they were giving the full amount received in the sale of some property. In reality they had conspired to keep some of the money for themselves. They acted according to their true selfish values. The lack of integrity in this case takes the form of a basic dishonesty.

Where have you seen this kind of a lack of integrity?

_____

_____

_____

_____

_____

What do you think the person's ultimate motivation was?

_____

_____

_____

_____

When Courage Fails

A second lack of integrity form is an inconsistency between one's actions on one side and one's words and values on the other. In this case a person presents his values through his words, but then he acts in an entirely different way (see figure 3).

This could reveal a great divergence between his "proclaimed" values and his "practiced" values. But it could also be that he simply did not have the courage to act according to his values.

> *In a chaotic environment a leader doesn't have perfect control. While leaders cannot offer control over the external environment that affects a company or a society, they can fill the needs of followers for stability by being trustworthy. Trust allows people to feel that there is order in their relationship with others. This is why there is so much concern over the ethics of leaders in all walks of life.*
>
> Joanne Ciulla
> "Ethics, Chaos, and the
> Demand for Good Leaders"
> *Teaching Leadership*

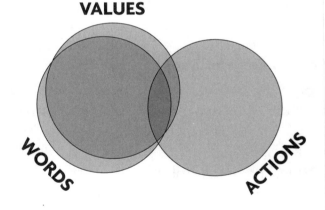

Figure 3
ACTION INCONSISTENCY

VALUES

WORDS

ACTIONS

Such lack of courage marked Peter when he denied Christ (Mark 14:66–72). After aggressively asserting his faithfulness to Jesus and commitment to stand firm even if everyone else deserted Him (Mark 14:29–31), Peter let his fear lead him to violently deny any knowledge of Jesus. There is no doubt that Peter's values were to support Christ and be faithful in following Christ. His assertions accurately reflected what he considered important. However, in the critical moment, his courage failed, and he was simply unable to act in harmony with his values.

Peter's case had a better end, for later in his life, after many years of faithful ministry, he had the courage to stand firmly for Christ in the face of his imminent martyrdom.

In what situation have you seen a lack of integrity that resulted from a lack of courage?

_____

_____

_____

_____

The Political Syndrome

The third form expressing a lack of integrity could be called the political syndrome. In this case, a person has a particular set of values. However, in an effort to be elected, he says what others want to hear and does what others want him to do. Being "elected" is just one expression of the motivation that causes someone to speak and act contrary to his or her values.

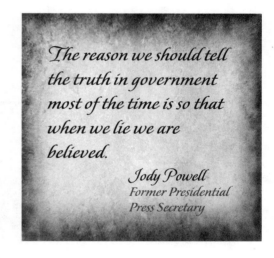

The reason we should tell the truth in government most of the time is so that when we lie we are believed.

Jody Powell
Former Presidential Press Secretary

In most cases the underlying motivation is something like being accepted, being successful, being liked, getting ahead on the job, keeping a job, getting one's way or other similar motivations. The result is personal inconsistency, and it is diagrammed in figure 4. The inconsistency appears as a discrepancy between one's inner values and outward expressions.

In what situations have you seen this kind of lack of integrity?

_____

_____

_____

_____

Figure 4
PERSONAL INCONSISTENCY

VALUES

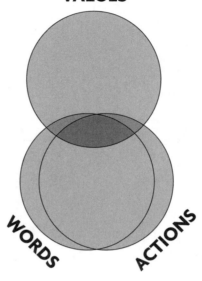

WORDS   ACTIONS

In order to be a leader, a man must have followers. And to have followers, a man must have their confidence. Hence, the supreme quality for a leader is unquestionably integrity. Without it, no real success is possible.

Dwight D. Eisenhower
President of the United States

When Integrity Fully Fails

Finally, there is a total lack of integrity in which no consistency occurs among a person's values, words, or actions. More than a lack of integrity, this is closer to a break with reality. Such a person is totally unpredictable and is out of touch with himself and probably unaware of what is happening.

In the first three cases, the person is somehow still acting in harmony with at least one segment of his values. Ananias and Sapphira certainly had a selfish value of personal recognition and approval. Peter had a value of self-preservation. The politician has a value in being elected. But the fourth case shows total inconsistency (see figure 5).

Figure 5
TOTAL LACK OF INTEGRITY
(Lack of Touch with Reality)

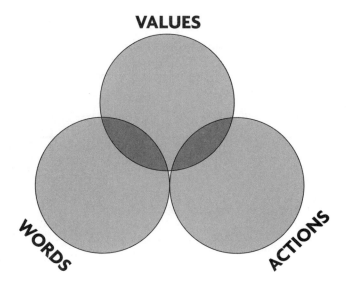

VALUES AND LEADERSHIP

In the past few decades people thought that because we live in a pluralistic society, it was important that education be "values-free." However, it was commonly assumed that there must be some accepted values that govern our actions. The same approach infected research and views on leadership. Many talked about leadership in terms of effectiveness in influencing others, regardless of the goals toward which they were influenced or the methods used in influencing them. According to this perspective, Hitler was technically an effective leader, whether you favored the results of his leadership or not.

In recent years, the situation has reversed. Leadership researchers are talking more and more about the need for values, but the society as a whole has abandoned belief in any absolute values. Today, values are situational and personal; that is, they bend and change according to the situation. They are whatever an individual person chooses them to be in his own life, and there are no absolute values that should apply to everyone.

The reality is that we all have values that we live by, whether we are conscious of them or not. Our values energize the motives that drive our actions. The important thing is that we consciously choose the values we live by.

Our values come from many sources, and we develop our personal set of values over a period of time starting with our early home life.

1. *Think back over your home life growing up.*
   a. What values were most important to your father?

   _____
   _____
   _____
   _____
   _____
   _____

   b. What values were most important to your mother?

   _____
   _____
   _____
   _____
   _____
   _____

   c. What values were most important to other family members?

   _____
   _____
   _____
   _____
   _____
   _____

> *We have a tendency to want to talk about the "substantive" things, the numbers or whatever. But our people also need to hear us talk about the normative things. Those are the real substance. As the leader, you must create a moral context for what you are trying to accomplish. . . . You have to keep going back to values.*
>
> *Gordon R. Sullivan and Michael V. Harper*
> *Hope Is Not a Method*

d. Which of the above values have you adopted as your own?

_____

_____

_____

_____

_____

_____

2. Think now of the heroes in your life, those people whom you respected greatly and wanted to be like.

   a. What values did your heroes exemplify?

_____

_____

_____

_____

_____

By 1952, the year Eisenhower entered into politics at age sixty-two, his character, as formed by heredity and experience, was set in concrete. It included the qualities of love, honesty, faithfulness, responsibility, modesty, generosity, duty, and leadership, along with a hatred of war. These were the bedrock.

    Stephen E. Ambrose
    Biographer of President Eisenhower

He was a man of too many paradoxes. Almost everything you find out about him you can find out a directly contrary quality immediately, and your problem is always which quality was real and which was assumed. Or maybe neither quality was real. Or maybe both were real, who knows.

    George Reedy
    Special assistant to
    President Lyndon Johnson

b. Which of their values have you adopted as your own? Why?

_____

_____

_____

_____

_____

_____

_____

_____

_____

_____

_____

3. *Our personal values also come from our sources of authority. For Christians, the foundational source of authority is the Scriptures. What are the top ten personal values you have adopted as a result of studying the Scriptures? List the values and their Scripture references below.*

(1) _____ **Ref:** _____

(2) _____ **Ref:** _____

(3) _____ **Ref:** _____

(4) _____ **Ref:** _____

(5) _____ **Ref:** _____

(6) _____ **Ref:** _____

(7) _____ **Ref:** _____

(8) _____ **Ref:** _____

(9) _____ **Ref:** _____

(10) _____ **Ref:** _____

The leadership body of a church also needs to have a clear set of values that give guidance to those in leadership regarding how they relate to each other, to the congregation, to the situations they must deal with. Remember that a group of elders must often deal with serious issues about which they do not all agree. And not everyone in the congregation will necessarily agree with how they choose to deal with an issue.

> *He who walks in integrity walks securely, but he who perverts his ways will be found out.*
> *Proverbs 10:9*

"The elders must humbly and lovingly relate to one another," Alexander Strauch noted in *Biblical Eldership*. "They must be able to patiently build consensus, compromise, persuade, listen, handle disagreement, forgive, receive rebuke and correction, confess sin, and appreciate the wisdom and perspective of others—even those with whom they disagree. They must be able to submit to one another, speak kindly and gently to one another, be patient with their fellow colleagues, defer to one another, and speak their minds openly in truth and love.[1]

4. *Think through any biblical directives that may apply, and then develop a list of values to govern the conduct of an elder board. Assume that you are an elder who has been given the responsibility of drafting a list of operating values for the elders to follow. (As an alternative exercise, you may use the list that follows this exercise, "Some Possible Elder*

THE LEADER'S VALUES AND GOALS

Board Values Derived from Scripture," and organize the statements into a more concise list of operating values.)

OPERATING VALUES
Elder Board, First Bible Church

_____
_____
_____
_____
_____
_____
_____
_____
_____
_____
_____
_____
_____
_____
_____
_____
_____
_____

SOME POSSIBLE ELDER BOARD
OPERATING VALUES DERIVED FROM SCRIPTURE

+ When faced with difficult issues, we will seek to avoid depending upon our own wisdom and resources and remember that God is "able to do exceeding abundantly beyond all that we ask or think" (Ephesians 3:20).

+ We will seek to act with "humility and gentleness, with patience, showing tolerrance for one another in love" (Ephesians 4:2).

+ We will be careful to "preserve the unity of the Spirit in the bond of peace" (Ephesians 4:3).

+ We will not sacrifice the unity of the Spirit for the promotion of our personal agendas (Ephesians 4:3).

+ We will remember that those on opposite sides of issues are also objects of the richness of God's mercy and the greatness of His love (Ephesians 2:4).

+ We will seek to grow in maturity ourselves and lead the congregation to grow in maturity, unity, and knowledge of Christ (Ephesians 4:13).

+ We will always endeavor to speak the truth in love (Ephesians 4:15, 25).

+ To be sure that we do not speak falsely about any person, we will seek to understand others by asking them directly about an issue (Ephesians 4:25, 29).

+ We will seek to speak to and about others in wholesome ways that build up and give grace (Ephesians 4:29; Colossians 4:6).

> *Therefore I, the prisoner of the Lord, implore you to walk in a manner worthy of the calling with which you have been called, with all humility and gentleness, with patience, showing tolerance for one another in love, being diligent to preserve the unity of the Spirit in the bond of peace.*
>
> *Paul to the church at Ephesus*
> *Ephesians 4:1–3*

+ We will give people the benefit of the doubt rather than jumping to conclusions (1 Corinthians 13:7).

+ We will be careful not to speak or act out of a spirit of bitterness or slander (Ephesians 4:31).

+ We will seek immediate resolution of issues/situations in which we experience anger (Ephesians 4:26).

+ We take seriously our responsibility to protect the congregation from false teaching; and we will do so with a spirit of humility, knowing that we ourselves are capable of error (Acts 20:30; Ephesians 4:14).

+ We will give careful, honest thought to our own feelings and motivations so as to avoid doing anything from selfishness or empty deceit (Ephesians 5:15, 17; Philippians 2:3, 12).

+ We will recognize that our unity is the target of Satan's attacks and that all conflict has an element of spiritual warfare (Ephesians 6:10–18).

+ We will seek to "conduct [ourselves] in a manner worthy of the gospel of Christ [so that we may stand] firm in one spirit, with one mind striving together for the faith of the gospel" (Philippians 1:27).

+ We will maintain a humble spirit and regard others as more important than ourselves and put their interests before our own (Philippians 2:3–4).

+ We acknowledge that being selected as elders does not mean that we have reached perfection (Philippians 3:12–13).

+ We will make the Word of Christ, the Scriptures, to be the standard of evaluation of our own thoughts and actions (Acts 20:32).

+ Recognizing that we are accountable to Christ, we take seriously our responsibility to lead by example (1 Peter 5:3).

+ We will allow no gossip, slander, or manipulation either in ourselves or in the congregation (2 Corinthians 12:20; Ephesians 4:31).

+ We will not allow divisions or a spirit of divisiveness to exist within the board or among the congregation (1 Corinthians 1:10).

+ We will not allow ourselves to become so concentrated on the business of running the church that we miss personal involvement in the lives of others (Acts 20:28; 1 Peter 5:2).

+ We will be careful not to accept unsubstantiated accusations against an elder or pastor. We will deal directly and quickly with accusations without partiality (1 Timothy 5:19–21).

Note

1. Alexander Strauch, *Biblical Eldership* (Littleton, Colo.: Lewis and Roth, 1995), 96.

INTIMACY

E I G H T

✦

APPROPRIATE OPENNESS AND VULNERABILITY

More leadership has failed from a lack of intimacy than from any other cause," Bob Briner and Ray Pritchard note. "Leaders, no matter how brilliant, cut their tenures short or accomplish less than they might otherwise when they fail to establish close relationships with a few key people, a core of followers. . . . Every time a leader tries to 'go it alone,' something less than the best occurs."[1]

THE INTIMACY SHOWN BY JESUS

Jesus made it a point to develop a close relationship with a few of His disciples. "He appointed twelve, so that they would be *with Him* and that He could send them out to preach" (Mark 3:14, italics added).

While Jesus maintained a ministry to the multitudes, He focused His attention progressively more on a smaller, select group of disciples. For the better part of three years, Jesus lived and ministered from within the intimate relationship with twelve men and a few other close disciples. Even among the Twelve, there were three who were brought into an even more intimate relationship with Christ.

Read the following passages and note some of the things Jesus did with this select smaller group:

Matthew 8:14 _____

Matthew 9:9–10 _____

_____

Matthew 9:35–38 _____

_____

Matthew 12:1–8 _____

_____

Matthew 13:36 _____

_____

Matthew 15:1–14 _____

_____

Matthew 16:13–28 _____

_____

Matthew 17:1–13 _____

_____

Matthew 17:14–21 _____

_____

Matthew 18:21–35 _____

_____

Matthew 19:27–30 _____

_____

Matthew 20:17–19 _____

_____

Matthew 24:1–14 _____

_____

Matthew 26:20–30 _____

_____

Matthew 26:36–37 _____

_____

Mark 1:29–31 _____

Mark 4:10 _____

_____

Mark 6:31–32 _____

_____

_____

John 11:17–44 _____

_____

John 12:22–23, 27 _____

_____

John 13:1–20 _____

Now look back over the list and summarize the relationship between Jesus and the disciples.

_____
_____
_____
_____
_____

1. *To what extent did Jesus share His emotions with His followers? On what occasions was this most evident?*

_____
_____
_____

2. *To what extent do you feel comfortable sharing your emotions with others?*

_____
_____

3. *What do you think makes you personally comfortable or uncomfortable sharing your emotions?*

_____
_____

4. How would you decide what is an appropriate level of emotional openness with others?

_____
_____
_____

LEADING BY EXAMPLE REQUIRES INTIMACY

The Scriptures are very clear about the kind of leadership Christians should use. Christian leadership is the opposite of the world's "power leadership" approach of "lording it over" those under their leadership. Elders are told in no uncertain terms that they are to lead by example (1 Peter 5:3). Numerous passages in the New Testament call believers to follow the example of godly leaders.

Leading by example often means modeling; the leader acts as a model for his followers. By observing the leader's actions, the follower learns what he is to be and to do. However, modeling is an inexact process. The follower observes the leader's action, but he does not know the motive for the action or the intended result. A follower could simply mimic the actions of the leader, without ever committing to the internal values that made the leader do them—unless, of course, he knows what those values are.

For modeling (or leading by example) to be truly effective, several things must be true. According to Larry Richards,[2] to be successful, the process of modeling requires:

1. frequent, long-term contact with the model(s),
2. warm, loving relationship with the model(s),
3. exposure to the inner states of the model(s),
4. the model(s) being observed in a variety of settings and situations,
5. the models exhibiting consistency and clarity in behaviors, values, etc.,
6. a correspondence between the behavior of the model(s) and the beliefs (ideal standards) of the community, and
7. an explanation of the lifestyle of the

> *He who is required by the necessity of his position to speak the highest things is compelled by the same necessity to exemplify the highest things.*
> *Gregory the Great*

model(s) conceptually, with instruction accompanying shared experiences.

Notice the third requirement: One must be willing to reveal his inner state if the modeling process is to be successful. This means that the leader must be willing to open himself up to others and reveal his thoughts, inner feelings, and motivations. Effective modeling requires such deep levels of intimacy. This is very much what Paul meant when he told the Thessalonian believers that he was well-pleased to have given them not only the gospel "but also our own lives" (1 Thessalonians 2:8). Literally, Paul says he shared his own "soul" with them.

5. *In what ways does Paul reveal his inner state in the following passages?*

Romans 9:1–5 _____
_____

2 Corinthians 2:1–11 _____
_____

2 Corinthians 10:1–11:33 _____
_____
_____
_____

6. *To what extent do you voluntarily give others access to your innermost thoughts as well as feelings?*

_____
_____
_____

What might hold you back from doing this?

_____
_____
_____
_____
_____

Usually it's some form of personal insecurity that holds us back from revealing our inner thoughts and feelings. We are afraid that what we reveal will not be accepted; or, worse, we will be personally rejected or criticized as a result. Because we feel that such rejection would be devastating to us, we hold back and refuse to allow others to know what is going on inside of us. This is why our earlier discussion of the leader's identity is so important. It is only when our personal identity is secure, because it is founded in our relationship to Jesus Christ, that we have the confidence to allow others to see what is happening within us. With our identity secure, we do not have to use other people to establish it. Rather we are free to be appropriately vulnerable with them.

INTIMACY REQUIRES VULNERABILITY

One cannot become intimate without being vulnerable. That is why so many people have no real experience of intimacy. Vulnerability is simply too frightening. Sometimes the hard-skinned, autocratic leader is simply covering up his own feelings of insecurity. So also is the nice-but-distant leader who will not allow himself to become close to anyone.

> *Leaders must develop a core group of followers in whom they confide and from whom they expect honest feedback and wholehearted support. Building this core may not be easy, there are fits and starts. Some chosen for it may not themselves be ready for the kind of relationship it requires. There may be some pain involved. Regardless, it is well worth it. In fact, quality long-term leadership is not possible without it.*
>
> Bob Briner and Ray Pritchard
> *More Leadership Lessons of Jesus*

Simply put, vulnerability is required because none of us is glorified yet. While we still live in the flesh, we still struggle with the flesh. And the flesh doesn't fight fairly. Just when we feel safest, suddenly we find ourselves involved in sin. Because our hearts are "more deceitful than all else and . . . desperately sick" (Jeremiah 17:9), we often cannot discern the subtle steps we take into temptation and failure.

This is the picture Paul paints in Galatians 6:1. The man who sins is "caught" in a trespass. The term "caught" means to be "overtaken" or "surprised." He doesn't understand how he got there. But note that he can be restored . . . if he is willing to listen to the friend who confronts him.

To be vulnerable means to be voluntarily defenseless. The person who is vulnerable is the one who has chosen to lower his guard and to allow others to see him as he really is and to confront him as necessary. Being vulnerable will help us deal with our deceit and failures, and it offers us the benefit of God's help and the help of friends as well.

Vulnerability Makes Us Open to God

David willingly lowered his defenses once he contemplated the fact that God knew everything about him and that God had been intimately involved in his life from its very beginning. He could not escape from God's knowledge of him and presence with him even if he tried.

To be known so thoroughly is a frightening thing. But David understood that God's desire for him was only good, so David chose to voluntarily open himself up completely to God and invite His search and correction (Psalm 139:23–24).

Read all of Psalm 139. Then take a few moments to reflect upon your relationship with God. Are there things you do not talk about with God? Things that you fool yourself into trying to keep hidden from God? Subjects you think about only while excluding God from your thoughts?

7. *What, if anything, is keeping you from making the same declaration of chosen vulnerability to God?*

_____

_____

_____

_____

Vulnerability Makes Us Open to Our Colleagues

Appropriate openness is a choice to be more transparent to others. It means that we relate in ways that are free of subtle attempts to hide our true thoughts, feelings, or motives from those we lead. As those who are vulnerable, we choose to lower our guard and allow others to see us as we really are.

8. *Think for a moment about the leaders you have known.*
   a. *Which ones would you describe as transparent?*

_____

_____

_____

   b. *When you have a sense that a leader is transparent, what feelings or responses does that generate in you?*

_____

_____

c. Do you have more or less confidence in such leaders? Why?

_____

_____

9. In what ways can you be more transparent in your relationships?

_____

_____

_____

Beyond a general transparency, we can choose to be more vulnerable to others. This involves a willingness on our part to listen to others with humility and respect for their ideas. The leader who respects only his own ideas is handicapping himself as a leader and preventing those he leads from using the gifts God has given to them.

One of the most helpful things leaders can do is to choose to be nondefensive in responding to criticism. This is no easy task, for sometimes we feel like our very life is threatened by the painful wounds of criticism (Proverbs 12:18a). Our natural response is to raise our defenses, but if we can choose to remain vulnerable, we can learn much from criticism, even that which is unjustified.

Vulnerability with Our Closest Friends

We should be most vulnerable to a few trusted friends. We choose to allow them a deeper, more unrestricted access into our lives. It is with these few friends that we may safely share our heaviest loads (Galatians 6:2). And it is from these few friends that we may gain the greatest help in growing consistently to maturity. To be vulnerable here is to invite accountability. Encouragement from these trusted friends is more uplifting because it is more confidently genuine. And correction from these is more helpful because we are more confident their words are intended for our good (Proverbs 27:6).

10. Who is there in your life that you feel free to be very vulnerable with? What is it about your relationship that makes you feel secure enough to be so vulnerable?

_____

_____

_____

_____

Notes

1. Bob Briner and Ray Pritchard, *More Leadership Lessons of Jesus* (Nashville, Tenn.: Broadman & Holman, 1998), 100.
2. Larry Richards, *A Theology of Christian Education* (Grand Rapids: Zondervan, 1975), 84.

N I N E

CHARACTER QUALIFICATIONS FOR CHURCH LEADERS

ALL LEADERS MAKE ONE CRITICAL DECISION consciously or unconsciously: They decide whether to use their power to serve themselves or to serve others. The choice is between servant leadership and self-serving leadership. Essentially, this is an issue of character.

Godly character is a necessary qualification for Christian leadership. Followers tend to mold themselves according to their leaders, regardless of the realm. This tendency is seen throughout the Scriptures. In the Old Testament, for example, when Israel had a bad king, the people tended to be sinful. When Israel had a good king, the nation tended to follow the Lord.

LEADERS ARE TO BE EXAMPLES

"Shepherds" have a profound impact on the direction and well-being of their sheep. Therefore, it is imperative that a leader possess a good character if he or she desires that his or her followers also have good character.

There is a normal expectation that a Christian leader represents what God desires everyone following him/her to be in both character and conduct. These expectations are often very high, and the Scriptures would concur that this is appropriate. Those inside the church as well as those outside look first to those who are recognized as leaders. When one who leads has a failure of character, several areas suffer: The world blasphemes the gospel, the ministry, the organization, the church, and Christianity as a whole. Sometimes believers even turn away from Christianity, or at least absent themselves from the fellowship of the church for a time.

For these reasons alone, a leader needs to be above reproach. Consider the great damage done by the very visible moral failures of well-known Christian leaders. What occurs on a national scale in such cases occurs very painfully and personally in a local congregation when a respected church leader fails.

THE MOST IMPORTANT QUALIFICATION FOR LEADERSHIP

Character is stressed biblically as the most significant qualification for leadership. This is highlighted in the New Testament statements of qualification for the leaders of the church, the elders. These qualifications are not presented as maximal qualifications, but minimal; that is, Paul expects to be able to find such people in church congregations. If this is the case, these biblical qualifications for leadership should provide a goal toward which all of us should strive. At the very least, these standards demonstrate how important character is to godly leadership.

THE SCRIPTURE ON CHARACTER QUALIFICATIONS FOR CHURCH LEADERS

The character qualifications for elders as church leaders are listed in 1 Timothy 3:2–7 and Titus 1:6–9.

Above Reproach . . .

In general, *elders* or church leaders must be *above reproach* (1 Timothy 3:2; Titus 1:7). The term literally means "not to be laid hold of."[1] That is, there is nothing in his life which can be seized upon to damage his reputation. He must exhibit consistent, mature Christian living that gives no grounds for public censure. Paul gives specific qualifications that cover the major areas of a Christian leader's life.

> *The only thing that walks back from the tomb with the mourners and refuses to be buried, is the character.*
>
> J. R. Miller
> *The Building of Character*

. . . in One's Personal Life

In his personal life the leader must be:

+ "temperate" (1 Timothy 3:2; "self-controlled" in Titus 1:8). The term refers to total abstention, being spiritually sober and clearheaded. He is calm, sober, possessing "the self-control necessary for effective ministry."[2] He is not in bondage to himself or to fleshly desires.

+ "prudent" (1 Timothy 3:2; "sensible" in Titus 1:8). Such a man is reasonable, sensible, and serious about life. He makes sound decisions because he exercises balanced judgment.

+ "not addicted to wine" (1 Timothy 3:3; Titus 1:7). The church leader is not "one who sits long beside the wine"[3]; he is not an excessive drinker.

+ "not pugnacious" (1 Timothy 3:3; Titus 1:7). A pugnacious man is a striker, "a bully."[4] In other words, a church leader is not quick-tempered, not violent tempered, nor given to acts of physical violence.

+ "gentle" (1 Timothy 3:3). God's church leader is gentle and kind, especially in contrast to a striker. He is "gracious, kindly, forbearing, considerate"[5] and does not insist on having his own way.

+ "peaceable" (1 Timothy 3:3). Such a leader can influence without fighting; he seeks peace rather than being aggressive. He is not given to selfish argumentation.

+ "not self-willed" (Titus 1:7). He is not "self-willed, stubborn, arrogant."[6] Nor is he insensitive or prone to forcing his ideas on others.

+ "free from the love of money" (1 Timothy 3:3; "not fond of sordid gain" in Titus 1:7). Money does not dominate him or his decisions. He is not motivated by a love of money, nor is he selfish with his material blessings.

+ "just" (Titus 1:8). In being just and upright, he is fair and impartial. The leader is able to make objective judgments based upon principle.

+ a lover of the good (Titus 1:8). He desires to do what is right, beneficial, and good; above all, he desires to do the will of God in every area.

. . . in One's Family Life

If the leader is married, his family life must be exemplary. The leader must be:

+ "the husband of one wife" (1 Timothy 3:2; Titus 1:6). Literally, this phrase means a "one-woman man." In other words, he is faithful to his wife in affection and action.

+ a good manager of his own household (1 Timothy 3:4; Titus 1:6). This man leads his own family in such a way that his family respects his authority as leader of the household. His leadership is expressed with dignity, not domination, and his children are believers. They are "not accused of dissipation or rebellion" (Titus 1:6). He has passed his values on to his children.

. . . in One's Spiritual Life

In his spiritual life, the leader must be:

+ "devout" (Titus 1:8). This term means holy, "pious, pleasing to God."[7] He is separated from sin.

+ "holding fast the faithful word" (Titus 1:9). Literally, he stays faithful to biblical teaching, living what he teaches, and being stable in his faith.

+ "not a new convert" (1 Timothy 3:6). He is a mature believer, not a new Christian. Thus he has demonstrated spiritual depth and stability over a period of time.

> *Integrity . . . is the willingness to do what is right even when no one is looking. It is the "moral compass" — the inner voice; the voice of self-control; the basis for the trust imperative in today's military.*
> *United States Air Force*
> *Core Values*

. . . in One's Relationships

In his personal relationships, he must be:

+ one who has a good reputation outside the church (1 Timothy 3:7). Those outside the church speak well of him; they respect his integrity and character.

+ "respectable" (1 Timothy 3:2). He is orderly in the fulfillment of all duties. His life is disciplined, well ordered, and worthy of emulation.

. . . in One's Ministry

In his ministry the leader must be:

+ "hospitable" (1 Timothy 3:2; Titus 1:8). Literally, this person is characterized by "loving strangers"[8] and being hospitable. He makes a point of having others in his home and is willing to share his blessings with others.

+ "able to teach" (1 Timothy 3:2). He is able to discern the truth of Scripture by study and able to communicate the truth effectively to others.

CHARACTER QUALITIES COUNT

Notice that most of the qualifications of elders have to do with character qualities, not ministry skills or spiritual gifts. This is critical, because the elders must provide an example of spiritual maturity for the church (1 Peter 5:3). While this is especially true of the elders, it is also true of other church leaders, no matter what level of leadership they provide.

The elders, or leaders, who function together in any part of the church ministry must also work together closely. Any selfishness, manipulation, or contentiousness will not only make it difficult to work together with the other elders but will also damage the church.

Since elders must determine the will of God for the church, any self-will, that is, inability of the elder to distinguish between his own will and God's will, makes it difficult for the group of elders to come to consensus. More than that, self-will inevitably causes disharmony among the elders—disharmony that will spread to the congregation.

PAUL AND THE ELDERS AT EPHESUS

Notice the depth of Paul's concern about the character and impact of church leaders upon believers in their congregations (Acts 20). When he met with the elders from Ephesus, men with whom he had spent three years in intensely personal ministry, he gave them a strong warning. Read Acts 20:17–38, focusing on verses 28–30. Then think through the following questions:

Who made these men elders (overseers)?

_____

What is their primary function? Explain in detail.

_____

_____

_____

_____

How would you describe what the apostle Paul is concerned about in verse 30? Who are these men?

_____

_____

_____

_____

And what is it they are doing that is causing problems?

_____

_____

_____

_____

> *Nearly all men can stand adversity, but if you want to test a man's character, give him power.*
> Abraham Lincoln

125

What do you think is the motivation behind their actions?

_____

_____

_____

It may be that Paul wrote his first epistle to Timothy, calling on the young pastor to remain in Ephesus to deal with exactly the kind of problems about which he had warned the Ephesian elders (in Acts 20:30). Evidently some of the elders of the church in Ephesus had begun to act selfishly in creating followings for themselves by propagating false teaching (see 1 Timothy 1:3,4). Among the important things Paul says in 1 Timothy is that the character of a leader is so important that, for the health of the church, leaders must be carefully evaluated by the standards of character, which he lists for them in 1 Timothy 3.

Look back over the list of qualifications. Identify two that you feel need the most improvement in your own life.

(1) _____

(2) _____

Now, think of two specific things you can do to grow in each area.

(1a) _____

_____

_____

(1b) _____

_____

_____

(2a) _____

_____

_____

(2b) _____

_____

_____

When will you start?

_____

_____

_____

Another helpful way of thinking through the character qualities of a church leader is to think of the impact of each quality on a leadership team (a board of elders or the worship team, for example). Evaluate the importance of each quality by completing the chart "The Personal Life of the Church Leader."

THE PERSONAL LIFE OF THE CHURCH LEADER

The leader is to be **above reproach** in the qualities listed below.	What does this quality contribute to a leadership team?	What would the effect be if a church leader did not have this quality?
In his **PERSONAL LIFE** the church leader must be:		
1. Temperate		
2. Prudent		
3. Not addicted to wine		
4. Not pugnacious		
5. Gentle		
6. Uncontentious		
7. Not self-willed		
8. Free from the love of money		
9. Just		
10. A lover of the good		

In his **FAMILY LIFE** the church leader must be:		
11. The husband of one wife		
12. A good manager of his own household		
In his **SPIRITUAL LIFE** the church leader must be:		
13. Devout		
14. Holding fast the faithful word		
15. Not a new convert		
In his **INTERPERSONAL LIFE** the church leader must be:		
16. One of good reputation outside the church		
17. Respectable		
In his **MINISTRY** the church leader must be:		
18. Hospitable		
19. Able to teach		

SEVEN IMPLICATIONS FROM THE SCRIPTURES

The following implications can be drawn from the qualifications mentioned in the 1 Timothy 3 and Titus 1 passages above:

1. If an elder has a contentious spirit, the people who follow him will inevitably become contentious—regardless of how greatly gifted and skilled the elder may be as a leader.

2. If an elder is not hospitable, over time the people will learn to be aloof, unfriendly, and cold.

3. If an elder loves money, he will subtly use the people and work for his own ends, and the people will tend to become lovers of money also. He will lead the

church to put emphasis on the wrong things—material things and the trappings of success—and those who are wealthy will have too much influence in the church.

4. If an elder is not just and devout, he will be unable to rightly discern critical issues and problems, causing the people to become unjust by growing insensitive to the truth.

5. If an elder is not sensible, balanced, and self-controlled, his judgments will be characterized by disorganization, aimlessness, and ugly extremes—as will be the tendency of the judgments of the entire congregation.

6. If an elder is not a faithful, one-woman husband, he will ultimately encourage others to be unfaithful.

7. If an elder does not faithfully hold to the Word, the people will not. Such an elder will be unable to guide the church through the fierce storms of satanic error and selfish deception.

All of this means that issues of character are the core issues of leadership. For no matter how gifted a leader may be, the extent of his character flaws will ultimately limit his effectiveness.

CHARACTER ISSUES TODAY

1. What are the character issues facing Christian leaders right now?
   a. List as many of those issues as you can.

_____
_____
_____
_____
_____
_____
_____
_____
_____

_____
_____
_____

> *Leaders in an organization need to impose on themselves that congruence between deeds and words, between behavior and professed beliefs and values, that we call "personal integrity."*
>
> Peter F. Drucker
> *Drucker Management*

b. Which of the issues above challenge you the most? Why?

_____
_____
_____

2. What are the cultural forces in present society that encourage character problems among Christian leaders?

_____
_____
_____

   a. Which are most difficult to deal with? Why?

_____
_____
_____

   b. What biblical principles would help church leaders deal with these cultural pressures?

_____
_____
_____

3. Can you list a Christian leader who has provided a good model for you in dealing with a character issue? Who?

_____
_____

   a. What was inspiring about his conduct?

_____
_____
_____

   b. Why did he have the spiritual strength to handle the character issue in a godly way? What were the critical elements which were responsible for his successful handling of the character issue?

> *Fame is a vapor, popularity an accident, riches take wing, and only character endures.*
>
> *Horace Greeley*

_____
_____
_____

Notes

1. Ralph Earle, "1 Timothy," *The Expositor's Bible Commentary,* F. E. Gaebelein gen. ed., vol. 2 (Grand Rapids, Mich.: Zondervan, 1978), 364.

2. *The New International Dictionary of New Testament Theology,* Colin Brown, ed. (Grand Rapids: Zondervan, 1975), 515.

3. Walter Bauer, W. F. Arndt, and F. W. Gingrich, *A Greek-English Lexicon of the New Testament and Other Early Christian Literature,* 2nd ed. (Chicago: Univ. of Chicago, 1957), 634.

4. Ibid., 675.

5. Earle, "1 Timothy," 365.

6. Bauer, Arndt, and Gingrich, *A Greek-English Lexicon,* 120.

7. Ibid., 589.

8. Earle, "1 Timothy," 364.

CHARACTER

T E N

FLAWS, STRATEGIES, AND CHARACTER DEVELOPMENT

UNTIL NOW WE HAVE BEEN FOCUSING UPON the positive aspects of our identity as Christians (chapter 4). We have looked at the unique strengths of our temperaments (chapter 5). We have also focused upon ways in which God has gifted us and the special abilities He has built into our lives (chapter 6). In our Life Stories we have seen how God has used the experiences of life to equip us to be leaders and develop our dependence upon Him.

All of this is very positive. But there is also a less positive side of each of us. The unwelcome truth is that while we are greatly gifted with many strengths, each of us is also dangerously flawed. Our characters are not all finished gold, for all of us are still under construction. Our gifts and strengths have corresponding weaknesses and limitations. And our responses to the experiences of life have not always been to grow closer to God. Sometimes we have developed sinful, protective strategies to stay safe and successful in the midst of life's uncertainties and difficulties.

THE BIG PICTURE

There are four aspects to our identity that we need to be aware of: our strengths, weaknesses, limitations, and flaws.

1. Strengths

Our strengths are God-given capabilities that allow us to make a unique and significant contribution to His purpose in the world. Ideally this is done through serving Him and others.

Our strengths may be found in the possession of certain spiritual gifts or natural talents. They may also be acquired competencies, things we have worked on to develop proficiency. For example, a person may have the gift of teaching. Or he may have the gift of exhortation and worked diligently to develop a skill in teaching. He may have a natural talent of speaking or expressing himself well. God brings all of these things together to enable the person to have a maximum impact. Of course, natural talents and spiritual gifts can also be used simply for personal reasons. But this was not their God-given purpose.

2. Weaknesses

Our weaknesses are capabilities we possess that for some reason are dormant. They are perhaps unrealized spiritual gifts or undeveloped natural talents. Given the proper development and nourishment, weaknesses can be turned into strengths.

A person may have the gift of teaching without ever having done anything to develop it. Perhaps he does not know how to study and therefore has a debilitating fear of being unprepared. With the proper training and development, his gift of teaching could become powerfully effective.

3. Limitations

Our limitations are simply those capabilities that we lack. They are measured by spiritual gifts God has *not* given us or natural talents which we do not possess. No matter how hard we try or how diligently we work, there are some things we will simply never do well.

While all believers must do things at which they are not gifted, individually we will never experience the same joy or satisfaction or level of contribution as others who are gifted in those things. For example, we are all called to give, but the believer with the gift of giving will experience a greater impact and satisfaction than those without the gift.

For some of us, taking voice lessons and practicing diligently may develop a better singing voice, but it will never rise to the level of one who has a natural talent in voice.

> *Leaders either shed light or cast a shadow on everything they do. The more conscious the self-awareness, the more light leaders bring. The more limited the self-understanding, the more shadows leaders cast.*
>
> Kevin Cashman
> *Leadership From the Inside Out*

4. Flaws

Our flaws are cracks in our character. Such character faults are much more serious than limitations. Limitations will prevent a person from being outstanding in a certain area. But flaws, if they are not properly dealt with, will derail one's entire life or ministry no matter how gifted or successful it may be.

Character flaws generally work secretly at the core of our being, creating weak spots. They can be covered up or managed until the stresses of life or ministry touch that weak spot so strongly that it collapses into some kind of moral failure. The failure may be large and public, an affair for example, or small and easily overlooked, like a reluctance to take a risk for fear of failure.

All of us have flaws; that is part of being human. Flaws are also part of God's process of maturing us. We should deal with our flaws, for these character issues contain the seeds of the destruction of our effectiveness as church leaders.

THE BASIC APPROACH

Stated simply, the basic approach to take in dealing with our strengths, weaknesses, limitations, and flaws is:

1. Focus on your strengths. Develop your strengths, refine them, express them, spend most of your time using your strengths. It is in the areas of your strengths that you will make the greatest contribution and receive the greatest satisfaction.

2. Work on your weaknesses. Improve in your areas of weakness. Do not give primary emphasis to this, but do what you must to grow in your areas of weakness.

3. Enlist staff to help compensate for your own limitations. Find someone to help do the things you will never do well. Learn to empower others to focus in areas of their giftedness.

4. Expose and deal with your flaws. For your personal growth and long-term ministry effectiveness, you must identify your character flaws and deal with them. Otherwise your effectiveness will always be in jeopardy.

HOW OUR FLAWS DEVELOP

Our character flaws have a three-level natural development (see figure 6).

Figure 6
HOW FLAWS DEVELOP

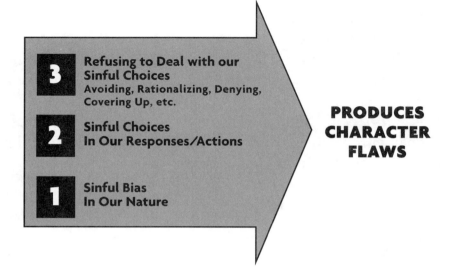

3 Refusing to Deal with our Sinful Choices
Avoiding, Rationalizing, Denying, Covering Up, etc.

2 Sinful Choices In Our Responses/Actions

1 Sinful Bias In Our Nature

PRODUCES CHARACTER FLAWS

1 On the lower level, we are all born with a sinful bias to our human natures. Because of Adam's rebellion against God, his sin has infected all mankind (Romans 5:19). That means we come into the world with a built-in warp in our character. We have a propensity toward sinful solutions to our life issues.

This sinful bias is so much a part of our nature that we hardly recognize it. In fact, it is buried so deep within us that the unbelieving world asserts that we are all born good, and it is only our environment that corrupts us. Jeremiah reminds us that: "The heart is more deceitful than all else and is desperately sick; who can understand it?" (Jeremiah 17:9).

The Scripture refers to the sinful aspect of our human nature as the "flesh." Notice the things the Scripture says about the flesh:

Matthew 26:41_____

John 6:63 _____

Romans 6:19 _____

Romans 8:8 _____

Romans 8:13 _____

Galatians 5:19–21 (What does the flesh produce in us?)_____

_____

How do the deeds of the flesh relate to the qualifications of an elder (see chapter 9 and 1 Timothy 3:1–7)? _____

_____

_____

_____

2 The middle level of the development of character flaws is created by our sinful response to various life issues. Most often it is a response to difficult or painful experiences.

For example, sometimes when a person grows up in a home with rigidly high standards, his response is·that he feels that he must always perform exceptionally well to be acceptable to other people. While this response may not seem that bad, it still represents the person's commitment to control his life circumstances so that he can find satisfaction apart from trusting in God. In other cases, the flesh responds to difficult situations by producing less acceptable kinds of character failures, including

+ the need to always be right,
+ a need to always be in control,
+ an inordinate need for attention, approval, appreciation,
+ a need to be needed,
+ workaholism, the feeling of never doing enough,
+ the feeling of never being good enough,
+ using other people for personal gain,
+ unwillingness to take a risk,
+ unwillingness to taking a stand on issues for fear of rejection,
+ divisiveness, and
+ being cold, aloof, distant (a preemptive strike against the fear of being rejected).

3 These wrong choices, bad as they are, could be dealt with by an honest admission and confession of them as sin. At that point they would be a relatively normal, though regrettable, human failure. What turns them into character flaws is the third level, when we refuse to deal with either the sinful choices or the underlying reasons behind them.

Avoiding, rationalizing, minimizing, denying, covering up, and shifting blame to someone or something else are all well-used strategies for refusing to deal with our own personal issues. Do this long enough, and dangerous cracks open up in our character.

Such flaws will destroy a leader and demolish his ministry. Furthermore, they will cripple the church. The solution is to become aware of them and deal with them before they can cause the destruction that Satan desires.

HOW YOU USE YOUR TEMPERAMENT TO TRY AND MAKE LIFE WORK FOR YOU

The various temperament types have characteristic ways of dealing with difficult or painful situations. Each of these strategies is a way to make life work apart from trusting in God to provide what you need to survive the situation and handle it constructively.

RESPONDING ACCORDING TO TEMPERAMENT

TEMPERAMENT TYPE	D	I	S	C
SEDUCTION Because of your temperament, you are tempted to be a:	**Workaholic** (Quantity)	**Charmer**	**Nice Guy**	**Workaholic** (Quality)
CONFRONTATION Your temperament naturally uses this confrontation style:	**Intimidation**	**Loud and Quick**	**Retreat and Destroy** (Attack others secretly to protect yourself)	**Major in the Minors** (Overwhelm with Minutia)
WITHDRAWAL Your temperament leads you to use this strategy to withdraw from others:	**Stress Out** (Brood)	**Chill Out** (Put on a happy face)	**Check Out** (Emotionally disengage)	**Hide Out** (Avoid contact, focus on work)

A PERSONAL ASSESSMENT

Take some time now to think through your own life to be reminded of your strengths, weaknesses, and limitations and become aware of your flaws.

Strengths

1. *Consider your temperament.*
   a. What is your temperament blend?

   _____

   _____

b. What are the strengths of this blend?

_____

_____

2. Consider your spiritual gifts. What are they?

_____

_____

_____

3. Consider your natural abilities. What natural abilities have you noticed in yourself? What have others noticed about you?

_____

_____

4. Consider your developed competencies. What skills or abilities have you worked hard to develop?

_____

_____

Weaknesses

1. Your temperament blend also has some weaknesses.
   a. What are they?

_____

_____

   b. Where have you seen these temperament weaknesses in your experience?

_____

_____

2. Your spiritual gifts also may have some weaknesses associated with them.
   a. What are they in your gift mix?

_____

_____

   b. Where have you seen these weaknesses occur in your experience?

_____

_____

Limitations

1. *Your own temperament poses limitations.*
   a. *Look at the temperaments (in chapter 5) that do not describe you. What are you not suited by your temperament to do?*

   _____

   _____

   _____

   b. *Have you had difficulty in relating to people or responsibilities because you do not have the strengths of these other temperaments? In what circumstances did this occur?*

   _____

   _____

   _____

2. *Your lack of certain spiritual gifts poses limitations.*
   a. *Note just a few of the spiritual gifts that you do not possess.*

   _____

   _____

   _____

   b. *Have you ever struggled trying to exhibit some of these gifts and not been successful?*

   _____

   _____

   c. *In what circumstances have you ever wished for a spiritual gift you do not possess?*

   _____

   _____

3. *Your lack of certain natural abilities poses limitations. What natural abilities have you longed for without receiving? Or what natural abilities have you sought without success?*

   _____

   _____

   Other believers have these abilities. This is an opportunity for you to function together as the body of Christ is intended to function.

Flaws

1. *On the lowest level, flaws develop by our sinful bias. Consider the personal expressions of your sinful nature.*

   a. *What basic aspects of the flesh do you struggle with most?*

   _____

   _____

   b. *Where do these tend to show up in your life or leadership relationships?*

   _____

   _____

   _____

2. *On the third level (see figure 6), character flaws thrive as we refuse to deal with our sinful choices or motives. Consider how you may be using defenses against life experiences.*

   a. *Look back over your Life Story Charts and Worksheets. Notice especially difficult or painful times in your life. As a result of those experiences, how did you attempt to protect yourself from such painful experiences in the future?*

   _____

   _____

   _____

   _____

   b. *Do you have a sense of developing unhealthy patterns of relating as a result of these experiences? Explain.*

   _____

   _____

   _____

   _____

FOUR STEPS TO DEALING WITH FLAWS

Here are four steps to dealing with flaws in your life:

1. Identify them.

   ✦ Recognize them before they occur; that's half the battle.

   ✦ Since they often grow out of our unhealthy responses to painful situations, develop the courage to revisit those situations in order to change our ways of handling them.

✦ Learn to be ruthlessly honest with yourself so you can recognize when you are denying or rationalizing or shifting blame to someone else in order to protect yourself.

2. Take them to the Lord.

✦ Honestly acknowledge them as sin.

✦ Thank Him that His blood covers them all.

✦ Ask for His strength to break the pattern when they occur.

3. Be alert to them.

✦ Identify "trigger" situations in which they commonly occur.

✦ Seek God's help and strength in those situations.

4. Get into an accountability relationship.

✦ Develop a few relationships in which there is a high trust level so that you can reveal your struggle without fear of rejection.

✦ Commit in these relationships to hold each other accountable for specific issues and to support each other in dealing with them.

E L E V E N

RELATIONSHIPS IN THE LEADER'S FAMILY

THE TIME SPENT IN KNOWING YOURSELF BETTER, knowing your gifts and abilities, and seeing how God has prepared and equipped you to lead is intended to help you become a more effective leader. It is not meant to produce self-centered leadership. Biblical leadership always exists to accomplish a purpose beyond the leader. And the accomplishment of this purpose involves leaders and followers working in relationship with each other. Understanding yourself more deeply enables you to relate more authentically and constructively to other people.

Part of that is accomplished by your interaction with your family. They have great insights into who you are. Equally important, you can learn the roles of leading and serving in your family. We will look at both later. First, let's look at the relationship between Jesus and His group of followers, the twelve disciples.

JESUS AND THE DISCIPLES (JOHN 13–16)

One of the best examples of the importance of relationship between a leader and followers is found in the relationship between Jesus and His disciples. In earlier chapters we have noticed the time Jesus and the Twelve spent together, the joint activities they engaged in, and the times of rest and relaxation or prayer together. But the quality of relationship that Jesus created between them is probably best seen in the passages that describe His last hours of intimate conversation with them before the Cross (John 13–16).

Read through the four chapters of the gospel of John and make some notes about the leader-follower relationship that Jesus created between Himself and His followers. Do this section by section and record your observations in the space provided below.

After making some observations about the leader-follower relationship, try to summarize some principles of relationship from each passage.

John 13:1–20: Washing the Disciples Feet

Observations:

_____

_____

_____

_____

Principles:

_____

_____

John 13:21–30: The Betrayal

Observations:

_____

_____

_____

_____

Principles:

_____

_____

John 13:31–38: The New Commandment

Observations:

_____

_____

_____

_____

Principles:

_____

_____

John 14:1–31: Hope for the Future

Observations:

_____

_____

_____

_____

Principles:

_____

_____

John 15:1–8: The Vine and the Branches

Observations:

_____

_____

_____

_____

Principles:

_____

_____

John 15:9–27: "I Have Called You Friends"

Observations:

_____

_____

_____

_____

Principles:

_____

_____

John 16:1–24: Kept from Stumbling

Observations:

_____

_____

_____

_____

Principles:

_____

_____

John 16:25–33: "In Me You May Have Peace"

Observations:

_____

_____

_____

_____

Principles:

_____

_____

THE STARTING POINT FOR CHURCH LEADERSHIP: FAMILY RELATIONSHIPS

Your ability to lead in the church will depend largely upon your ability to relate to people in ways that encourage (not command) their following. Interestingly enough, the Scriptures indicate that there is one set of relationships that provides a litmus test for the ability to lead the church well: the relationships in your immediate family, with your spouse and children (1 Timothy 3:4–5).

Leadership in the family is a challenging yet realistic training ground for leadership in the church. Family leadership requires one to truly lead by example, for in no other leadership situation is the character and consistency of the leader more visible to the followers. (See 1 Peter 5:3 for the requirement that elders lead by example.) Therefore, if a man cannot lead his wife and children successfully, how can he be expected to lead in the church? In both situations, the transparency and integrity of the leader is essential.

This does not mean that a church leader must be married and have a family. Paul himself was not married, and while he normally had a more itinerant ministry, he led the churches in Antioch and Ephesus for multiyear periods. However, without the family experience as a reference, an unmarried person must be given enough time for his other relationships to show the character of his leadership before being taken into the leadership structure of the church.

The Scripture contains similar family and relational requirements for women who have a leadership role in the church, leading ministry to other women (1 Timothy 3:11; Titus 2:3–5). The important element in all these situations is that leadership is tested in family and other relational settings before the person is brought into the leadership of the church.

Now is a good time to review the quality of those relationships, for because of our unconscious commitment to internal consistency, you will most likely lead others the same general way you lead in your family.

FOR HUSBANDS AND WIVES

Read Ephesians 5:25–6:4 and answer the questions below. Husbands should answer questions 1–5; wives should answer 6–8. Talk them over with your spouse to see if she or he agrees.

1. *If you are a husband, to what extent would your wife say that you love her like Christ loves the church (5:25–27)? What concrete things have you done recently that demonstrate such love?*

    _____
    _____
    _____
    _____

2. a. *To what degree would your wife say that she knows and understands what you are thinking?*

    _____

    b. *To what degree do you share your inner feelings with your wife?*

    _____

    c. *Would she agree with your assessment? Why or why not?*

    _____

d. To what degree does your wife feel that she is understood and listened to by you?

_____

e. To what degree do your children feel understood and listened to?

_____

3. a. To what degree does your wife feel encouraged and empowered to be who God has gifted her to be? (cf. Ephesians 5:28–29)

_____

b. Does your involvement in her life make her feel lifted or held back? Why?

_____
_____
_____

4. a. Spend some time this week talking together about the values you share for your family life. What things are most important to you?

_____
_____
_____
_____
_____

b. Are you spending your time in ways which support these values?

_____

c. What changes need to be made in your family life?

_____
_____
_____
_____

5. a. How would you evaluate your performance in providing godly leadership to your family? (Circle one)

Outstanding   Very Good   Average   Not So Good   Failing

b. *In what areas do you need to improve?*

_____

_____

_____

_____

c. *What is the single most important thing you could do to improve your leadership in your family?*

_____

d. *What is keeping you from doing it now?*

_____

6. a. *If you are a wife, to what extent would your husband say that you show him respect? (In Ephesians 5:33, Paul uses the term "respect" as another way of saying "submit to.")*

_____

b. *What concrete things have you done recently to show him respect?*

_____

_____

_____

7. a. *To what degree does your husband feel that he is understood and listened to by you?*

_____

b. *To what degree do your children feel understood and listened to?*

_____

8. *Discuss with your husband your thoughts to his responses to the questions in 4 above.*

T W E L V E

✦

RELATIONSHIPS IN THE CHURCH

ALL LEADERSHIP IS A FUNCTION OF THE interaction between the three elements of any leadership act: the leader, the followers, and the specific situation in which they interact. The situation brings the need for leadership and the specific conditions in which leadership will be provided. The leader brings to the situation his knowledge, experience, reputation, power, and his own personal needs, desires, and aspirations. The followers bring their own set of desires, aspirations, and needs, along with their personal abilities, experience, knowledge, and expectations. In the end, the followers' willing involvement is necessary for the leadership to be successful.

All of this makes leadership a fairly complex intersection of relationships between the leader and followers. In fact, in the church, more than any other organization, the quality of relationships between leaders and followers is at the heart of successful leadership.

MOTIVATING FOLLOWERS IN THE CHURCH

In a business situation, a follower will put up with a lot of poor leadership because it is easier to bear the difficulty than to find a new job with the same pay and benefits. However, people in the church do not have the same external forces keeping them in the church. It is much easier to find a new church than to find a new job. So, when leadership is poor, people may simply move to another church. As we will discuss in a later chapter, followers have power also. It is the responsibility of church leaders to lead them to commit their power to the fulfillment of the church's mission.

Similarly, the willingness of followers to participate is much different in the church setting than at work. Leadership in a church situation depends much more on influence than control. In fact, the control option simply does not exist. There are too many other churches in which a person can serve, too many other options to spend one's time in a more satisfying way. As a consequence, the quality of relationship between leader and follower is a greater factor in church leadership than in other, more structured leadership situations.

THE IMPORTANCE OF RELATIONSHIPS

Leadership is not self-expression for its own sake; it's self-expression that makes a difference, that enriches the lives of others. Leadership does not exist in a vacuum—it always operates in a context, in relationships.

Kevin Cashman
Leadership from the Inside Out

Whether others in the church will follow our lead depends largely upon the quality of our relationship with them. Good leadership skills are very important, but none is so important as the ability to develop and nurture relationships. The pastor or elders may present the most wonderful vision for the church, but unless they can build the willing support required to implement the vision, the vision will remain only an abstract idea without ever becoming a reality.

Every leader must build the network of relationships needed to give life to a vision. After all, if the leader can realize a vision by himself, it is not much of a vision! Though it is not often said this way, a leader is dependent upon his followers.

THE KEY TO RELATIONSHIP QUALITY

All of us come to any relationship with a strong set of personal needs. Primary among them are the need to be loved or accepted and the need to feel significant. The need for acceptance is met when we feel loved and accepted for who we are, that is, unconditionally. When we feel truly loved, we feel secure, and we feel free to focus on others outside of ourselves. As long as we feel unloved and unaccepted, we will obsessively focus on ourselves and on relieving the pain that comes with feeling unaccepted.

The need for significance is satisfied when we sense that our lives have meaning, that we make an important contribution to something greater than ourselves, that it matters that we are alive. When we do not feel significant, we tend to act in ways that we think will give us the sense of significance that we desperately need.

These two needs are so powerful that they dominate everything we do. Sometimes people talk about the dominant role played by a person's self-image. But, in reality, self-image is largely the function of the two needs of acceptance and significance being met. If a person feels loved and significant, his self-image will most likely be very positive.

The importance of this is that a relationship in which a person is legitimately made to feel accepted and significant or appreciated will be a strong, healthy relationship. When a leader builds such a relationship with his followers, his leadership will likely be quite successful. As Myron Rush puts it,

> *The basic driving force of human behavior is the desire for acceptance, understanding, appreciation, and recognition. The need for significance is such a powerful aspect of our personality that it motivates us to identify with success and just as powerfully motivates us to avoid failure and conflict.*
> *Les Carter and Jim Underwood*
> *The Significance Principle*

Relationships evolve around personal needs. People need each other. No one is really self-sufficient. . . . Met needs build relationships. . . . Unmet needs erode and destroy relationships.[1]

There is ample biblical warrant for such an approach to leadership and relationships. It should be noted that no person can fully meet another person's need for acceptance or significance. Being perfectly loved and truly significant comes only through a trusting personal relationship with Jesus Christ. He alone loves us perfectly, a fact proved visibly by His willingness to leave heaven, live among us, and ultimately die in our place on the Cross (Romans 5:8). He did this while we were still living selfishly in rebellion against Him. And He alone gives us the opportunity to spend our lives in ministering to others in His name. Nothing else in human accomplishment will last forever.

THE GOAL OF LEADERSHIP IN THE CHURCH

Leadership in the church is a ministry to people. Legitimate leadership is never an exercise in self-promotion or the exercise of personal power for the sake of the leader. Church leadership must always act in fulfillment of biblical goals for ministry. Below are just three passages out of many that present goals for ministry. What is the goal in each case?

Colossians 1:9–12 _____

_____

_____

Colossians 1:28–29 _____

_____

_____

1 Timothy 1:5_____

_____

_____

Modern secular leadership theory has begun to recognize the need for a similar function of leadership. Writers speak in terms of "transformational leadership" in which the result of leadership is that the lives of those led are benefited in some way. They are enabled to grow as persons, or their lives are enriched in some positive way. In other words, things must be transformed for the better if leadership is to be judged as "good." Other writers speak about the kind of leadership that "adds value" to the organization and to those led.

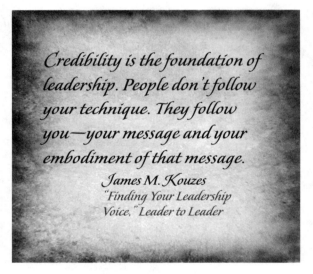

Credibility is the foundation of leadership. People don't follow your technique. They follow you—your message and your embodiment of that message.
James M. Kouzes
"Finding Your Leadership Voice," Leader to Leader

Biblical leadership is servant leadership. The leader acts for the benefit of others, not for some selfish benefit to himself, nor for the purpose of getting his way or seeing his own ideas adopted. The greater goal, in simple terms, is "What will help my church better fulfill its God-given purpose?" and "What will help the people I lead grow to be more like Christ?" How often have you seen a self-serving, insensitive leader push through his own agenda for the church while leaving a trail of wounded believers behind him?

Biblical leadership is quite different. There is an abiding concern for the quality of relationship between church leaders and followers. Read the following passages of Scripture, noting the relationship concepts that are presented. Then summarize any principles of relationship that you discern from each passage. Pay particular attention to the larger context of each passage.

Matthew 5:23–24 _____

_____
_____
_____
_____

Principles:_____

_____
_____
_____

Romans 12:3–5 _____

_____
_____
_____
_____

Principles:_____

_____
_____
_____

Romans 12:9–10 _____

_____
_____
_____
_____

Unfortunately, many driven leaders fail to comprehend how nothing is accomplished without engaging in relationships and appreciating the unique contribution of many, many people.

Kevin Cashman
Leadership from the Inside Out

Principles:_____

_____
_____
_____
_____

Romans 14:19–21 _____

_____

_____

_____

Principles: _____

_____

_____

_____

Romans 15:2–3 _____

_____

_____

_____

Principles: _____

_____

_____

_____

Galatians 5:26 _____

_____

_____

_____

Principles: _____

_____

_____

_____

Galatians 6:1–5 _____

_____

_____

_____

Principles:_____

_____

_____

_____

Philippians 2:3–4 _____

_____

_____

_____

Principles:_____

_____

_____

_____

IMPROVING YOUR LEADERSHIP RELATIONSHIPS

What can you do to improve your leadership relationships? Here are five key principles, including action steps (and responses) for the first three principles.

1. Understand yourself clearly.

First, take a personal inner inventory. Answer the following questions, which look at motivations and goals.

What are your motivations; why are you interested in leading?

_____

_____

_____

_____

_____

What are your personal goals in accepting leadership responsibility?

_____

_____

_____

_____

A reality check: To what extent are you leading out of a desire to meet your own needs?

_____
_____
_____
_____

Look back at chapter 5 under "Understanding Your Relational Style" and note the sentences you completed at the bottom of page 81. What did you learn about your relational style in that exercise?

_____
_____
_____

Second, learn to "hot check" your motives in the midst of a leadership situation; that is, be emotionally mature enough to step outside of yourself and analyze your emotions in the midst of an intense situation. If you simply act on the basis of your unevaluated emotions, you probably feel confident that you are right—but you may actually be rigidly unwilling to entertain the possibility that you might be wrong.

2. Learn to be sensitive to the needs of your followers.

Remember that every person in a church comes with a set of personal needs, with the core needs of acceptance and significance. These needs are at least in the background of every interaction the person has with you.

Often they are legitimately in the foreground. For example, when a person has a particular issue with which they need help, a struggling child or a dying parent, those needs are up front. But the core needs are there in every interaction. If you get exasperated and "blow off" a person's question, you have impacted that person's core need for acceptance and significance without even realizing it.

Will Schutz observed that people come into any relationship situation with three questions related to inclusion, control, and openness. The three questions they ask are:

> *Whether a leader is in a Christian or secular setting, there is no difference. Confidence must be earned every day; credibility is no longer automatic; and competence is an open question.*
> David McKenna
> *Power to Follow, Grace to Lead*

✦ Inclusion: Am I in or out?

✦ Control: Am I on top or on the bottom?

✦ Openness: Am I open or closed?[2]

To what extent do you think people come into the church situation with these questions in the back of their minds? Elaborate on your answer.

_____

_____

_____

_____

_____

_____

_____

_____

_____

_____

3. Learn to listen.

The ability to listen is crucial to solid relationships and a sense of trust. Begin by giving the other person your full attention. Look directly at the person. Be sure your body language—how you sit or stand—communicates interest. Do not interrupt the speaker.

Three other tips for listening well are:

✦ Withhold judgment until the person has finished speaking. Do not begin framing your answer while the person is still talking. Wait until you are certain you understand his position.

✦ Ask clarifying questions to be sure you understand. Ask if there is more they want to say.

✦ Resist the impulse to become defensive; learn to recognize defensive feelings within yourself.

> *Authentic listening . . . is about being generous—listening with a giving attitude that seeks to bring forth the contribution in someone versus listening with our limiting assessments, opinions, and judgments.*
> *Kevin Cashman*
> *Leadership from the Inside Out*

4. Learn how to express genuine approval and acceptance to others.

Every person wants to feel accepted and valued by those important to him or her.

As leaders, when we make people feel they're part of the team and express sincere appreciation for their efforts, they will be motivated to help further.

5. Learn how to handle difficult relationship issues.

Concerning this final step, note that Matthew 5:23–24 implies that even among people who are spiritual, there is the possibility of fractured relationships. We will deal with this issue in the later chapter on conflict resolution.

Notes

1. Myron D. Rush, *Richer Relationships* (Wheaton, Ill.: Victor, 1986), 15, 17, 19.
2. Will Schutz, *The Human Element* (San Francisco: Josey-Bass, 1994), 25ff.

T H I R T E E N

DEVELOPING VISION FOR YOUR LIFE

LEADERSHIP IS FUNDAMENTALLY DIFFERENT from management. Although the two are often confused, they have radically different purposes. The purpose of management is to make things run well or efficiently. Management sets up orderly procedures for getting things done. Leadership, on the other hand, determines what gets done. Leadership sets the direction, develops the strategies to get where it wants to go, and mobilizes the people and resources to get there.

In a sense, leadership is about chaos; management is about order. Leadership shakes things up by setting a new direction. Management attempts to smooth things out by creating orderly processes to reach the goals necessary to realize the vision. Both are necessary.

For example, leadership and management operated side by side in the life of Moses. Moses as a leader was given a mission from God to lead God's people out of Egypt (Exodus 3:10). As he took steps to accomplish this mission, he created chaos both for the Egyptians and for his own people. The Israelites were uprooted from their homes and way of life, which, though difficult, was also desirable enough that some weeks later they would look back on it with longing for what they were missing.

Some time later, Moses became overworked trying to judge all the disputes among the million or so people wandering in the Sinai desert. His father-in-law, Jethro, suggested a management structure involving

> *The single defining quality of leaders is the capacity to create and realize a vision.*
>
> *Warren Bennis*
> *On Becoming a Leader*

civilian judges. The structure made Moses more efficient and effective in carrying out change (Exodus 18:13–27).

Any leader must also do some management. But he must not be sidetracked from doing the things that leaders do. Being a leader in a local church is the same. Church leaders must perform some management duties, but they must manage without neglecting their leadership functions.

The primary function of leadership is direction setting, and the key to setting a direction is developing a vision for the future.

Today every leadership book, both secular and religious, recognizes the importance of vision as a function of leadership. Vision is defined in many different ways, but all of the definitions come down to the idea that vision is a mental picture of the future state of a person or an organization. George Barna defines vision for ministry in the following terms: "Vision for ministry is a clear mental image of a preferable future, imparted by God to His chosen servants, based upon an accurate understanding of God, self, and circumstances."[1]

Others use similar terms but qualify the definition more completely. In *Visionary Leadership*, Burt Nanus writes: "Quite simply, *a vision is a realistic, credible, attractive future for your organization*. It is your articulation of a destination toward which your organization should aim, a future that in important ways is better, more successful, or more desirable for your organization than is the present."[2]

Kouzes and Posner define vision simply as "an ideal and unique image of the future."[3]

> *While leaders come in every size, shape, and disposition—short, tall, neat, sloppy, young, old, male, and female—there is at least one ingredient that every leader shared: concern with a guiding purpose, an over-arching vision. They were more than goal directed, they were vision directed.*
>
> *Warren Bennis and Joan Goldsmith*
> *Learning to Lead*

Others describe a vision as "a waking dream," because a vision is a conscious dream of what the future could be like.

Why We Need Vision

A vision may be a personal vision describing your own future, or it may be a corporate vision that gives definition to what you believe God wants your church or ministry to be in the future. Either way, a clearly stated vision provides several benefits. Among them are the following:

1. It provides energy for fulfilling the church's mission. Vision is the spark that ignites excitement, the fuel that drives accomplishment.

2. It provides focus to the person's or the church's ministry.

Concerning focus and energy, a clear vision tends to unite people around common goals and generates energy toward accomplishing those goals. Such vision also focuses and energizes by (a) *concentrating one's attention directly on the needs of people* to whom God has called the minister, promoting a servant leadership, (b) *focusing our attention and effort on* what we or the church will be and do in *the future,* and (c) *emphasizing action toward the fulfilling of goals.* With a clear vision we can set right priorities and move beyond the press of daily demands in order to take steps to fulfill the vision.

Four other benefits derive from a clearly stated vision:

+ A vision *motivates us to accomplish* something of value. A vision gives the larger goal that infuses individual efforts with a higher value.

+ A vision *raises expectations and standards.* A vision sets high goals and calls us toward fulfilling those goals. High goals bring out the best in people.

+ A vision *gives hope.* It lets us see what the future could be like and how we can fit in to that new day.

+ A vision *enables us to be proactive* rather than *reactive.*

For these reasons, a sense of vision for the future is a powerful motivating force for our lives, both personally and organizationally. To deepen our understanding of the visioning process, let's look at the biblical account of Nehemiah.

LESSONS FROM THE LIFE OF NEHEMIAH

Read the account of the development of Nehemiah's vision to see what you can learn about the envisioning process in a person's life and ministry. The account is found in Nehemiah 1–2.

What was the historical situation in Nehemiah's day?

_____

_____

_____

What was the "triggering event" in Nehemiah's life?

_____

_____

_____

_____

What was it that grieved Nehemiah? Why?

_____

_____

_____

_____

What was the process followed in the development of Nehemiah's vision?

_____

_____

_____

_____

_____

_____

_____

How would you state his vision clearly and succinctly?

_____

_____

_____

_____

The personal vision that Nehemiah developed became a guiding light for his life. In this sense, his envisioned future began to determine his current actions as he focused his energies on the fulfillment of the vision.

There are other examples of personal visions in the Scriptures. Consider the apostle Paul.

What statement of personal vision is included in Paul's words in Romans 15:20–21?

_____

_____

_____

_____

A PERSONAL VISION STATEMENT

Before working on an organizational vision statement for your church or ministry, it will be helpful to clarify your own sense of vision for your personal life. To do this, work through the following questions and exercises.

1. *Look over your Life Story (chapter 3) and write in the space below the themes that are evident in God's working in your life. What patterns are there in God's preparation of you? What repeated experiences did He allow in your life to teach you special lessons?*

_____

_____

_____

_____

_____

_____

2. *Now review the strengths of your temperament pattern (chapter 5) and your spiritual gifts and natural strengths (chapter 6). Summarize them in the space below:*

Temperament: _____

_____

_____

Spiritual Gifts: _____

_____

_____

Natural Abilities: _____

_____

_____

3. *a. In what ways have you seen God use your gifts and strengths and abilities so that you have felt a deep sense of fulfillment and enjoyment? What has God uniquely equipped you to accomplish?*

_____

_____

_____

3. b. *Have these experiences generated any sense of direction for your life? Have they helped to clarify what you would like to give your life to? If so, what?*

_____

_____

_____

_____

4. *What are the values that are most important to you? (Review chapter 7.)*

_____

_____

_____

_____

_____

5. *What needs in the world most motivate you to be involved? What is there in the field of your life that you believe something absolutely must be done about?*

_____

_____

_____

_____

_____

6. *Another way of thinking about your life vision is found in answering the question: "How do you want your obituary to read? If you could write an obituary that would describe the impact of your life, what would you want it to say?"*

_____

_____

_____

_____

_____

_____

7. *What dream or cause are you willing to die for?*

_____

_____

_____

_____

8. *Take some undisturbed time to reflect on your answers to the above questions, an hour or two in the evening perhaps, after everyone else has gone to bed. Ask God to bring to mind the themes or issues that you feel most passionately about. Jot down your thoughts so you won't forget them. Then begin to formulate short, clear statements that describe your dreams for various aspects of your life. "When I come to the end of my life, here's what I would most like to see accomplished in . . .*

✦ my personal life:

_____
_____
_____
_____
_____
_____

✦ my relationship with the Lord:

_____
_____
_____
_____
_____
_____

✦ my relationship with my spouse:

_____
_____
_____
_____
_____
_____

✦ my children:

_____
_____
_____
_____
_____
_____

CHARTING A BOLD COURSE

_____
_____
_____
_____
_____
_____

✦ my ministry:

_____
_____
_____
_____
_____

When you have completed these statements, look back over them. Carry on a conversation with God about them, asking whether the statements truly reflect the dreams that are most important to you. Ask Him also to help you bring these dreams to reality.

Notes

1. George Barna, *Without a Vision, the People Perish* (Glendale, Calif.: Barna Research Group, 1991), 29. The visioning process in chapters 13 and 14 is developed from the concepts introduced in Barna's book.

2. Burt Nanus, *Visionary Leadership* (San Francisco: Jossey-Bass, 1992), 8.

3. James M. Kouzes and Barry Z. Posner, *The Leadership Challenge*, 2nd ed. (San Francisco: Jossey-Bass, 1987), 85.

168

F O U R T E E N

DEVELOPING VISION FOR YOUR MINISTRY

THE FIRST CRITICAL DECISION A CHURCH (or ministry) has to make is the *decision of authority*. The authority decision is the process of answering the question, Who will the church serve?

There are several possible answers to this question. It could serve its pastor or elders or some other powerful person or group in the church. On the other hand, it could serve the culture in which it exists, doing only those things that the culture deems acceptable. Ideally, a church will recognize Christ as the head of the church (Ephesians 1:22) and consciously decide to serve Him. This brings with it a decision to allow the Word of God to be the instrument of God's authority over the church.

The second critical decision is the *direction decision*. In its various elements, this decision boils down to the question, "What does the One we serve want us to accomplish for Him?" This is the question of *purpose* and *vision*. God has a purpose for His church. He also has a vision for each local church, a vision that describes how He wants that church to fulfill the purpose in its unique sphere of influence.

It is the responsibility of the leaders of a

> *The first responsibility of a leader is to see a vision which addresses the question, "What are we trying to do for whom?" As simple as it may sound, the answer to this strategic question will make the difference between excellence and mediocrity in an organization, as well as in its leadership.*
>
> David L. McKenna
> Power to Follow, Grace to Lead

local church to discover God's direction for their church and express it in a statement of vision which can be communicated to the church body. The benefits of communicating a clear, compelling vision are enormous in the life of a church. Review the list of benefits given in the previous chapter (under "Why We Need Vision"); the same benefits accrue to a church or ministry organization.

VISION DURING *ALL* STAGES OF THE LIFE OF A CHURCH

The essence of leadership is stimulating and guiding the process of change through the development and communication of vision. This is particularly important when a church is founded. A vision spells out clearly why the church is being planted and what the church will accomplish. The vision will generate the enormous energy needed to start a church, and it will unite people to pool their resources and efforts together to see the church thrive. The excitement felt by those who come together to plant a church is fueled by the vision of what God will accomplish through the church. They can "see" the future in their thinking, and they find excitement and energy in being part of that future.

Significantly, a clear vision is also essential throughout the life of a church, though often in different ways. At critical points in the life of an existing church or organization the vision must be renewed. All churches reach plateaus in energy or effectiveness at various times. Some of the times are predictable, for example, the plateau that occurs at an attendance of approximately two hundred. Other plateaus are connected with internal problems or changes in the economic or cultural conditions in the society in which the church exists.

After some time on the plateau (see figure 7, "Stages in the Life of a Church and Vision"), if the vision is not renewed, the church will begin to decline. Ongoing visioning is therefore essential to the continued growth of the church or ministry. Circumstances and culture are continually changing. The vision that was effective at one point in the church's history may not fit the current situation. If the vision is not renewed, the church becomes out of touch with the new circumstances and changing needs of people. The only stability possible is stability in the midst of continuous change. Life is never static.

VISION AS A UNIFYING FACTOR IN THE CHURCH

A church ministry is made up of several different ministries to various segments of the congregation. Each of these ministries is important in itself, but something must pull them all together. A clear and compelling vision for the whole church should be used to bring all the various ministries into alignment.

Figure 7

STAGES IN THE LIFE OF A CHURCH AND VISION

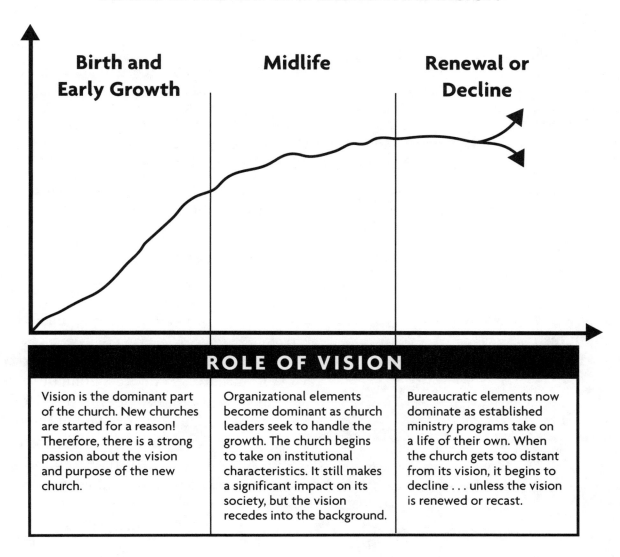

Birth and Early Growth	Midlife	Renewal or Decline
ROLE OF VISION		
Vision is the dominant part of the church. New churches are started for a reason! Therefore, there is a strong passion about the vision and purpose of the new church.	Organizational elements become dominant as church leaders seek to handle the growth. The church begins to take on institutional characteristics. It still makes a significant impact on its society, but the vision recedes into the background.	Bureaucratic elements now dominate as established ministry programs take on a life of their own. When the church gets too distant from its vision, it begins to decline . . . unless the vision is renewed or recast.

Without a unifying force, it is natural for each ministry leader to feel like his or her ministry is the most important. And each leader will have some level of vision of where he wants the ministry to go. Without proper leadership in the church, it will be easy for the various ministries to head in their own directions, with disastrous effects on church unity.

CHARACTERISTICS OF AN EFFECTIVE VISION

A good vision has several important characteristics:

1. It's anchored in reality. A good vision must be connected to the real needs of people; it cannot be the private dream of one person.
2. It offers a view of the future that is desirable enough to inspire people.
3. It becomes the property of the church or ministry group. The leaders and the people of the church must come to own the vision as their own.
4. A vision statement is unique to a given church. It describes how that particular church will fulfill the mission Christ gave to His church.

A COMPLEX PROCESS

The development of vision involves a complex but exciting process. The five steps followed by Nehemiah can be generalized to guide the process of developing a vision for ministry.

First, Nehemiah spent significant time in prayer and reading the Scriptures to discern God's desire. Second, Nehemiah understood his own strengths and abilities. He had access to the king and the respect of the king. He had personal wealth and connection with those in Jerusalem. Third, he had an understanding of the strengths, abilities, and limitations of the people and resources he had available upon his return to Jerusalem. Fifth, he distilled in his thinking a vision of what Jerusalem could be with its walls rebuilt physically and its people rebuilt spiritually. He expressed this vision to the leaders in Jerusalem (Nehemiah 2:17–18).

The five steps Nehemiah used are valid today. However, note that these "steps" should not be thought of as discrete actions, each of which must be fully completed before going on to the next step. There is value in working

> *We mustn't pretend that vision is always the result of an orderly process. It often entails a messy, introspective process difficult to explain even by the person who conceives the vision. Vision formation is not a task for those who shun complexity or who are uncomfortable with ambiguity.*
>
> *Burt Nanus*
> *Visionary Leadership*

on them in the order they are given, but they should be continuously evaluated and updated. Certainly it is important to continue to pray and study God's Word throughout the entire visioning process. The development of vision requires analytical skills, imagination, judgment, and the willingness to ask and answer lots of questions. As Nanus has noted, the process is complex, and at times it involves introspection.

STEPS IN THE PROCESS

Read through the following steps in the visioning process. Think specifically about your church or ministry as you do so.

Step 1: Gain a Clearer Understanding of God's Desires

A fuller understanding of God's purposes for the universal church will help you understand His purposes and desires for your church. Here are five ways to get a better understanding:

1. Pray individually and corporately. Ask God to give direction and understanding as you work through the process of developing a vision for your church. Ask Him to reveal to you what He desires your church to do. Practice fasting or other spiritual disciplines you desire as part of this process.

2. Study the Scriptures. Study passages of Scripture that reveal God's purpose for the church. Study the key passages in the New Testament on the church. Be sure to include the following passages (there may be other applicable passages which you may want to study also):

   + Matthew 28:19–20
   + John 3:16
   + 2 Corinthians 5:18–21
   + Ephesians 1:3–12
   + Ephesians 4:11–16
   + 1 Timothy 2:4

3. Synthesize the teaching of these passages and write a mission statement for your church. Remember, a mission statement differs from a vision statement.

Mission	Vision
The broad purpose for which *any* church exists	A specific, detailed statement of the unique way that the mission will be accomplished by *your* church
Timeless, biblical	Local, situational
Fits all churches	Fits your church uniquely
Concerned with *purpose*	Concerned with *direction*

Take some time now and try to write a mission/purpose statement for your church or ministry.

_____

_____

_____

_____

_____

_____

_____

_____

_____

_____

_____

_____

_____

_____

_____

_____

_____

_____

_____

_____

_____

WHEN YOU HAVE COMPLETED YOUR STATEMENT, GO TO THE NEXT PAGE.

A SAMPLE MISSION STATEMENT:

The Mission of the church is

to

penetrate the world

(Matthew 28:19)

and

make disciples

(Matthew 28:19)

by

leading people to faith in Christ

(Matthew 28:19; 2 Corinthians 5:18–21)

and

building them up to maturity

(Matthew 28:19)

through

the ministry of all the gifted members of the church

(Ephesians 4:11–16)

to the glory of God

(1 Corinthians 10:31).

Notice that the above mission statement could apply to any church. It is timeless and biblical. This is a biblical statement of what God wants churches to do. Your mission statement should look reasonably similar to this one. The vision statement which you write later in the process will describe the unique way your church or ministry will fulfill this general mission statement. Other churches will have different vision statements as God leads them to accomplish His mission in situations different from yours. Each is valid as long as it is within the scriptural bounds of Christ's mission for the church.

4. Reflect. Spend some time quietly reflecting on what you have learned about God's plan for the church. Ask God to direct your thoughts and sharpen your understanding. Throughout the process of developing the vision, ask yourself the question: "What is the most effective thing our church can do to accomplish this mission in our area of ministry?"

5. Seek wise counsel. Talk with mature believers in other churches about the mission and vision of their church. Seek out wise members of your own congregation and ask for their counsel about the vision of your church.

Step 2: Understand Your Unique Strengths, Abilities, and Limitations

Next, understand your own strengths and abilities as a leader, as well as your limitations. If you are the pastor of the church or leader of a ministry team, much of the responsibility for determining and fulfilling the vision rests upon you. This is why God made you a leader! The vision will be closely connected to who you are as a person; it will be influenced by how God is working in your life, by your own gifts, abilities, strengths, and weaknesses.

Since you will be the primary (though not the only) person articulating the vision and leading people in its fulfillment, you should experience a strong commitment to and identification with the vision. If your personal vision is in harmony with the church's vision, and your gifts, abilities, and interests fit with the church's vision, you will experience a strong sense of fulfillment and satisfaction as you work toward the fulfillment of the vision. However, if your personal vision diverges from the church's vision, or your gifts, abilities, and interests do not fit the church's vision, you will experience significant dissatisfaction and stress. Under these conditions, many pastors find it necessary to move to another ministry, and many other ministry leaders do the same or drop out of the church altogether.

It is therefore essential that in the process of developing the vision for your church or ministry you carefully consider your own interests, gifts and abilities, strengths and weaknesses. The following questions are a beginning:

1. Your motivations
    + Why are you in the ministry?
    + What are your personal goals in ministry?
    + Whose glory are you seeking?
    + What are you seeking to accomplish in the visioning process?
    + In what situations do you feel most "alive?"
2. Your values
    + Which attributes of character are most important to you?
    + What are the core values that are the foundation for your personal life and ministry?
    + What are you the most passionate about? What do you dream about doing or accomplishing? What do you feel that you *must* do?

3. Your strengths, gifts, and abilities

+ What are your spiritual gifts? How have you been able to use these gifts in ministry?

+ What special abilities do you have? Artistic? Music? Preaching? Writing? Others?

+ In what activities or ministry have you experienced the most satisfaction? What do you enjoy doing?

+ In what activities or ministries have you been most successful?

+ For what ministry activities do you consistently receive positive feedback from others?

4. Your weaknesses

+ In what activities or ministry responsibilities do you feel that you struggle?

+ What things do you dislike doing? What things do you avoid?

+ For what aspects of ministry do you not feel suited?

5. Your spiritual life

+ How intimate and satisfying is your relationship with God now?

+ Where in your life have you recently experienced God's faithfulness?

+ Is your relationship with God growing in a positive direction? Why or why not?

+ What sins do you struggle with the most?

+ What things do you try to hide from God, others, or even yourself? What would happen if you were honest with God about these things?

+ How deeply can you trust in the goodness of God? Why?

+ Which passages of Scripture impact your life most strongly?

6. Your ministry

+ How satisfied are you with the direction of your ministry at the current time? Why?

+ How would you like to see your ministry develop in the next five years?

+ How comfortable are you in your relationships with others? Is it easy for you to talk with others about personal issues in their lives? Why or why not?

+ On what aspects of your ministry do you spend most of your time?

+ What ministry goals do you have for the next year?

+ How will you recognize success in your ministry?

Remember, these questions are only a beginning. You should continuously be evaluating your own life and ministry. This is an essential element in the process of growth.

Step 3: Understand Your Congregation's Unique Strengths, Abilities, and Limitations

Once you recognize your strengths, abilities, and limitations, do the same evaluation for your congregation. Every congregation has important resources available to fulfill the vision. These resources include people, finances, facilities, skills, information, history, and level of community respect. No two congregations are the same; the particular grouping of resources makes a congregation unique and equips it for a specific role in the building of the kingdom of God.

Seeking answers to the following questions will help clarify the unique contribution your congregation is equipped to make.

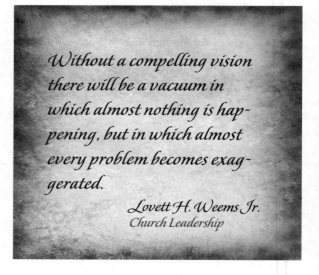

Without a compelling vision there will be a vacuum in which almost nothing is happening, but in which almost every problem becomes exaggerated.

Lovett H. Weems Jr.
Church Leadership

1. What are the characteristics of our congregation?
    + What is the membership? the attendance?
    + What is the age profile of the members?
    + What are the trends in membership and attendance?
    + Are we growing? Holding steady? Declining?

2. What are the special strengths of our congregation? What things are we pleased with? What do we do well? Where have we seen God's blessing?

3. What are the weaknesses of our congregation? What things do we wish were different? What do we not do well?

4. What are the interests and needs of our members?
    + What are their dreams, their hopes?
    + What are their particular stresses?
    + What are the program needs?
    + What are the facility needs?
    + What are the staffing needs?

5. What is the history of our congregation?

+ How was it founded?

+ Who were the early leaders? What were they like? What stories are popular about them?

+ What were the major ministry accomplishments of the church?

+ Construct a "Life Story" of the church. Adapt the Life Story process used in Chapter 3 to graphically depict the historical development of the church. What does this tell you about the church? What approaches to ministry characterize the church? What crises influenced the church's thinking?

6. What is the current situation of our congregation? One writer has defined vision in this way: "Vision is the ability to see the opportunities within your current circumstances."[1]

+ What are the current strengths and weaknesses of our leadership team?

+ What is the atmosphere of the congregation? Warm? Cold? Cooperative? Lively? Dull? Uncertain? Powerful? Dynamic?

+ What unique opportunities exist in this congregation?

+ What unique strengths do we have to build on?

7. What special influences are there in our congregation?

+ What effect have recent cultural, social, or political changes had on our church?

+ What new opportunities for ministry exist in our area?

+ What "holdovers" from earlier days are now nonfunctional and need to be eliminated? (They may be attitudes, beliefs, and/or programs.)

Step 4: Develop an Awareness of the Needs of the People Outside.

Part of the visionary process is to determine the needs of people you will minister to outside the church. What are the special needs of the community?

> *Leadership can never be understood apart from mission and vision. Leadership never exists for itself or for the glorification or even personal development of the leader. Leadership exists to make possible a preferred future (vision) for the people involved, which reflects the heart of the mission.*
> *Lovett H. Weems Jr.*
> *Church Leadership*

Their needs will become "doorways to ministry." People may think they are not interested in "church," but they are interested in satisfying their felt needs. For example, hurting marriages become an opportunity to minister to people who might not otherwise come to church.

As you consider the particular community in which the congregation exists, answer these questions:

+ What is the community like?
+ What are the needs of people?
+ What pressures are they facing? Where are people hurting?
+ What are their values, beliefs, and attitudes? Which values control their lifestyles?
+ What cultural changes are happening in the society?
+ Understand the competing distractions of your cultural context: television, sleeping late, tiredness, desire to raise economic level, need to provide for family, sports, hobbies, family time, etc. Find out why people choose other options over involvement in the church.
+ What are their dreams?
+ Who are the people who have no relationship with the church?
+ What special people groups exist in the area of your church? For example, are there apartment dwellers, university students and faculty, business people, poor people, or prisoners?

If possible, do a community survey, asking people for their perception of personal and community needs. Ask what ministries they would be interested in at the church. Respond to such surveys by changing programs or other aspects of church life; this will strengthen the church's service to the community.

Beyond your immediate community, remember to consider the world at large. Scripture indicates that the mission of the church extends to the entire world (Matthew 28:18–20). Determine (1) the needs and the hopes of people and (2) specific regions where the gospel has not penetrated. Then answer this question: "What can our church do to carry out its ministry with greater effectiveness to those beyond our community and state?"

As you consider the needs of people around you, you should begin to sense a commitment to minister to a certain group of people. Perhaps the group is defined geographically, or perhaps by age or occupation. As you consider the various possibilities along with the strengths and weaknesses of your church, God will lead you to focus on a particular group of people. Try to identify this group clearly.

Remember that no one church can meet all the needs that exist in society. Focus on those people and needs God has equipped your church to minister to and trust Him to raise another church (or churches) to minister to the others.

Step 5: Write a Vision Statement for Your Church.

The climax of the visionary process is writing and refining the vision statement. The process of developing a vision for your church involves bringing together (in the context of prayer, Bible study, and honest seeking of the Lord's direction) the biblical mandates that define the timeless mission of the church and the situational realities in which your church exists and ministers. The visioning process is described in the chart below.

Figure 8
THE VISIONING PROCESS

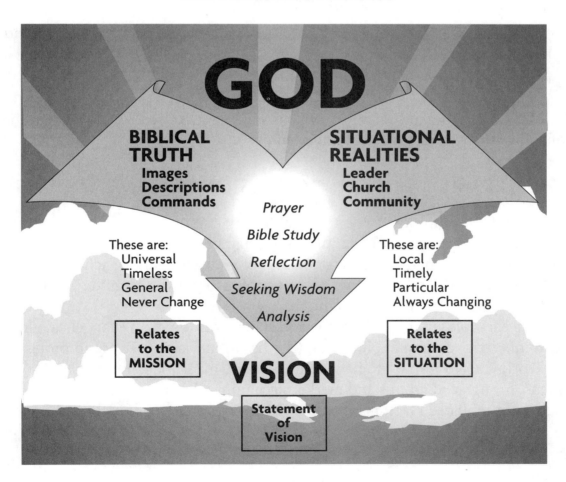

Adapted from Lloyd M. Perry and Norman Shawchuck, *Revitalizing the 20th Century Church* (Chicago: Moody, 1982), 22.

Now, write out your vision statement as concisely as possible. As you do, be sure your vision statement:

1. identifies the people you believe God is calling you to minister to, your target audience.
2. clarifies the purpose of your ministry to these people. What are you planning to accomplish with them?
3. identifies the elements which make your church distinct from others in the area. What characteristics or purposes set your church apart from others?

Make the statement as clear and compelling as possible. Be sure it:

1. uses clear, graphic language that communicates positive images.
2. uses terms that are active rather than passive.
3. paints an attractive mental picture that people will want to identify with and become a part of.
4. is concise, preferably less than fifty words.

Be ready to rewrite and refine the vision statement, as you would any important document, so the wording is clear and specific.

EXAMPLES OF CHURCH VISION STATEMENTS

Once you have completed your statement, review those of other churches; they may suggest modifications (either additions or change of focus). Avoid the temptation to simply adopt the general mission statement of your favorite megachurch, however. Let God use His Word and the needs of the people around you to guide you into crafting a vision statement that fits your church.

Here are examples of three church vision statements. First, an evangelical, denominational, inner-city church in New York City has as its vision: "To equip professionals in New York City to impact their web of relationships, focusing on reaching non-Christians through cell groups and marketplace ministries that address urban needs."[2]

The community need factors influencing this vision statement include:

✦ This church is in a crowded urban area surrounded by apartment buildings, office buildings, and small businesses.

+ Their target audience is the business and professional people who live around them.

+ They realize these people are hungry for the kind of interpersonal relationships cell groups provide.

+ Such people will be initially attracted through some need or connection in their business or professional life. The church has "marketplace ministries" aimed at the needs of businesspeople.

+ *The Doorway to Ministry:* A strongly felt need for relationships and the stresses and demands of business and professional life.

Second, an independent evangelical church located near a major university with 35,000 students has the vision: "To reach the university community in our city through lifestyle evangelism and build them up through involvement with the Word of God and personal relationships with church families so that they will be equipped for ministry throughout the world."

The community need factors influencing this vision statement include:

+ This church is located in a residential area where several thousand students live. The entire city is not very large, so the church is within easy driving distance from most of the city. Therefore, the primary target audience is university students and faculty.

+ They realize that students are at a critical point in their lives, living away from home for the first time and experimenting with more adult relationships. Most are not from Christian homes, and many are not from healthy families.

+ Most students have not had much teaching from the Scriptures.

+ Students from this respected university obtain jobs all around the world.

+ *The Doorway to Ministry:* Students are at a natural point of interest because of the transitions in their lives; they are highly group oriented.

Third, an evangelical church being planted in a middle-class community has the vision: "To plant a culturally relevant church with a Great Commission vision, which empowers people to communicate Christ through significant relationships with God, other believers, and nonbelievers. The dream is to raise up a community church which reaches out to an unchurched community."

The community need factors influencing this vision statement include:

+ This church is being planted in a residential community near a large metropolitan area. Most people who live in this community work in the nearby city.

+ They generally feel somewhat disconnected from other people and experience a desire for supportive relationships with others.
+ The church desires to build a sense of community (that is, the feeling of togetherness which comes from quality relationships) through which it can reach out to others in the area to offer them significant relationships with God and with others.
+ *The Doorway to Ministry:* The felt need for relationships is a determining factor in the lives of the people of this community.

TESTING YOUR VISION STATEMENT

Before your committee or leaders adopt a vision statement, be sure you can answer each of the following questions with a yes:

1. Does your vision statement clearly identify the target group that you desire to minister to?
2. Does your vision statement give a clear direction for the future of your ministry?
3. Does the statement provide a positive view of the future for the church such that people will want to be involved?
4. Does the statement give guidance regarding appropriate strategies to employ to fulfill the vision?
5. Is the vision statement specific enough to enable the church to make clear choices between several good ministry options?
6. Does the vision statement show your church to be unique and different enough to distinguish it from other churches?

Now, take some time and write a second draft of a vision statement for your church or ministry.

_____
_____
_____
_____
_____

Notes
1. Rick Warren, *The Purpose-Driven Church* (Grand Rapids: Zondervan, 1995), 28.
2. George Barna, *Without a Vision, the People Perish* (Glendale, Calif.: Barna Research Group, 1991), 133–34.

F I F T E E N

✦

COMMUNICATING YOUR VISION

CREATING A VISION FOR THE FUTURE MAY BE the most important single thing a leader does. But, as Oswald Sanders notes, unless the leader can communicate the vision effectively to others, the vision will have no impact, and the leader will have few followers.

One of the measures of leadership is the ability to secure a strong enough commitment to the vision that people are willing to give their time, energy, and resources to see the vision realized. Remember, the church is a volunteer organization. A few people will work sacrificially in the church because of their own commitment or need. But to get the kind of broad support needed to fuel an effective church ministry, the leader will have to present a compelling vision for the future. The first part of that process is to develop the vision; the second is to communicate the vision powerfully.

> *The man who possesses vision must do something about it or he will remain a visionary, not a leader.*
> *J. Oswald Sanders*
> *Spiritual Leadership*

THE VISION MUST BE ARTICULATED CLEARLY

It goes almost without saying that you, the leader, must clearly understand the vision yourself before you can communicate it clearly to others. Almost, but not quite—there are too many examples of cloud-obscured visions that progressed little further than a halfhearted presentation at a congregational meeting. "The key to gaining widespread commitment to a new vision, therefore, is to present the vision in such a way that people will want to participate and will freely choose to do so," Burt Nanus wrote in *Visionary Leadership*.[1]

Work through your vision statement thoroughly until it is precise and crystal clear. Review the process in the previous lesson, especially step 5, point 4 (page 182).

Notice how clearly Jesus expressed His vision. What is the key statement in each instance?

Luke 19:10 _____

_____

John 3:17 _____

_____

John 10:9–10 _____

_____

How would you state His vision?

_____
_____
_____
_____

For a different illustration, read the account of Nehemiah communicating his vision to the leaders of Jerusalem (Nehemiah 2:11–20). Concentrate on verses 17 and 18.

What are your observations about Nehemiah's communication process?

_____
_____
_____
_____
_____

THE VISION MUST BE COMMUNICATED PERSONALLY

Not only must you understand the vision clearly before you can articulate it clearly; you must also "own" it personally before it can be "owned" by others in your church or ministry. You can communicate with integrity and conviction only what you are personally committed to. Kouzes and Posner note that "the greatest inhibitor to enlisting others in a common vision is a lack of personal conviction."[2] If the vision has not made a visible difference in your own life, how can you reasonably expect it to make a difference in the lives of others? Your own demonstrated commitment to the vision is the most powerful communication of the value of the vision.

In short, the vision must be lived by you before others will give their lives to it. Your actions toward fulfilling the vision will be the strongest enticement for others to commit themselves to it.

> *The most universal fact emerging from our research was this: It is the personal vision of the pastor or church planter, and his or her ability to communicate that vision, that drives churches to growth.*
> Robert E. Logan
> *Beyond Church Growth*

Go back to Nehemiah's vision. How had he demonstrated his commitment to the vision before he asked for their commitment?

_____

_____

_____

How did Jesus show His commitment to the vision He presented?

_____

_____

_____

The leader must be a living illustration of commitment to the vision. You will show the reality and depth of your commitment to the vision in many obvious and not-so-obvious ways:

✦ *What you say about the vision and your involvement in it.* Part of this is what you say formally when you present the vision. But even more will be communicated by how you talk about the vision

> *Leaders live the vision by making all their actions and behaviors consistent with it and by creating a sense of urgency and passion for its attainment.*
> Burt Nanus
> *Visionary Leadership*

informally. If it has really captured your commitment, you will talk about it all the time in one way or another. You will connect other topics to their effect on the vision. You will talk about it with emotion and passion, as one talks about something which is of supreme importance to him.

+ *What you give your time to.* How you spend your time communicates loudly what is really important to you . . . no matter what you *say* is important.

+ *Whom you associate with.* If the vision is a high priority in your life, you will be spending a great amount of your time with those who share the vision and are involved in the fulfillment of the vision.

+ *How you use your resources.* How you spend your money, use your home, and share your possessions will show clearly what is important to you.

Think back over the vision you developed for your family or your ministry in previous lessons. List below some specific things you can do that will demonstrate your own personal commitment to the vision.

_____

_____

_____

_____

_____

THE VISION MUST BE COMMUNICATED CAREFULLY

Plan carefully how you will articulate the vision. The vision for your ministry should be written in as comprehensive a fashion as possible. But tell it very simply.

As you communicate your vision, tell stories, for stories are one of the primary ways to communicate vision. Jesus was a master at storytelling. His stories are called parables. In them, He took some of the most common, well-known experiences of life and used them to communicate truth powerfully. He talked about lost sheep, lost coins, a prodigal child, and many other things people were familiar with.

Carefully choose images that convey the idea contained in your vision. For example, a church can be an army, a community, a hospital, a flock, etc. Each image communicates different ideas to listeners. What ideas do you want to convey? The vision must be made "real" to others. Images and stories help to do this.

Again, think of your family vision or ministry vision. What stories or images could you use to communicate this vision?

_____

_____

_____

_____

_____

Help those you lead understand the vision. Here are four ways to do that:

1. Discuss the vision with as many people as possible.
2. Present the vision as an expression of the mission that God has given to the church or your family.
3. Refer to the vision statement when planning the ministry of the church.
4. Develop a summary document that presents the core elements of the vision clearly. For a family vision, this could be a chart easily understood by the children. For a church or ministry it would likely be a longer document that spelled out the essential elements of the vision.

To be effective, the vision must be shared and it must be omnipresent. That is, people must see it all the time and be continually reminded of it. The tidal wave of information that engulfs people today will sweep away your vision if it is not continually brought into their consciousness.

THE VISION MUST BE COMMUNICATED POWERFULLY

The most clearly articulated vision will produce only passing interest unless it somehow connects with the personal dreams people have for their own lives. Few will be attracted to a vision that they perceive to be only about the leader's dreams.

Look for ways to reach people at the heart level, the level of their primary personal needs; then show how those needs will be met by involvement in fulfilling the vision. What really excites people, what really provides meaning and generates enthusiasm, are these value-related opportunities:

+ A chance to be tested, to make it on one's own
+ A chance to take part in a social experiment
+ A chance to do something well
+ A chance to do something good

✦ A chance to change the way things are [3]

Each one of us wants a chance to be involved in accomplishing something greater than we are—something that has great value. A worthwhile vision will help us have that sense of significance.

THE VISION MUST BE COMMUNICATED FREQUENTLY

For a vision to be successful, it must capture the attention of those needed to fulfill it. Part of capturing attention is the dramatic presentation of the vision. Another part is repetition and variety. The vision must be continuously before the people. It must be seen from as many perspectives as possible, and it must become an integral part of the thinking of the group.

No matter how grand the dream of the individual visionary, if others do not see in it the possibility of realizing their own hopes and desires, they will not follow. It is incumbent upon the leader to show others how they too will be served by the long-term vision of the future.

James M. Kouzes and
Barry Z. Posner
The Leadership Challenge

An Exercise: Imagine that you are the leader of your church's missions ministry. You and the leadership team have developed a vision describing what you want to see God do through that ministry. The vision statement you have decided upon is:

Going Forth With the Gospel in Prayer and in Person: The members of our church will be contributing to God's missionary program by regular prayer, supporting missionaries, taking short-term missionary opportunities outside the United States, and sending out vocational missionaries.

Now, think about the possibilities for ways you could communicate this vision to the people of your church. List as many specific possibilities as you can think of in ten minutes. (You may use a separate piece of paper if you wish.)

_____

_____

_____

_____

_____

_____
_____
_____
_____
_____
_____
_____
_____
_____
_____

THE TRUST FACTOR

The character issues we discussed in earlier sections of this course play an important role in communicating your vision. Any vision worth presenting will call for significant personal sacrifice. No matter how skillful your communication, if your audience does not have a high level of trust in you, they will not commit themselves to the vision you present nor make the sacrifice required to fulfill the vision. Leadership skills always occur in a character context.

FINAL THOUGHTS

If you are communicating a ministry vision, enlist some people personally, then use them to help promote the vision to others.

Use the vision statement when planning; use it when evaluating; use it when motivating. In other words, use it wherever possible. Not only will this give the vision more exposure; it will also demonstrate its importance as it is used to measure performance and allocate resources.

Notes

1. Burt Nanus, *Visionary Leadership* (San Francisco, Calif.: Jossey-Bass, 1992), 135.
2. James M. Kouzes and Barry Z. Posner, *The Leadership Challenge* (San Francisco, Calif.: Jossey-Bass, 1987), 124.
3. David Berlew, "Leadership and Organizational Excitement," *Reflections* 2 (fall 2000), 20.

S I X T E E N

+

UNDERSTANDING YOUR CHURCH'S PURPOSE AND CULTURE

T HE CHURCH IS A DIVINELY ORDAINED INSTITUTION, but an individual congregation is made up of saved sinners who are all still in the process of becoming more like Christ. That single fact puts the torch to neatness.

As a leader in your church, you must have a clear understanding of the church and of your local congregation. Two perspectives must inform your understanding. The first is biblical; the second is cultural.

A BIBLICAL UNDERSTANDING OF THE CHURCH

In order to provide good leadership, a church leader must have a clear understanding of the biblical principles that guide the church. The Scriptures provide a historical account of the founding of the church and of the early years of its expansion into the rest of the world. The Scriptures also provide instructions and principles applicable to the church in any age or location. Take some time now to review some of the Scripture passages relating to the following important guiding principles of the church.

1. The *Purpose* of the Church

Read the following passages and note the purposes indicated for the church:

+ Matthew 28:19–20 _____

✦ Acts 1:8 _____

✦ 1 Corinthians 14:26 _____

✦ 2 Corinthians 5:17–21 _____

✦ Ephesians 3:21 _____

✦ Ephesians 4:13–16 _____

✦ Philippians 1:9–11_____

✦ Colossians 1:28 _____

✦ Hebrews 13:15–16_____

Although there are many more passages that could be listed, these cover the main areas of purpose. Now, summarize the purpose of the church.

_____
_____
_____
_____

In chapter 14, "Developing Vision for Your Ministry," you wrote a purpose statement for your church. How does your summary above compare? What areas of difference are there?

_____
_____

2. The *Organization* of the Church

God designed the church to have a simple but effective organization at the local church level.

Who is the head of the church (Ephesians 1:22; 5:23)?

_____

What are some of the practical implications of this?

_____
_____
_____
_____

What is the role of the human leaders of the local church?

a. The elders and pastors
Acts 20:28_____
Acts 20:17, 35_____
1 Thessalonians 5:12_____
1 Timothy 3:2 _____
1 Timothy 5:17_____
Titus 1:9_____
1 Peter 5:2, 4_____
1 Peter 5:3_____

b. The deacons
Acts 6:1–7_____
1 Timothy 3:8–10, 12–13 _____

c. The women in leadership
1 Timothy 3:11_____
Titus 2:3–5_____

What is the general purpose of the human leaders of the church (Ephesians 4:11–16)?

_____
_____
_____

3. The *Practices* of the Church

The passage in Acts 2:42–47 gives a snapshot of early church life. Read the passage carefully.

Based on Acts 2:42–47, what were some of the activities the church engaged in when they met together?

_____
_____
_____
_____
_____

As we study church life in the New Testament, we need to note carefully which practices are prescribed for the church throughout the church age and which were culturally limited to the first century. This distinction involves the difference between "form" and "function." Biblical functions of the church are transcultural activities that every local church should do, no matter in what century or culture it exists. On the other hand, forms are the specific ways the functions are carried out in a given historical situation. Forms will differ from culture to culture.

For example, one biblical function is evangelism. All churches, whenever and wherever they exist, should be involved in evangelism. However, the evangelism function can be expressed in many different forms: preaching in the temple (in Peter's day), door-to-door evangelism, evangelistic services in the church, friendship evangelism, passing out tracts, mass meetings, etc.

Which of the activities mentioned in the Acts 2 passage above are functions?

_____

_____

_____

Which are forms?

_____

_____

_____

The basic principle to remember is this: Functions never change; forms should change as often as necessary to insure that they fulfill the function they are expressing.

A CULTURAL UNDERSTANDING OF THE CHURCH

It is important to note that every church creates its own unique culture as it develops. The role of that culture is far more powerful than most of us imagine, and church leaders who do not understand this powerful force will find themselves meeting resistance they do not understand. There is probably some reluctance to think of a church as developing an "organizational culture." After all, isn't the church an "organism," a living body, not merely an "organization"?

Actually, it is both. The reality is that any group of people who commit to meet and work together is, or becomes, organized in some fashion. Certainly the Scriptures call for some specific organizational elements in churches. The end result is that every church has its own distinctive way of seeing things, relating internally, and understanding the world around them.

"Culture" is really a set of basic assumptions and beliefs that are shared by the members of a church. These basic assumptions deal with how the members relate to each other and how they view the world around them. Edgar Schein formally defines group culture as "a pattern of shared basic assumptions that the group learned as it solved its problems of external adaptation and internal integration, that has worked well enough to be considered valid and, therefore, to be taught to new members as the correct way to perceive, think, and feel in relation to those problems."[1]

HOW A CHURCH CULTURE DEVELOPS

The culture of a church is "jump-started" at its founding. The founding pastor has a powerful influence on the church culture. It is the founding pastor, or perhaps founding leadership group, that sets out the guidelines for the church, and therefore establishes its culture. The early leader(s) of the church defines the way the church will relate inwardly to its members; he also defines how the church will understand and relate to the world around it. The founder usually sets the vision for the church and tells people (from the Scriptures, of course) how they are to function together, what the leadership structure will be, and how they are to view the world around them. Schein's observation (see right) is another warning about the dramatic importance of character issues in a leader.

At the beginning, these views may not be fully developed, but they become more clearly developed and more deeply held as time goes on. When an issue or a problem arises, someone (often the leader, especially in the early days) offers a solution. If the proposed solution solves the problem, then the next time a similar problem develops the same solution is used. Before long, that particular approach to solving the problem becomes accepted as "the right way to do things," or it becomes embedded in "the way we do things around here." After a while, it becomes so commonly accepted that people no longer think of it specifically; it is simply part of the fabric of church life.

Church culture is not specifically prescribed in the Scriptures, though many things

> *Leaders not only embed in their organizations what they intend consciously to get across, but they also convey their own inner conflicts and the inconsistencies in their own personal makeup.*
>
> *Edgar H. Schein*
> *Organizational Culture and Leadership*

are that ultimately make up the culture of the church. Scripture mandates worship, prayer, evangelism, discipleship, and pastoral care, for instance, and the approaches used by a particular church become part of that church's culture. Members use both Scripture and the heritage of the particular kind of church they form to create a church's culture

For example, there are some specific cultural elements associated with Bible churches, or Presbyterian churches, or Fellowship churches, or "seeker-friendly" churches. But the ingredients also include the views and experiences of the people, especially the leaders of the church, their shared experiences, and the characteristics of the society around them.

LEVELS OF CULTURE

Culture is like an iceberg; some elements of culture are visible above the surface, but lots more is hidden from view below the waterline. Figure 9, "Three Levels of Culture," shows the three levels, only one of which is visible to the congregation.

Figure 9
THREE LEVELS OF CULTURE

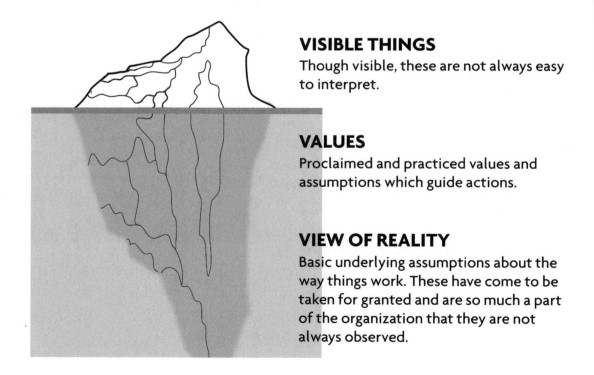

VISIBLE THINGS
Though visible, these are not always easy to interpret.

VALUES
Proclaimed and practiced values and assumptions which guide actions.

VIEW OF REALITY
Basic underlying assumptions about the way things work. These have come to be taken for granted and are so much a part of the organization that they are not always observed.

Level 1: The Visible Things

The "visible things" include a wide variety of physical things or visible patterns of relationships. All of these things communicate something about your church. Analyzing them will give you important insights into your church culture.

1. *What do the external buildings and grounds communicate about your church and the patterns of relationships?*

   _____

   _____

   _____

2. *What do the auditorium, office, classrooms, and meeting rooms say about your church? What "feel" do they give? (Note: Even the fact that you call it the "auditorium" or the "sanctuary" communicates different messages!)*

   _____

   _____

   _____

3. *What the allocation of space to various ministries communicate about your church and its values?*

   _____

   _____

   _____

4. *What do the location and neighborhood surroundings say about your church?*

   _____

   _____

   _____

5. *How do people dress when they come to the church services? What does this say about your congregation?*

   _____

   _____

   _____

6. *What is the atmosphere of the Sunday services?*

   _____

_____
_____

Who participates in worship?

_____
_____
_____

What style of music is used?

_____
_____
_____

7. *What do the written documents of the church communicate about your church? What "feel" do they give? Scan some of the literature available to all (weekly bulletin or newsletter, information brochures, ministry description pamphlets, etc.).*

_____
_____
_____
_____

8. *Get a copy of your church constitution and read it. What form of government does it prescribe? Who has the power in the church according to the constitution? Is there a difference in reality?*

_____
_____
_____
_____

9. *Find church literature relating to the vision of your church. How clear is the vision? Do people in the church know what the vision of the church is?*

_____
_____
_____
_____

10. *How do people in the congregation talk to each other? What language do they use? (Lots of Christian jargon? Personal? More impersonal?) What do they talk about most?*

_____
_____
_____
_____

11. *How is respect shown and value communicated to people in the church?*

_____
_____
_____
_____

12. *How do people associated with the church behave in the church services? during the week? How do they behave toward each other? toward outsiders?*

_____
_____
_____
_____

Level 2: The Values

Values describe the things that are most important to us. They determine the way we think things "ought to be." Values come in two distinct varieties: proclaimed and practiced. Proclaimed values are the values we say we hold. Practiced values are the values we actually live by.

For example, a deacon who is struggling in his marriage has stated that he believes divorce to be wrong and unbiblical. But he later divorces his wife and marries another woman. His proclaimed values are: "Divorce is wrong; Christians ought to remain together and work out their differences. God's power is sufficient to bring about change or the grace and strength to endure the situation." But his practiced values are: "I ought to be free to seek happiness with whoever I think will provide it for me; my personal feeling of happiness is more important than biblical commands. If working out the differences between us takes too long, I am justified in looking for someone else."

1. *Does your church have a published list of core values? If so, list some of the proclaimed values of your church and/or its leadership. If not, ask the pastor and some of the elders, then list them below:*

_____
_____
_____

201

2. *Now list some of the practiced values of your church or its leadership. (You will have to infer some of these from actions you have observed.)*

_____

_____

_____

_____

_____

_____

_____

Level 3: The View of Reality

Level 3 is the deepest level of culture and the most difficult to uncover. At this level reside the basic assumptions or beliefs about how the people of the church see reality. It relates significantly to how they view the society around them, in which they exist, both individually and together as a church. It also relates to how they view human nature (both of believers and unbelievers) and relationships.

Basic assumptions in these areas are in part passed down from others and in part developed through the church's struggle (as noted earlier) with its two primary problems:

1. When a church is founded, the initial leaders build their basic assumptions into the framework of the church. In this way, these basic assumptions are incorporated, often without critical examination, into the life of the church.

2. When confronted with a problem, church leaders look for a solution. When this solution to the problem works repeatedly, it comes to be understood as an expression of "the way things really are." The fact that there might have been other solutions is gradually forgotten, and the repeated solution begins to be taken for granted.

Over a period of time, these basic assumptions are so accepted that they "go underground." They are so implicit that they are not readily visible. They therefore become very difficult to confront or challenge. When they are made visible, they are difficult to change because they are such a part of the church that to challenge them is almost to challenge the church itself.

For example, an unstated basic assumption might be that mature Christians "have it all together and do not have serious problems because they trust God and live according to biblical principles." The effect on people in the church is that everyone puts on a good "front" when they come to church, and no one is very transparent with others for fear of being exposed as an immature (or "unspiritual") Christian.

This assumption is epidemic among Christian leaders, for church leaders are surely supposed to have it all together. That's why they are leaders, right? This assumption has a devastating effect upon both leaders and followers.

What might be some of the effects of such an assumption on church leaders or church people?

_____

_____

_____

_____

_____

_____

TWO CRITICAL PROBLEMS FOR SURVIVAL

Any church must solve two critical problems. Both are related to the survival of the church. The first is the problem of "How do we survive as a church in our external environment?" The second is the problem of "How do we have to relate to each other inside the church in order to accomplish our purpose and survive?"

The external problem relates to how the leaders and the church view the external environment. That is, they must answer the question, "What must we do to grow and conduct effective ministry in our current environment?" Churches often develop a unique culture as "teaching" churches, or "social" churches, or "Spirit-filled" churches, or "fellowship" churches depending upon their understanding of the Scriptures and the culture around them, as well as upon the leaders' own temperaments and personalities.

The external problem is complicated by the continually changing culture that surrounds the church. Clearly there are generational changes, but there are also social changes, ethnic changes, and economic changes, among others, in the area around the church. At the beginning of the twenty-first century the pace of change has accelerated to the point that a local church must continually sharpen its vision, reevaluate its culture, and focus its ministries in order to be able to minister effectively to a rapidly changing external culture. The days of lengthy ministry stability are gone.

The internal relationship problem revolves around what it will take to develop internal relationships that permit the group to survive by performing effectively and maintaining internal harmony. These issues have to do with who holds power in the church, how easily newcomers are incorporated into the body, what the criteria for acceptance are, and how relational problems are dealt with.

As a church grows, its leaders influence the development of a group culture. Solutions to the external and internal problems come to be shared and accepted by the entire group and are passed down to new members as the "right way" of thinking and acting. Before long they become submerged in "the way we do things here."[2]

SURVIVING IN THE EXTERNAL ENVIRONMENT

In order to survive in the external environment in which the church exists, the congregation must come to agreement on several types of issues. Among them are: (1) the church's mission and vision; (2) the strategies and goals to fulfill the mission; (3) the means used to reach the goals; (4) the proper measuring of its success in reaching the goals; and (5) making corrections when the goals are not met.

1. The Mission and Vision of the Church

A church must be able to build a shared understanding of its biblical mission and for the unique vision that will enable it to fulfill Christ's mission.

Like other organizations, churches seem to have multiple functions, which are sometimes in competition. For example, churches exist to worship God, to evangelize the world (or the part of it near the church), to build up believers to do the work of the ministry, to provide fellowship opportunities for members, to minister to the lost and hurting, etc. People also come to church for various other purposes: to have a group of friends in which they feel secure and accepted, to have a group for their teenage kids to belong to, to make social or business contacts, to learn about the Bible, to have an opportunity to exercise power over others, etc.

In the previous two lessons, you have thought about vision and communicating vision. In question 9 above, you looked at the documents which express the vision of your church. Now answer these questions:

1. How strong is the agreement on the vision in the congregation?

_____

_____

_____

_____

2. Are there subgroups in the congregation who disagree with the vision? If so, who are they, and what is their level of support in the congregation?

_____

_____

3. *Why do you think they are opposed to the vision of the church? Do they simply not under-stand it? Are they promoting a different vision? What could be done to gain their support for the vision?*

_____

_____

_____

_____

2. The Strategy and Goals to Fulfill the Vision

The church must also develop a functional agreement on the strategies and specific goals which will be used to fulfill the vision. Without this, there will be constant friction from people offering different strategies.

3. The Means Used to Reach the Goals

Congregations must also come to agreement on the means that will be used to accomplish the goals. One question of means has to do with staffing. For example, is the next person hired a youth pastor or an outreach pastor? There will certainly be a subgroup (usually of parents) that strongly favors hiring the youth pastor first. Others will want the outreach pastor position filled first.

Or, if part of the strategy of the church involves evangelism, what style of evangelism will be used? Door-to-door? Big event, mass evangelism? Friendship evangelism? Evangelistically oriented Sunday morning services?

4. How to Measure Success

There must be general agreement on the criteria used to measure the church's success at fulfilling its goals and realizing its vision. In other words, how will the church know when it is successful? What defines success? Is it growing attendance numbers? If so, what percentage growth defines success? Or perhaps it's personal growth. How can you measure personal growth? Here are two questions to help determine how your church measures success:

1. *What do you think is the measure of success used at your church?*

_____

_____

_____

2. *By what criteria do you evaluate your pastor or church staff? Are they aware of the criteria?*

_____

_____

_____

_____

5. How to Make Corrections

What will happen if the church's goals are not being met? There should be an understanding of the acceptable steps to be taken if goals are not met.

There are two possible solutions (sometimes used in combination). Please answer these two questions:

1. *Will you automatically see it as the pastor's fault, get rid of him, and find someone else you think can do the job? Why or why not?*

_____

_____

_____

2. *Will you rethink the strategy? Recalibrate the goals? What?*

_____

_____

_____

SURVIVING WITH INTERNAL HARMONY

Sometimes it is more difficult for a church to stay together internally than it is to successfully minister to those outside of the church. In order to function successfully together, the church must resolve at least the following internal issues: (1) how to speak the same language; (2) the price of belonging; (3) the means of gaining power in the church; (4) the expression of intimacy and friendship; (5) standards of conduct; (6) rules of engagement; and (7) inside stories.

1. Speaking the Same Language

Members of the church must be able to communicate with understanding. Christians use a lot of special language. Some of it is biblical and theological; some of it is simply part of Christian culture. For example, what does it mean when someone says, "John is spiritual"? or "Sally is committed"?

What are the common "Christianese" phrases used around your church?

_____

_____

_____

Is there general agreement on what these phrases signify? _____ Yes _____ No.

How does this language affect nonbelievers and visitors?

_____

_____

_____

2. The Price of Belonging

Requirements for being a church member differ from church to church; so does the atmosphere. The following questions help you explore the "price of belonging" at your church.

What are the criteria for official membership in the church? On what basis are people accepted or rejected? What requirements are placed on new members?

_____

_____

_____

What is the atmosphere of your new member classes? Warm and welcoming? Careful and evaluating?

_____

_____

_____

What must a person do to become accepted into the unofficial inner core of the church?

_____

_____

_____

3. Gaining Power and Status

Every church has a process or a set of rules which determines how a person gets, keeps, or loses power or status in the church.

What process does a person have to go through in your church to get into a position of power?

_____

_____

_____

Who are the most powerful people in your church? Rank them starting from the most powerful.

_____

_____

_____

Who is the "power broker" in your church—who does one have to be on the good side of in order to gain influence in your church?

_____

_____

_____

How long do people stay in power in your church? How long do elders continue to serve?

_____

_____

What causes people to lose power in your church?

_____

_____

_____

4. Acceptable Expressions of Intimacy and Friendship

There are rules that govern all relationships, especially relationships between the sexes, and the manner in which openness and intimacy are to be handled acceptably in the context of the life and work of the church.

How personally vulnerable are your church leaders willing to be with the congregation; that is, how much of themselves, their hopes, dreams, successes, failures, fears, and struggles are they willing to share publicly?

Pastoral Staff:

1	2	3	4	5	6	7	8	9	10

Closed/uptight   Somewhat open   Very open and vulnerable

Elders:

1	2	3	4	5	6	7	8	9	10

Closed/uptight   Somewhat open   Very open and vulnerable

Other Leaders:

1	2	3	4	5	6	7	8	9	10

Closed/uptight   Somewhat open   Very open and vulnerable

How personally vulnerable are those in the congregation willing to be with each other?

Congregation:

1	2	3	4	5	6	7	8	9	10

Closed/uptight   Somewhat open   Very open and vulnerable

How do men in the church express friendship with other men in the church?

_____

_____

_____

How do men and women express friendship in the church?

_____

_____

5. Standards of Conduct

Acceptable and unacceptable behavior is governed by criteria that determine what behavior gets rewarded, what gets punished, and, ultimately, what results in exclusion from the church.

What behavior is publicly praised, appreciated, or rewarded in your church? What do the pastor or elders praise publicly?

_____

_____

_____

What kinds of things would cause a person to be excluded from your church?

_____

_____

_____

6. Rules of Engagement

Churches have stated or unstated rules about how conflict is to be handled in the church. Some churches have an unwritten rule that no visible conflict should be allowed (believing that Christians don't have conflict). Other churches seem to thrive on loud, verbal disagreements. Because conflict is often so painful, there is a strong temptation to disallow conflict and act as though it does not exist.

How does your church handle conflict? What are the rules?

_____

_____

_____

What is expected of a person who disagrees with a major direction of the church? who disagrees with a decision of the elders? who disagrees with the pastor?

_____

_____

_____

7. Inside Stories

"Inside stories" about the church, especially about the early days of the church or crisis times in the church's history, give meaning to some critical events. Such stories give significant insight into the culture of the church. Culture is very hard to discern; therefore we need all the data we can get. Early incidents that are remembered in stories tend to be incidents that exert a powerful influence on the culture in later years.

What are some of the best stories still remembered and told about the early days of the church? What do they tell you about the church?

_____

_____

_____

_____

_____

_____

What are some of the often-told stories about how the church successfully surmounted past times of crisis?

_____

_____

_____

_____

FINAL NOTE: THE IMPORTANCE OF CULTURE

Understanding the culture of your church is a critical element of leadership. No matter how compelling your vision, if the culture of the church is not supportive of the vision, the vision will not become a reality. The leader's task is to build a culture that will enable the church to fulfill the vision.

Notes

1. Edgar H. Schein, *Organizational Culture and Leadership* (San Francisco: Jossey-Bass, 1991), 12. In this chapter, we have applied Schien's excellent analysis and categories to a church culture.
2. Lovett H. Weems, *Church Leadership* (Nashville: Abingdon, 1993), 99.

SKILLS

S E V E N T E E N

✦

PLANNING CHANGE TO FULFILL THE VISION

ALL CHANGE IS SCARY. MOST OF US, IF OFFERED a choice, would opt for long periods of stability. Unfortunately, those days are gone for good. In these first years of the twenty-first century, change is being forced on us at an overwhelming rate. Most of us can barely keep our heads above water.

Consider just one technological change. Forty years ago, engineers used slide rules to make their calculations. Most of today's engineering students have seen a slide rule only in a museum or in their father's memorabilia. We've gone from slide rules to handheld electronic calculators (early 1970s) to desktop computers today—desktops that share the stage with mobile laptop computers that have the computing capacity of earlier "supercomputers."

THE IMPACT OF CHANGE

Technology is driving massive cultural changes as well. For example, cellular phones allow us to keep in touch anywhere. But now we have to decide whether we want to be contacted anywhere, at any hour of the day.

Meanwhile, news reporting has accelerated from *Movietone News* showing newsreels of events that had taken place days or even weeks earlier to real-time coverage of the 2003 war with Iraq featuring correspondents with troops moving into enemy territory, with sights and sounds of artillery and air-raid sirens. The extent of our awareness of things outside of our own lives, and our mental and emotional involvement with them, has multiplied dramatically.

Technological changes bring great benefits, but with such massive changes there is

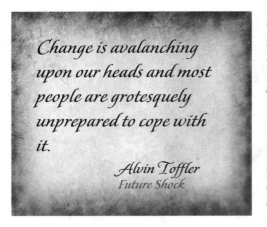

> *Change is avalanching upon our heads and most people are grotesquely unprepared to cope with it.*
>
> *Alvin Toffler*
> *Future Shock*

also a huge mental and social price to pay. No wonder some people are looking for islands of unchangeableness in the midst of a tidal wave of changes. *Many people want their church to be the island of unchanging tranquility and security in their lives.*

More change occurred in the twentieth century than in all the previous centuries. Alvin Toffler first spelled out the impact of such swift and massive changes in his book *Future Shock*. Future shock occurs when people are asked to absorb the simultaneous or cumulative impact of too much change. When the changes are too complex to handle and the disruptions to life are too great, people feel future shock, and they want some relief from the pressures of change.

OUR CHANGING CULTURE AND THE CHURCH

Surfing on the waves of technological and social change, each new generation is more different than the previous generation. A clash of generations has developed in society and to a lesser extent in our churches as younger generations see things differently and have different values and expectations than the older generations—and as postmodernism has taken hold, beginning in the late twentieth century.

Much has been written recently about postmodernism, and much effort is being made to understand postmoderns. However, this is only one part of a larger picture. Other factors are having an equal impact on our society. Christianity (especially Protestantism) was for many decades the de facto established religion of the United States. But the church no longer has the preferred status it once enjoyed. The rise of pluralism since World War II eroded the dominant role the church enjoyed under traditionalism. No longer is there a dominant Christian cultural consensus. Multiculturalism is increasing at such a rapid rate that by 2030 there will be no clear ethnic majority in the U.S. The church in the U.S. has depended upon a dominant cultural majority. America itself is becoming more "Europeanized" and is characterized by the secular, pluralistic, and pragmatic.

The church in America must more and more see itself as a missionary movement to its own culture. This means, among other things, that we will have to become better at changing our forms and methods in order to accomplish the functions of relating the gospel to the culture of our day. When we do that, there are two pitfalls we must avoid.

First, we must be wary that we do not become so much like our current culture that the transforming truth of the gospel is lost amid such adaptations. If we become too much like the culture, not only will we have lost the distinctiveness of the gospel in the world, but we will also find that we have adopted the values of the unbelieving world we are trying to reach.

On the other hand, if we under-adapt to the culture, we lose the opportunity to speak to those who are immersed in the culture. But we also fall prey to a different set of cultural values that appears to be spiritual on the outside but is actually lifeless and destructive on the inside. In order to reach out to postmoderns, one must "flirt" with selling out to the spirit of the postmodern age. If we refuse to do this, you and I are in danger of becoming Pharisees; yet we must not sell out in the process.

Note that one of the primary charges against Jesus was that He enjoyed too close a relationship with those in the culture rejected by the self-righteous Pharisees. Study the following passages to see how Jesus responded to this charge.

What was the issue in each of the following encounters with the Pharisees?

Luke 5:27–32 (early in Jesus' ministry)

_____

_____

Luke 15:1–7 (late in Jesus' ministry)

_____

_____

Luke 19:1–10 (late in Jesus' ministry)

_____

_____

In that day, eating a meal together, with the table fellowship involved, was entirely too close a relationship for the scribes and Pharisees to accept. Throughout Jesus' ministry, they criticized Him for "selling out" to the spirit of the world about them. Our withdrawal from the culture about us puts us in danger of being more like the Pharisees than like the Lord who told us to go into all the world and make disciples (Matthew 28:19–20).

So, like it or not, change is being forced upon us. And the option to remain isolated and unchanging does not really exist. We have to continuously remind ourselves that the Christian life itself is all about change.

1. *Describe the change during the course of the Christian's life (2 Corinthians 3:18):*

_____

_____

_____

2. *Describe the change at the end of the Christian's life (1 Corinthians 15:51–52):*

_____

_____

_____

THE NATURE OF CHANGE

Human Dynamics of Change

Why is change so difficult? Why is there so much resistance to change? It helps to understand the nature of change. *Stability is about control.* We are comfortable when we feel like we are in control of our life and our future.

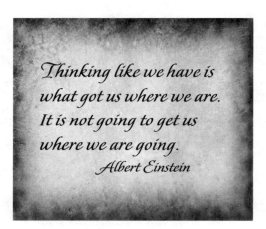

Thinking like we have is what got us where we are. It is not going to get us where we are going.
—*Albert Einstein*

We don't necessarily have to know the future (though we often wish we did), but we want to feel that we have resources to deal with it. We develop a comfortable sense of being in control in the present. We know where we fit in; we have developed the strategies and the resources we can count on to deal with the present situation. So we feel relatively comfortable in the status quo.

However, once we find out that the future is going to be different, that the status quo is going to change, suddenly our sense of being in control is shaken. Will we be able to handle the new requirements or demands? Will we survive?

Sometimes, even if the status quo is very difficult, we develop strategies for dealing with it. And when a change for the better comes along, we resist it because we do not have any strategies yet to deal with the change. Even a difficult or painful situation that we have learned to deal with is preferred to a new, better situation that we have no idea how to deal with. *Change is about being out of control.*

Think of a time when you were dealing with a major change. Perhaps it was leaving home to go away to college. Maybe a job change requiring a move to a new part of the country. Maybe it was an even more difficult or painful change. Write your answers to the questions below.

1. *What was the major change you are thinking about?*

_____

_____

_____

_____

2. *What were your feelings about the change? Did you experience feelings of loss of control? Did you wonder whether you could negotiate the change successfully?*

_____

_____

_____

_____

3. *Why was this a particularly difficult change?*

_____

_____

_____

_____

4. *What was happening in your life at the same time as this major change? Were other changes happening around the same time? Or were you in a period of stability before the major change?*

_____

_____

_____

5. *How was the change finally resolved? What helped you to deal with the change? What did you learn from the experience?*

_____

_____

_____

_____

Feelings About Change

People have intense feelings about change, and these feelings are fairly universal.

1. People feel *uncomfortable*. Significant change always requires us to think and act

differently. We have to learn new ways of doing things. We have to get to know new people or familiar people in new relationships. Any time we have to try something new we feel awkward at first and often quite uncomfortable with the new expectations and demands.

2. People feel *alone*. Even if a large number of people are going through the same change, we tend to feel alone. The familiar moorings of the status quo are gone, and we feel adrift. Our personal focus is naturally, "How will I make it in the new situation?" That focus tends to push us into feeling alone. And people come from different experiences: some from a period of stability, others from many changes they have had to adapt to. The differences foster the feeling of aloneness.

3. People feel a sense of *loss*. Every change involves giving up the status quo; therefore, something we depended upon is lost. Sometimes the loss is simply a stable situation in which we had grown secure. Other times, the loss is extremely significant and painful. The loss of a job or the loss of a loved one creates a painful experience that can challenge our very lives. People tend to measure change on the basis of what they lose or what they have to give up. Often we need to mourn the loss before we can move forward.

4. People feel *inadequate*. Significant change requires us to act in ways we have not acted before. We have to learn new ways of doing things; we have to establish new relationships. Beyond the initial awkwardness, we feel inadequate to do something about which we have not had the opportunity to develop confidence. And sometimes we get angry at ourselves for our feelings of inadequacy.

5. People feel *overwhelmed and uncertain*. Change has a cumulative effect. The more change required, the more overwhelmed people feel. If their lives are currently full of change, the toll adds up very quickly on a new change. They begin to feel uncertain, overwhelmed, and confused. Many people begin to have difficulty making decisions; they become immobilized. There is a limit to the amount of change people can handle well.[1]

The Role of Culture

In the previous lesson, we discussed the role of culture in general and in the church. What is important to remember here is that culture is one of the primary elements providing people a sense of security and control. Culture has developed through what has worked in the past, and it will therefore resist change. In fact, *the impact of church culture (or organizational culture) will almost always be to hinder change.*

The longer a church exists successfully, the deeper and more powerful its culture becomes. The culture sets a pattern of basic beliefs about the nature of reality, time, space, people, relationships, and acceptable forms of ministry and leadership. The culture provides a sense of internal consistency and order and will affect almost everything that is done in the church.

Any significant change will usually upset that sense of internal consistency and require adjustments to the group's basic assumptions. Unless the church culture itself is changed, very little significant or lasting change can take place. Note how critical this is to the fulfillment of a vision. Since vision always involves change, the church culture must be brought into harmony and support of the vision or else there will be continual conflict. In other words, fulfilling a vision requires the development of a new church culture. If this does not happen, the vision will not be realized.

The vision and values come alive within the culture. Most leaders assume that change comes about without changing the culture. But the vision must be incorporated within the culture before any significant change can take place.[2] In *Managing at the Speed of Change,* Daryl Conner warned, "Whenever a discrepancy exists between the current culture and the objectives of your change, the culture always wins."[3]

THE PROCESS OF CHANGE

We need to think about change as an unfolding process rather than a single event. The "beginning" and "end" of a major change may be separated by months or years. We are conditioned by our culture to want quick solutions. Television seduces us to think that all issues can be resolved in thirty minutes. Instead, we must remember that change is a continual, fluid *process*—not a discrete *project*.

The change process has three phases:

a. The *present state* is the status quo—an equilibrium position that will continue until some force disrupts it. The present state is certain and comfortable. Few people want to leave it. Even if it is a bad situation, they have grown used to it and learned how to deal with it.

b. The *transition state* is the phase during which we disengage from the present state and develop new attitudes and behaviors that can take us to the desired state. The transition state is chaotic, uncertain, and uncomfortable. It is often accompanied by high stress and conflict. Frequently, in the midst of the uncertainty of the transition, people want to go back to the present. They tend to idealize the present state.

c. The *desired state* is what we want the future to be.

We must recognize that this process is so daunting that it will be undertaken only under certain conditions.

Condition 1: Pain

People will leave the status quo only when the pain of staying there is greater than the pain of leaving. The uncertainty and fear of the unknown is so great that people do not want to leave their comfort zone. They have to become convinced that remaining in the comfort zone of the present will somehow become uncomfortable. And they need to accept the discomfort of ambiguity as a natural part of transition. They have to believe that remaining in the status quo is far more expensive than the cost of transition.

Therefore, we must come to realize that change will be expensive. And we have to accept that we will pay, whether we change or not. Making the change and fulfilling the vision will have its price. But refusing to change will also have its price in the long run, and its price is generally higher.

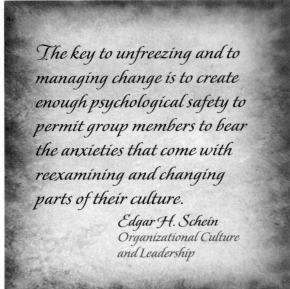

The key to unfreezing and to managing change is to create enough psychological safety to permit group members to bear the anxieties that come with reexamining and changing parts of their culture.

Edgar H. Schein
Organizational Culture and Leadership

It therefore takes a critical mass of information that justifies breaking out of the status quo. This requires *a strong sense of urgency*. Only then will people accept significant change. People must become aware that the resulting cost of refusing to change will ultimately be too uncomfortable to accept.

For example, consider Wind Ridge Community Church, planted forty-seven years ago in a predominantly middle-class neighborhood. During the past fifteen years the area has changed dramatically. The main street upon which the church property is situated has become entirely commercial. Older houses have been demolished to make room for convenience stores, auto repair shops, liquor stores, and many kinds of small specialty shops. The apartments and houses remaining are in bad repair. The community is now a transition area through which many ethnic groups move as they are assimilated into the larger culture. Many of the store signs are in Chinese or Vietnamese. The church has been experiencing a shrinking attendance over the last five to seven years.

A long-term planning committee established two years ago has recommended that the church find new property and relocate or change its focus dramatically to minister to the various ethnic groups that now surround the church. The pastor is publicly advocating the relocation. However, a large number of families are becoming vocally resistant. Please answer the following questions.

What do you think is happening here?

_____

_____

_____

_____

_____

What needs to happen?

_____

_____

_____

_____

_____

Condition 2: Remedy

In order to change, we have to see a new situation which is desirable and obtainable. Our view of the desired state has to be as clear and attractive as possible so that its desirability outweighs the uncertainty of leaving our comfort zone in the present state. In addition, we need to see an understandable plan which we are confident will get us there. This relates to a *compelling vision* and *workable strategy*.

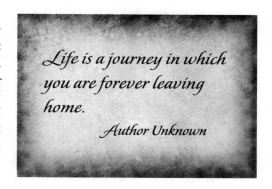

Life is a journey in which you are forever leaving home.

Author Unknown

NECESSARY ELEMENTS IN INTRODUCING CHANGE

We note seven elements in bringing change into the local church. They are: (1) establish the need for change, (2) develop the vision for change, (3) develop a workable strategy, (3) build support for change, (5) implement the necessary change, (6) solidify the change, and (7) deal with resistance to change.

1. Establish the Need for Change

To establish the need for change, give a clear rationale for leaving the present state. There are several means to move people from the comfortable status quo to the uncomfortable transition. Essentially this means the leaders must convince them that trying to stay in the present state is, or will be, even more uncomfortable than leaving.

Honest evaluation is where you start. Encourage people to honestly evaluate the church and its ministry. Are we accomplishing our purpose? Are people coming to faith in Christ? Are people growing in their relationship with Christ and with each other? Are we having an impact on our community? on our world? Are we growing? Ask as many penetrating questions as possible. Be ready for the unrest this creates.

Second, be sure to *clarify the mission*. One aspect of evaluation is to revisit your understanding of the mission of the church. A church can become very comfortable simply being a club where the members are focusing on their own needs and desires. Understanding the fullness of Christ's mission for the church can be a helpful antidote to the comfortable complacency of a selective understanding of the mission of the church. (This is a good spot to review your work on the mission of the church in chapter 14.)

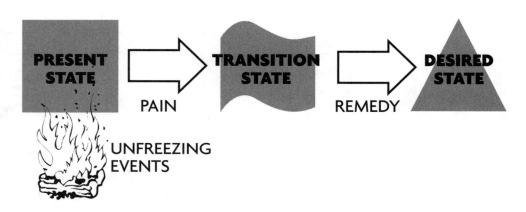

Third, whenever possible, use unfreezing events to stimulate the desire for change. Often a prime unfreezing event, such as pastoral staff changes or major changes in the community, have people wondering about the status quo. The event may be dramatic. For example, one church welded to its long-time location was able to move after the sanctuary burned down as a result of an electrical short. These events shake people out of complacency and cause them to reevaluate the present.

2. Develop the Vision for Change

To develop the vision for change, present a clear vision of a future, one exciting enough to justify leaving the present. A clear, compelling, desirable vision is probably the strongest incentive for people to shift their focus to the future and leave the comfort of the present. (Your work on vision in chapter 14 is important here.)

Take special care in selecting those who will be part of the Visioning Team. Some call this group the "Vision Community."[4] Whatever you call the visioning group, it is essential that this group develop a real team relationship. They will have to work together, support each other, and speak with a united voice in the midst of the uncertainty of change. It only increases the anxiety levels when the visioning team appears to be divided. The visioning team has a real leadership function; it is not just a think tank.

The initial role of the visioning team is to be a means through which the leader is in touch with the needs of the followers. The later role of the members of the visioning team will be that of primary sponsors for the vision to the congregation.

The vision that is developed needs to be clear enough, strong enough, and appealing enough to pull people forward into the future.

> *A vision is powerful because it speaks directly to the heart—to unconscious yearnings to be great, to serve, to make a difference, to be involved in something meaningful, to pursue a dream, to achieve a higher purpose. A vision bypasses the rational ego to connect with deeper subtle potentials.*
>
> Richard L. Daft and
> Robert H. Lengel
> Fusion Leadership

3. Develop a Workable Strategy for Change

To develop a workable strategy for change, you should show clearly the process for reaching the future.

Strategic planning is the key phrase for the process of determining the necessary steps to reach the envisioned future. This will be discussed in more detail in the following lesson. The key role of planning in change is to provide the confidence which comes from seeing the actions that will be taken in order to realize the vision. This helps make the accomplishment of the vision much more probable in the minds of people and enables them to begin to see what role they might play in the process and in the envisioned state.

4. Build Support for Change

One of the clear measures of leadership is the ability to secure a commitment to the vision strong enough that people are willing to give their time, energy, and resources to see the vision realized. Develop a critical mass of support for the change. Some helpful actions in building support include the following:

1. *Communicate twice as much as you think is necessary.* Communicate the vision clearly and passionately so that people can understand it and will be excited about seeing it fulfilled. Review the lesson on "Communicating Your Vision" in

chapter 15. Clear, frequent communication will help alleviate a crucial source of resistance—uncertainty about the future.

2. *Model your own commitment to the changes required to fulfill the vision.* This relates to the issue of trust. When asked to commit themselves, their time, their resources, people will follow only those leaders in whom they have a high degree of trust. One of the most important ways that a leader builds that trust is to demonstrate his or her own commitment to the vision. This was at the heart of Peter's exhortation to the elders when he called upon them to be examples to those in the church (1 Peter 5:1–3). Trust in the leader builds the confidence that diminishes the insecurity associated with change.

3. *Build a team.* Team building for change starts with those who are asked to be a part of the visioning team. These visioning team members, respected as they are in the congregation, need to be the first "sponsors" of the change. Beyond the initial visioning team, recruit other respected and influential people to join together to advance the vision. Ask yourself, "Whose help is critical to have in order for us to realize the vision?"

Concerning the visioning team, develop a group of a size to enable reasonable representation of the congregation while still enabling discussion and decision making. Members of the group must be highly respected by the congregation and in touch with a sizeable segment of the congregation. The goal is not to try to blend every group's views into the result, but it is critical to be aware of the various groups in the church as the process develops.

As sponsors, team members will sanction change, letting others know that the change is important enough to justify the initial difficulty it will bring. Sponsors legitimize the change.[5]

Any worthwhile vision will require great, focused effort over a long period of time. Team members will add their unique gifts and strengths to the process and be able to share the load and encourage each other for the long haul.

4. *Celebrate every success that helps fulfill the vision.* Celebrate or recognize with approval every action that helps make progress toward fulfilling the vision. Give public commendation as progress is made; celebrate all "wins," big and small; have public celebrations when goals are achieved; express personal appreciation to those who work to fulfill the vision.

5. Implement the Change

Implementing the changes needed to fulfill the vision will empower the vision.

Do what is necessary to gain the support of the ruling group of the church or ministry. Ideally, some of the ruling group are part of the visioning process and will be sponsors of the changes needed to implement the vision. Talk to the others personally and seek their wholehearted support. Use sponsors to do this as well. The ruling group will need to authorize the funds needed to pursue the vision.

Do not forget to express value for those existing aspects of the ministry that are contributing to the vision. The point is not to change everything or devalue existing ministries. The point is to fulfill the vision.

Get serious about Ephesians 4. Delegate and empower people to work in the areas of their giftedness. As the strategic plan is developed, recruit people to work on the objectives and goals needed to fulfill the vision. Give them the encouragement, authority, and support they will need to accomplish their goals.

Begin a process of developing the leaders needed to fulfill the vision. Provide the training needed to implement new ministry approaches. Seek out the best conferences and seminars; send representatives who will be responsible for teaching others what they learned.

6. Solidify the Change

Implanting the vision in the organizational culture is critical. This process begins by aligning all elements of the ministry to the vision. Visions not only make clear what you should do, but they also give helpful guidance about what you should not do. Those programs and actions that do not contribute to the fulfillment of the vision must be eliminated. We should not be callous about the impact of eliminating things (every program has its committed supporters), yet we cannot let marginal programs hinder progress toward realizing the vision.

Develop a "permission-giving" culture that rewards initiative and creativity aimed at fulfilling the vision. Make sure there is understanding and commitment to the vision, then turn people loose to do innovative things. Develop general guidelines wherever possible so that people will have the freedom to be creative. Where necessary, have strict guidelines and policies such as for qualifications for nursery and children's workers, who is allowed to drive on youth ministry trips, etc. But do not let the church or ministry become bound by a big policy manual. You will need to negotiate this with the ruling body of the church or ministry. To give permission to others to act often means that the ruling body must give up some of its power to control.

Think through the core values in light of the vision. Generally, core values do not change. Furthermore, core values influence the development of vision. However, once the vision is developed, it would be helpful to evaluate the core values in light of the vision. Are there any conflicts? Are there any new core values that need to be incorporated?

Remove obstacles; change standard procedures if they hinder action to fulfill the vision. Teach regularly that all programs have an end date, or at least a reevaluation date. Reallocate power in the organization so that those committed to fulfilling the vision have the power to act.

Focus on functions rather than forms. Keep the functions; change the forms whenever necessary to accomplish the functions.

7. Deal with Resistance to Change

Understand that, in the nature of things, resistance to change will always occur. This is true both of changes with difficult implications ("negative" changes) and "good" implications ("positive" changes). The resistance may take overt forms in which the resistance is visible, openly expressed. Or it may take covert forms in which the resistance is hidden, but nevertheless real. How should you respond to resistance?

Most people resist change not for fear of discovering the future, but for fear of discarding the past.
Win Arn
The Fine Art of Change

1. Accept the inevitability of resistance and welcome it. Resistance that goes underground because it is not welcomed becomes far more dangerous and disruptive. It will lead to serious conflict. Because resistance may help you identify weaknesses in the plans, pursue the thoughts behind the resistance thoroughly to learn what you can from them. Some resistance will melt away because the resistor just wanted his view validated by being thoroughly understood and considered.

2. Deal with the emotions behind resistance. To some extent these will often relate to a sense of loss. With the change to something new, there is always something lost, something that must be given up. Legitimate grief is associated with this loss. This is where the comforting side of leadership is needed.

3. Do not put people into a position from which they would have a hard time retreating. For example, do not present a major change to the congregation first. People's first reaction to change is usually negative. If this negative reaction is expressed publicly, they will have a hard time backing away from it later for fear of "losing face." Build strong support among individuals and important groups

first, before going public with the change. Use the sponsors to help develop support in one-to-one meetings.

4. If the change is significant, anticipate resistance from those most powerful in the church or ministry. Remember, those in the most powerful positions got there under the old status quo. So some may regard the change as diminishing their roles or positions in some way. Help those leaders see the important role they can play in the future. The change may not be that significant, yet people can feel the change is a challenge to their leadership since they did not do it before. Such resistors must believe that the past is still valued. If at all possible, connect the need for the change to changed present and future conditions, not to failure in the past.

EXERCISE: AN EXPERIENCE OF CHANGE

Think of an actual situation in your church or ministry in which a significant change was introduced. Analyze the change situation in light of the principles of this lesson. What could have been done differently to be more effective? Be prepared to discuss your analysis.

Note: Introducing change is the acid test of leadership. This is where the leader's demonstrated character, the trust he/she has earned, and all the leadership skills come into play. This is what leadership is all about. This is what leaders do! This is what distinguishes leadership from management (an important discipline in its own right).

STRATEGIC PLANNING

Strategic planning is simply long-range planning in which the leader develops the details of a strategy that will realize the vision. What makes it "strategic" is that it is tied to fulfillment of the vision. The planning process breaks the general strategy into discrete objectives, goals, and action steps that all contribute to the realization of the vision.

In any spiritual ministry, the planning process begins with God. If God does not guide the specific directions and provide the needed resources, the ministry vision will not be realized. No vision worthy of commitment can be realized solely by human effort. While detailed plans are essential to the success of any major ministry vision, planning is never a substitute for dependence upon God (Proverbs 16:9; 19:21). On the other hand, dependence on God does not rule out the need for carefully considered plans (Proverbs 16:3; 21:5).

There are some common objections to strategic planning. Most reflect the fact that many people do not want to do the work of planning. Perhaps they do not yet see the connection between planning and better results. Still others resist planning because once goals are stated specifically, success or failure becomes measurable. And, once success or failure becomes measurable, people and ministries become accountable. This objection is seldom stated openly because it is a character issue.

One legitimate concern regarding strategic planning is the pace of change. Some object to long-range planning because conditions are changing so rapidly that long-range plans will be obsolete before they have a chance to be realized. The force of this objection can be dealt with in several ways. First, be reasonable in how far ahead you are planning. A twenty-year plan can legitimately deal with some issues, buildings perhaps, but not others like specialty ministries that may be obsolete in a few years.

Second, maintain a flexible approach to the plans made. Realizing the pace of change, reevaluate plans periodically. Acknowledge up front that plans are subject to change if there are significant environmental changes. Do not let anyone become so tied to specific plans that they are unwilling to change as needed. Plans often have "sponsors" who have an emotional commitment to a particular element of the plan.

It is important to remember, and remind people periodically, that functions do not change, but forms do. The purpose and values of the church remain the constant; but specific ministries, methods, and approaches are all subject to change when they no longer contribute significantly to fulfilling the purpose.

THE PROCESS OF PLANNING

From Vision to Action Plans

The basic principle of planning is that planning works backwards from the vision of what is to be accomplished. This is one reason why a clear vision statement is so important.

PLANNING
Work BACKWARD from the VISION

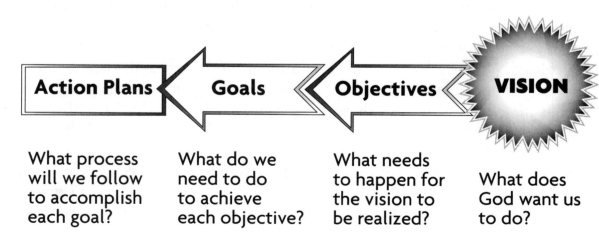

Action Plans	Goals	Objectives	VISION
What process will we follow to accomplish each goal?	What do we need to do to achieve each objective?	What needs to happen for the vision to be realized?	What does God want us to do?

A Note on Terminology

Different approaches to leadership and management use terms differently. This is especially true of terms such as "goals" and "objectives." The important thing is not which view is correct; it is rather to be consistent in the definitions and approach you choose. Then use it! We will use the following definitions to describe the parts of the planning process.

The *vision* is the image of the desirable future state for the church or church ministry. The vision is developed by bringing together the biblically mandated mission with the actual ministry context in which the church or ministry exists. The vision answers the question, "What does God want us to do?" By describing the desirable future state, the vision provides the direction for planning. Developing a strategy for realizing the vision involves choosing objectives, goals, and action plans that will contribute to making the vision a reality.

Objectives are selected that will make the vision a reality (i.e., "realize" the vision). The vision is broken down into specific, measurable accomplishments that, taken together, will realize the vision. Objectives answer the question, "What needs to happen for the vision to be realized?" Objectives describe major things that we want to achieve. Objectives are usually long range.

Goals are selected that will achieve each objective. Each objective can be broken into smaller parts that, when accomplished, will achieve the objective. Goals answer the question, "What do we need to do to achieve each objective?" Goals are more specific than objectives; they are also measurable. In fact, good goals have several critical characteristics:

+ Good goals are *realistic*. They can actually be accomplished. It is motivational if they are challenging and require an exercise of faith to accomplish. But unrealistic goals discourage people.

+ Good goals are *specific*. They are clear and understandable; they describe a definite accomplishment.

+ Good goals are *measurable*. They are specific enough to be able to be measured. For example, "Make three calls to prospective nursery workers" is better than "Work on getting more nursery workers."

+ Good goals are *time sensitive*. There is a specific time by which the goal must be accomplished.

+ Good goals can be *delegated*. Responsibility for accomplishing the goal can be assigned to a person. If the goals are specific and measurable the person assigned responsibility will be able to accomplish them.

Action plans are made to accomplish each goal. Action plans involve specific steps that must be followed to accomplish each goal. Action plans answer the question, "What process must we follow to accomplish each goal?" Action plans are normally temporary activities that mark the first activities taken toward reaching the objectives that will fulfill the vision.

A planning worksheet may be used to make specific action steps for each goal. The worksheet is a simple way to become intentional and more thorough in your planning process. Use one worksheet for each goal. A sample "Planning Worksheet" is included at the end of the chapter.

Once the planning is done, execution of the plans starts with the action plans for each goal.

EXECUTION
Work **FORWARD** toward the **VISION**

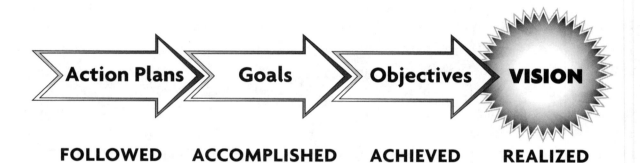

A Planning Exercise

The staff and elders of Central Valley Bible Church have recognized the need for a ministry to young couples. The church currently has a large population of singles, mostly professionals in their late twenties and early thirties. From this group there is a continuous stream of young couples getting married. These couples and those recently married would benefit from a ministry which helped them in the months of premarital adjustment and in their first few years of marriage.

The staff and elders have provided the following vision statement:

The Young Married Ministry will help young couples build strong Christian marriage relationships by providing biblically based instruction, personal encouragement, and authentic fellowship to take them through the adjustment to marriage to maximizing their ministry for Christ as a couple.

1. *Using the vision statement given above, determine the four most important objectives which need to be achieved. What major things need to happen for the vision to be realized?*

    Objective 1 _____
    _____

    Objective 2 _____
    _____

    Objective 3 _____
    _____

    Objective 4 _____
    _____

2. *Choose one of the objectives and determine what goals must be accomplished in order to achieve that objective.*

    The Objective _____
    _____

    To achieve this objective, we need to accomplish the following goals:

    Goal 1 _____
    _____

    Goal 2 _____
    _____

    Goal 3 _____
    _____

    Goal 4 _____
    _____

    Goal 5 _____
    _____

3. Finally, choose one of the goals and use the "Planning Worksheet" on the following page to develop an action plan that will accomplish the goal. NOTE: Make a photocopy of the worksheet, as you will want to keep the original for use with your own future planning.

PLANNING WORKSHEET

Goal: _____

Responsible Person: _____

Date: _____

WHAT ACTION STEPS WILL WE TAKE TO ACCOMPLISH THE GOAL?	WHO WILL BE RESPONSIBLE FOR THIS ACTION STEP?	DATE TO BE CHECKED	DATE TO BE COMPLETED	WHAT RESOURCES WILL BE NEEDED?	WHAT WILL THE RESULT BE?

Notes

1. Adapted from Ken Blanchard, "Seven Dynamics of Change," *Executive Excellence* 9 (June 1992): 5–6.

2. Lovett H. Weems, *Church Leadership: Vision, Team, Culture, Integrity* (Nashville: Abingdon, 1993), 100.

3. Daryl R. Conner, *Managing at the Speed of Change* (New York: Villard Books, 1992), 176.

4. For example, see Jim Herrington, Mike Bonem, and James H. Furr, *Leading Congregational Change* (San Francisco: Jossey-Bass, 2000).

5. Connor, *Managing at the Speed of Change*, 105ff.

E I G H T E E N

COMMUNICATING EFFECTIVELY

COMMUNICATION IS THE LUBRICANT THAT enables church members to work together smoothly. Communication builds and maintains the relationships necessary for the church to accomplish its mission. The greatest vision for ministry will not accomplish anything if it cannot be communicated clearly and if the leaders and people cannot communicate adequately with each other in the process of working together.

SOME IMPORTANT POINTS ABOUT COMMUNICATION

1. Communication is a complex process.

The success of communication depends upon reaching a common understanding. Communication may be defined as "the process we go through to convey understanding from one person or group to another."[1]

Of all the leadership skills, communication is most taken for granted. It is so easy to think that because we have talked with someone we have communicated with him. However, we have not actually communicated with him unless we have reached a common understanding. When the meaning he understands is the meaning we meant to convey, only then have we truly communicated.

2. Communication takes place on many levels.

Anything one person says to another is filtered through many grids. The speaker's grid includes his own past experiences of communication, how he feels about the message he is communicating, what he perceives the listener's attitudes to be, and his own personal needs. Talking is such an integral part of life that we are usually unaware of the grids that shape our communication attempts.

The listener has the same filters working: his own past experiences with the speaker, what he perceives to be the speaker's intentions, how he feels about the subject of the message or the context in which it is given, and his own personal needs. As a result, people tend to hear what they expect to hear or what they want to hear. What we do not expect or want to hear is screened out. This is called "selective perception." Our tendency to selective perception is the source of many misunderstandings and conflicts in the church.

For example, selective perception is the reason why two people can be a part of the same church meeting and afterward describe it in entirely different terms. It is also the reason why people on different sides of a conflict can promote totally opposite descriptions of the same events. Neither group is lying; its members simply saw what they expected to see and interpreted others' actions according to their own grid.

3. Communication is risky, so people engage in it carefully.

Rejection of a person's words is experienced as rejection of the person. Most people fear rejection to such an extent that they take care to communicate in "safe" ways. Above all, they use ways that will not expose them unnecessarily to the possibility of rejection. Often people hold back from saying things they fear will bring a painful response. Or they say what they think the other person wants to hear. At other times they attempt to appear neutral and uninvolved, and consequently they are distanced from the possibility of being hurt by the response. For example, avoiding the risk of personal responsibility, a church member may come to an elder and say, "I've heard some rumblings in the congregation about the pastor's preaching. Maybe you should ask around."

Every leader leads by team building. Whether the team we build is really dependable will be based largely on our communication skills.

Calvin Miller
The Empowered Leader

Many of the factors that affect a specific communication experience have nothing to do with that particular communication at all. They are simply brought into the communication experience as baggage by the participants.

4. Nonverbal communication is, in many situations, as important as verbal communication.

Nonverbal communication consists of facial expressions, gestures, body positions, physical mannerisms, and actions. These are commonly called "body language." Body language is usually involuntary. It is therefore more spontaneous. People generally do not consciously control their body language, especially their facial expressions. This means that body language, which one does not usually control, is often a more accurate reflection of the speaker's thoughts than are his words, which he normally does control carefully.

For example: You have an idea for a new, much-needed (in your opinion) ministry in the church. After church one Sunday morning, you find an elder in the foyer and begin to present your idea to him. As you are speaking you notice his facial expressions and posture. What messages do the following actions give?

> *Body language communicates the majority of the emotional content of any message. In fact studies show that 55% of the emotional content of any message is communicated non-verbally.*
>
> *Myron Rush*
> *Richer Relationships*

He stands with his arms crossed over his chest and looks directly at you. His face shows neither a smile nor a frown; he says "uh-huh, . . . uh-huh" several times.

_____

_____

He stands, shifting his weight back and forth; his eyes seem to focus somewhere past you; every so often he mumbles "uh-huh, yeah."

_____

_____

He smiles, nodding his head as you talk. He seems to look right into your eyes. He says "uh-huh, yeah," several times.

_____

_____

After you have said a few sentences, he asks you to sit down with him on a bench in the foyer to continue your discussion.

_____

_____

THE COMMUNICATION PROCESS

Now look carefully at figure 10, "The Process of Communication," and notice the steps involved in communication.

How does this process affect an actual message? Consider the following scenario: Mary, a Sunday school teacher for fifth-grade boys meets with Elliott, the elder responsible for the church education program. Referring to the diagram, here are the eight steps in action:

1 Mary is having some trouble with the boys in her class. They are very energetic and hard to control, making it difficult to conduct a lesson. Mary wants to have another adult assigned to her class to help her. So she forms her message.

2 Mary says, "Elliott, the boys in my class are driving me crazy! It's so hard to teach them anything. You've got to get me some help!"

3 Elliott hears Mary say ". . . boys . . . driving me crazy! . . . hard to teach them. . . . You . . . get me some help!"

4 He assigns a meaning to her words.

+ Scenario 1: Elliott has had a rough week at work. He hasn't had any time to give to the Sunday school program for a couple of weeks. And he has a big project presentation first thing Monday morning. So he assigns the meaning to Mary's words: "Mary can't control her class, but she doesn't want to deal with it. She wants to pass the buck to me and make me deal with it."

+ Scenario 2: Elliott knows that Mary has been teaching the fifth-grade boys class successfully for three years. There must be something new going on. Even though he doesn't have time to deal with the situation now because of the stress at his work, he assigns the meaning: "Mary seems to be in a difficult spot and needs some help."

Figure 10
THE PROCESS OF COMMUNICATION

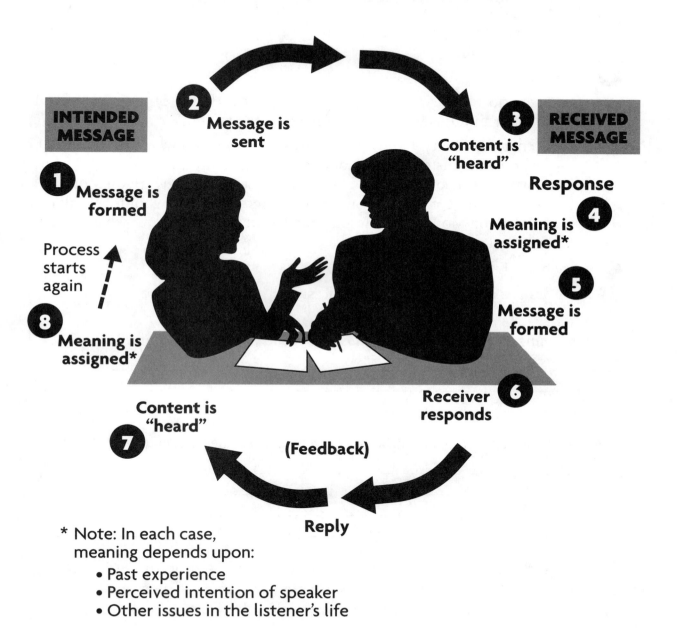

INTENDED MESSAGE

2 Message is sent

3 **RECEIVED MESSAGE**

Content is "heard"

1 Message is formed

Response

4 Meaning is assigned*

Process starts again

5 Message is formed

8 Meaning is assigned*

6 Receiver responds

Content is "heard"

7

(Feedback)

Reply

* Note: In each case, meaning depends upon:
- Past experience
- Perceived intention of speaker
- Other issues in the listener's life

SOURCE: Adapted from Edward R. Dayton and Ted W. Engstrom, *The Art of Management for Christian Leaders* (Waco, Tex.: Word, 1976), 111.

5 So Elliott forms a message.

+ Scenario 1: "I've got to get this woman off my back. I don't have time for this stuff. She needs to get control of her class!"

+ Scenario 2: "I don't have time to handle this now, but it's clear that Mary needs some help. I need to set up a time to talk with her after I finish my presentation."

6 Elliott says:

+ Scenario 1: "Mary, you've got to be tougher with those boys! Get control of them and they will respect you and listen to you."

+ Scenario 2: "Mary, I know it is really frustrating you when your class acts up and won't listen. It sure sounds like you could use some help. I want to work with you on this. I have a big presentation at work on Monday, and I have to concentrate on that this afternoon. But, would you call me at home on Monday or Tuesday night, and we'll talk about what we can do to get you some help?"

7 Mary hears Elliott's words.

8 Mary assigns a meaning to Elliott's message.

What meaning do you think Mary would assign to his message in scenario 1?

_____
_____
_____

What meaning do you think Mary would assign to his message in scenario 2?

_____
_____
_____
_____

Notice that the conversation took a different course based on the "grid" through which Elliott passed Mary's words in order to assign a meaning to them.

To get further insight, study these four examples of communication in the Scriptures.

1. *Read the account of the men from the tribe of Benjamin (Saul's tribe) who joined David at the stronghold in Ziklag (1 Chronicles 12:16–18).*

a. What is the context in which this communication takes place? What is the significance of these men being from the tribe of Benjamin?

_____

_____

_____

b. What is the atmosphere of David's communication with them?

_____

_____

c. How would you rate David on the clarity of his communication? Why?

_____

_____

d. How well did David speak to the needs of these men?

_____

_____

e. What important communication principles do you observe in this incident?

_____

_____

_____

_____

2. Read the story of Rehoboam's aborted opportunity to become king of all Israel upon the death of his father, Solomon (1 Kings 12:1–20).
   a. How would you describe Rehoboam's communication in vv. 12–14?

   _____

   _____

   b. What could he have done differently?

   _____

   _____

   _____

3. Analyze Jesus' conversation with the woman at the well from a communication perspective (John 4:5–42).

a. *What is unusual about the context of their conversation?*

_____

_____

b. *What needs did the woman have? Did Jesus speak to these needs? If so, how?*

_____

_____

_____

c. *What would you say about the integrity of Jesus in this conversation? How was His integrity seen?*

_____

_____

_____

d. *Do you think the woman felt "heard" by Jesus? Why or why not?*

_____

4. *Read the account of Jesus' communication with His disciples at the conclusion of the Last Supper (John 14:1–24).*
   a. *What needs in His disciples was He attempting to meet?*

_____

_____

_____

   b. *What important qualities of Jesus' communication are seen in this example?*

_____

_____

_____

_____

_____

BUILT UPON TRUST

"For effective communication to take place it must be OK to tell the truth, the whole truth, to clarify feelings and to work at dispelling misconceptions. This means sharing good things as well as things felt to be negative."[2] We generally say only what we are sure will be acceptable. Thoughts that are perceived to be negative or not desired will not be shared because of the fear of adverse reaction.

Unless the truth can be communicated, there is no possibility of truly useful communication. This means that the primary requirement for true communication is a relationship of trust between the speaker and the listener.

One of the most important responsibilities of pastors and other church leaders is to create that climate of trust in the church. Church leaders at every level must encourage open communication of key issues and problems by all members of the church. This gives people permission to communicate. One of the most destructive developments in a church occurs when people begin to talk secretly about problems.

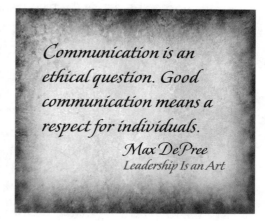

Communication is an ethical question. Good communication means a respect for individuals.
Max DePree
Leadership Is an Art

All church leaders must model an accepting and nonjudgmental response to members' communication. This tells people it is "safe" to communicate. Pastors especially must support and encourage members to work and communicate together in the ministry of the church. This creates a positive effect by empowering them to share responsibility for the successful fulfillment of the church vision.

ENHANCED BY CULTIVATING COMMUNICATION SKILLS

With trust as the foundation, communication is enhanced by practicing communication skills. Here are nine skills that promote effective communication.

1. Have a clear purpose.

Effective communication starts with a clear purpose for the communication. Before you can communicate effectively, you must know what you want to communicate. Communication is more than just talking. If you do not really understand what you are trying to say, you will not be able to communicate it to others. The more important your communication, the more carefully you should think through and plan what you will say.

2. Speak with integrity.

When you provide a model of open communication by sharing your own ideas and feelings, you will communicate trust to your listener. People will usually be only as open as they sense you being with them. Allow yourself to express the emotions you feel about the message you are communicating.

When strong, straight words are needed, say them. But say them graciously (Ephesians 4:15). Remember, the goal is not to "get it off your chest" but to say what is in the best interests of the other person, even if it is hard to do so.

3. Listen well.

Practice the art of "active listening." Active listening refers to the process of becoming thoroughly attentive to the speaker's words and thoughtfully interacting with him in ways that aid your understanding of his message. Active listening is an expression of your value for the person. It means that you unselfishly put your own interests on hold for a time while you concentrate on the speaker's needs and words.

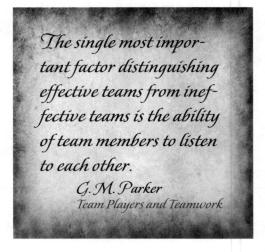

The single most important factor distinguishing effective teams from ineffective teams is the ability of team members to listen to each other.
G. M. Parker
Team Players and Teamwork

Some of the important elements of active listening are the following:

+ Stop talking. You cannot listen when you are talking, intent on expressing your own thoughts.

+ Communicate attentiveness by looking directly at the person.

+ Draw out the other person with questions or comments that invite him to explain further. These responses tell him you are processing what he is saying, and they open the door for the person to say more. For example, (1) reflect to the speaker what he is saying by repeating his words: "You are saying, '. . .'."; (2) ask for clarification: "Do you mean that . . .?"; and (3) interpret the speaker's words back to him: "I understand you to be saying that . . ."

+ Respond with acceptance and encouragement of the person's emotions.

4. Be appropriate.

Recognize different levels of communication. Not all communication has to be deep. There is value in surface communication as a means of opening up the opportunity for deeper relationship. Relationships progress through various levels with an appropriate depth of communication at each level. However, in order to minister to people, church leaders are often required to communicate at a personal depth far beyond the level of relationship they have developed with the listener. When a person is relating to you at a deep level, your words will be very powerful.

5. Plan.

Plan your communication. Try to be as explicit and clear as possible. Choose your words and actions carefully to convey what you want to communicate. Seek to be creative and personal in your communication. Consider how the other person thinks. To what approaches does he respond best?

6. Be considerate.

Be tactful. Think ahead about how the other person will respond. What are his needs, stresses, hopes, fears? Think about how you would respond if you were in his place. Phrase your communication in ways that will be sensitive to your listener.

The basic principle is found in Ephesians 4:29. What does this passage say about the purpose of our communications?

_____

_____

Ask yourself: "What does this person need from our conversation?"

+ comfort?
+ information?
+ encouragement?
+ understanding?
+ validation by being listened to?
+ confrontation or correction?
+ accountability?
+ a chance to air his frustration?

7. Communicate more than you think you need to.

"Be as redundant as possible."[3] Let me repeat: Be repetitive, recurrent, habitual, and persistent. It is better to err on the side of too much communication than too little. A church thrives on frequent communication.

8. Develop a feedback system.

Feedback is a way of gaining help to know whether the message the listener received from you is the same message that you intended to communicate. In other words, are you communicating what you think you are communicating? Invite others to tell you how they are experiencing you and what they understand from your communication.

A key approach to obtaining helpful feedback is to ask questions. For example, ask the listener, "What did you understand me to be saying?" To determine both the tone and meaning you conveyed, ask, "How did my words come across to you? What do you think I was saying? Another good question is, "What can I do to communicate this more clearly?"

The best feedback is specific, descriptive, and focuses on behaviors that can be changed. When you receive such feedback, be careful not to react defensively. If you do, people will be afraid to give you honest feedback. And honest feedback is the only one worth having.

Ask your spouse to help you in developing your feedback system. Ask your spouse to communicate clearly by observing how you communicate together and with others.

9. Develop a communication plan for your church or ministry.

The benefit of a communication plan is that it helps avoid slipups in communication. Develop the plan to provide regular, timely information to those who should be informed. It will certainly help avoid the embarrassment and loss of support that often comes when some important person or group was left uninformed.

+ Staff and elders should have regular communications with the congregation.
+ Pastoral staff communication with elders and deacons should aim toward keeping elders and deacons informed of developments and plans in the church. It should also seek to build a closer working relationship.
+ Leaders of any church ministry should set up regular communication with those involved in their particular ministry. It is very discouraging to feel "left out of the loop."

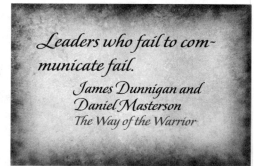

Leaders who fail to communicate fail.

James Dunnigan and
Daniel Masterson
The Way of the Warrior

A COMMUNICATION EXERCISE

Be ready to discuss this situation in your group: You are an elder at Central Bible Church. Lately there has been some conflict between the music minister and some of the people in the congregation. After the morning service a woman stops you in the foyer of the church building and starts telling you her thoughts about the music in the worship service that morning. What can you *do* to communicate to her that you are *listening* to her and *hearing* her?

REFLECTION

Think of a recent situation in which you had difficulty in communication. Perhaps someone misunderstood your words. Perhaps the person wanted you to communicate more to him or her. Whatever the situation, think back over your communication process.

Where did the problem start?

_____

_____

_____

What could you have done differently?

_____

_____

_____

What can you learn from this incident?

_____

_____

_____

Notes

1. Myron Rush, *Richer Relationships* (Wheaton, Ill.: Victor, 1983), 115.
2. E. K. Morrison, *Leadership Skills* (Tucson, Ariz.: Fisher Books, 1983), 90.
3. Ted W. Engstrom and Edward R. Dayton, *The Art of Management for Christian Leaders* (Waco, Tex.: Word, 1976), 114.

N I N E T E E N

HANDLING CONFLICT CONSTRUCTIVELY

CHURCH CONFLICT IS ONE OF THE MOST PAINFUL experiences in the life of a church as well as in the individual lives of those involved. Long-term friendships can be shattered, distrust can infect ministry relationships, and ugly accusations can leave lingering wounds. Because of mishandled conflict, people will leave the church, some in sadness and disillusionment, others in self-justifying anger. However, as painful as conflict can be, it would be unhealthy if there was no conflict in a local church. Complete calm is no more a measure of spiritual maturity than a bright new paint job is a measure of the structural integrity of a termite-infested house.

UNDERSTANDING CONFLICT

Understanding some basic principles of conflict can help give us a healthier perspective on conflict. The causes of conflict in a church can be boiled down to two major sources.

First, church ministry always involves change, and change produces conflict. When you think about it, the single primary goal of all ministry is change—change on a personal level and on a corporate level. God's goal in each of our personal lives is to make us more like Jesus Christ (2 Corinthians 3:18; Romans 8:29). All of us have experienced inner conflicts in this process, and sometimes those spill out into interpersonal conflicts. But ministry is also about corporate change. That is, churches have to change continuously in order to minister effectively to a changing world. Ministry forms and methods that worked a few years ago have lost their effectiveness. But, we have grown

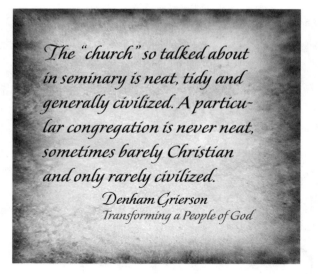

The "church" so talked about in seminary is neat, tidy and generally civilized. A particular congregation is never neat, sometimes barely Christian and only rarely civilized.
Denham Grierson
Transforming a People of God

comfortable with those forms and feel insecure in letting go of them, so we resist change. And conflicts occur.

Second, none of us is glorified yet. Each of us still struggles with a fallen nature. Therefore there will be times when you and I do not act in a loving manner. Sometimes we are threatened by change and lash out at others to protect ourselves. We let legitimate differences become personal issues; we attack the person instead of interacting with the idea. We withdraw and hold ourselves aloof from those we need to interact with the most.

These are spiritual issues and character issues. This is why again the spiritual and the character issues are at the very core of leadership.

A QUICK SURVEY OF EARLY CHURCH CONFLICT

The reality is that conflict has always been a part of church life. Sometimes we look longingly at the early church as described in Acts 2:43–47 and think that those conditions of unity and unselfish sharing continued for a long time. Unfortunately those early experiences of excitement and unity did not last long, and there is an understandable reason why they did not. In fact, you could say that the early church was a mess! And the scriptural account clearly depicts the early church conflicts and struggles in technicolor reality.

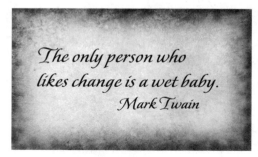

The only person who likes change is a wet baby.
Mark Twain

Church conflict is part of the fabric of church life from Acts to Revelation. To get a feel for the kinds of conflict, look at the following passages and interact with the Scripture through the questions posed below.

Acts 6:1–6

What was the cause of the conflict or the issue which sparked the conflict?

_____

_____

What happened?

_____

_____

How was the conflict resolved?

_____

_____

What can we learn about church conflict from this example?

_____

_____

_____

Acts 11:1–18

What was the cause of the conflict or the issue that sparked the conflict?

_____

_____

What happened?

_____

_____

How was the conflict resolved?

_____

_____

What can we learn about church conflict from this example?

_____

_____

_____

Acts 15:1–35

What was the cause of the conflict or the issue that sparked the conflict?

_____

_____

What happened?

_____

_____

How was the conflict resolved?

_____

_____

What can we learn about church conflict from this example?

_____

_____

_____

Acts 15:36–41

What was the cause of the conflict or the issue that sparked the conflict?

_____

_____

What happened?

_____

_____

How was the conflict resolved?

_____

_____

What can we learn about church conflict from this example?

_____

_____

_____

Galatians 2:11–14

What was the cause of the conflict or the issue that sparked the conflict?

_____

_____

What happened?

_____

_____

_____

How was the conflict resolved?

_____

_____

What can we learn about church conflict from this example?

_____

_____

_____

TRUTHS ABOUT CONFLICT

There are misconceptions about conflict that we should recognize—and truths that dispel those misconceptions. First, *conflict is not always sin*. Conflicts can arise from simple misunderstandings. Conflicts can arise from personality differences, differences in experience, or differences of perspective. In such cases, if the conflict is handled properly, there is no sin involved.

Second, *conflict is a complex issue*. It is often difficult to discern clearly the reasons for the conflict. Often the parties to the conflict are unaware of their own motives. After a while, after cycles of justifying to themselves or others why they acted as they did, the truth gets lost. Rationalizations assume the aura of reality, and "what really happened" is probably unrecoverable. Selective perception plays a role in conflict. People see in situations and actions what they expect to see or what they want to see. What does not fit with their bias is rejected or overlooked. This is why two people can give contradictory accounts of the same meeting, and both passionately believe they are describing reality.

Third, *conflict can be resolved*. A relationship with Jesus Christ provides the power to solve the conflict. Relationship with Christ provides the fulfillment of our deepest needs, so they do not have to be motivators of strategies that cause conflict with others. This takes us back yet again to issues of spiritual pilgrimage and character. By this point in the course it should be clear that character and spiritual pilgrimage issues play a role in every leadership action or skill. We lead out of who we are.

REASONS THAT CONFLICTS DEVELOP IN A CHURCH

When we recognize that conflict is a complex issue, we wonder, *How can I resolve it*? Part of the answer is to recognize the causes of conflict. Here are seven reasons for conflict in the church.

1. Personality Differences

People have different temperaments, different experience bases, and different preferences. The conflict between Paul and Barnabas may have been based in different temperaments. Paul was the goal-oriented driver; Barnabas the people-oriented encourager.

Of course to suggest that Paul was not people-oriented would overlook the depth and sensitivity of the many relationships he valued. See Romans 16, for example. But in this case, Paul was adamant that one who had "deserted" them on an earlier trip could not be trusted. Barnabas thought that John Mark could be salvaged for the ministry. It was a difference in values and perspective.

2. Differences in Approach to Ministry

In fact, the only sin which we never forgive in each other is difference of opinion.

Ralph Waldo Emerson
Society and Solitude

Sometimes these are generational differences. Each generational group has different experiences and different worldviews. These include a different set of values. While a younger generation may hold to the same basic set of biblical values as the older generation, it may express them differently. This becomes a form-function problem. Both generations may value the same function (worship, for example) but value different forms of expression.

When a church is first formed, the current culture creates a stable, predictable environment and provides meaning, identity, and a pattern of relationships and communication. Generations later, the church's culture has become so well embedded and traditional that it serves only to reinforce the assumptions and values of the older, more conservative elements of the church.

At this point a "rebellious counterculture"[1] is often created by the younger, more externally oriented elements in the group, and the total group culture begins to suffer from loss of integrity. Conflicts begin to erupt into the open. The counterculture does not necessarily always come from the younger group; it can come from any significant church group that does not believe its needs are being met in the current situation.

The younger generation wants new music, a more open worship; the older generation holds on to the ministry forms that have provided stability, security, and meaning in the past. This tension can lead to a church split. In an extreme situation a massive replacement of people may take place. From a positive perspective, a genuinely new cultural approach to church ministry may develop.

Other times conflicts come from cultural differences. The inclusion of Gentiles into the church is an illustration of such a conflict (Acts 10:9–11:18). At times conflicts are caused by differences in leadership style.

3. Power Struggles

All churches have limited resources, both of finances and time. The person who is egocentric views his area of ministry as more important than that of others. He then competes with others for funding or time "up front." Or he may mistakenly view everything as a "closed system"; that is, there is only a fixed amount of everything. He then views any praise and attention given to someone else as being unavailable to him. Those who embrace an "open system" believe praise, recognition, and attention can expand to whatever amount is needed.

Sometimes the power struggles are more sinister in nature. Many people exercise various types of power in the church; and sometimes they conflict with each other. Power itself is so alluring that it has been called "the ultimate high." The exercise of power is so appealing that we are more drawn to it than any of us would like to admit. Churches tend to allow people to obtain and abuse power fairly easily. What is often not tolerated in the secular world is overlooked in the church, because believers, out of a misunderstanding of "turning the other cheek" or a desire to avoid uncomfortable situations, are less willing to confront those who seek power. Churches are always in need of workers and leaders, and sometimes church leaders are not careful about whom they allow to take leadership roles.

> *Self-deception about one's behavior and motives is a potential hazard for all who are in positions of authority. A taste of power whets one's appetite for more of it.*
> *James E. Means*
> *Leadership in Christian Ministry*

The abuse of power is conceived invisibly in our normal need for self-esteem. God intended that our primary source of self-esteem would be our relationship to Himself as His specially created and greatly loved children. But we often substitute human means, which the world promotes as paths to self-esteem, such as accomplishments, positions of power or influence, wealth, social status, or possessions. When we begin to take ourselves too seriously, or think more highly of ourselves than we ought to think (Romans 12:3), we enter into danger. We begin to confuse our desires with the will of God. And we begin to view other people as means or obstacles to the accomplishment of our own ends.

How can we recognize the abuse of power? Calvin Miller suggests five evidences of power abuse.[2]

1. Giving up those disciplines we still demand of underlings.

2. Believing that others owe us whatever use we can make of them.

3. Trying to fix things up rather than make things right.

4. Closing our minds to every suggestion that we ourselves could be out of line.

5. Believing that people in our way are expendable.

4. Loss of Focus on the Purpose of the Church Ministry or Loss of Vision

When the church loses sight of its ministry vision, competing individual visions come into conflict. The power issues discussed above add volatility and intensity to this mix. Different views of the purpose of the church also bring conflict. Is the church an army, a hospital, a counseling center, a social gathering, or an activity center?

Much harm is done in the church because we forget the corrupting nature of power. It is easy to want to control others for our own advantage.

Calvin Miller
The Empowered Leader

5. Differences in Values

Values conflicts do not normally yield to a clarifying of the facts, because facts are not the issue. Conflicts driven by differences in values can be acknowledged but rarely solved.[3]

6. Theological Disagreements

Even people who are close to each other sometimes disagree on how to interpret the Scriptures. Most differences of this type occur in the application of theology to current issues such as:

+ the role of women in the church,

+ divorce and remarriage and church leadership,

+ worship styles and forms,

+ the ministry of the Holy Spirit and the exercise of gifts, and

+ sanctification, grace, and legalism versus liberty.

Unfortunately, theological disagreements often degenerate into personality conflicts. And sometimes personality conflicts are disguised as theological disagreements. This is because it is considered more acceptable to disagree theologically than to have a personality conflict. True theological conflicts are significantly fewer than the number claimed.

7. Certain People Who Are Prone to Conflicts

Through the years I have observed several churches during times of intense conflict. From these I have compiled a listing of "Destructive People in the Church," who are described at the end of this chapter. Be aware that these people exist in every church.

CONFLICTS FOLLOW A PREDICTABLE CYCLE

Church conflicts follow a pattern of escalation to higher levels of intensity and antagonism. Each conflict cycle has at least seven stages, depicted in figure 11.

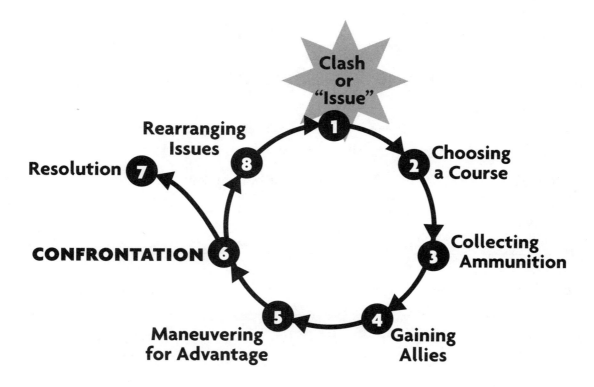

Figure 11
THE CONFLICT CYCLE

All conflicts start with a clash between two people or an "issue" that becomes the cause for a conflict. One key to conflict resolution is to break the cycle at the earliest stage possible. The further the conflict develops, the more difficult it will be to resolve. At stage 2, people are asking, "What is my role in this situation?" or "What should I do about the problem I see?" If problems could be confronted at this stage, before the list of injustices starts growing, they could be solved fairly easily. Once a person decides to fight, he begins to collect ammunition (stage 3), usually in the form of a list of injustices or wrongs committed by the opponent. He then goes about using this list to gain allies in the conflict (stage 4). Others are made aware of the opponent's wrong actions and enlisted as allies to help right the wrongs of the opponent. The group then maneuvers for advantage in order to insure that the confrontation takes place on ground on which they have the advantage.

Think of a recent conflict in your church and trace it through the cycle of conflict:

1 What was the clash or "issue" that precipitated the conflict?

_____
_____
_____

2 What initial choice did the principal party make about dealing with the precipitating event?

_____
_____
_____

3 What kind of ammunition did the person collect?

_____
_____
_____

4 How did he or she recruit allies to his or her cause?

_____
_____
_____

5 What maneuvers did he use to gain advantage?

_____
_____
_____

6 *What happened at the confrontation?*

_____
_____
_____
_____

7 *Was the problem resolved, or did they readjust their issue and continue the conflict?*

_____
_____
_____
_____

8 *List two things you learned from this conflict.*

_____
_____
_____
_____

LEARNING FROM CONFLICT

Conflict can actually be very healthy in a church. Conflict often unfreezes a situation by making people analyze their basic assumptions, unshakable positions, and traditional methods of ministering and relating to each other. Conflict also motivates the sharing of opinions and feelings which may have been denied or hidden but which still influence people in their responses to others.

Conflict often enhances communication. It can create channels of communication that have not existed before and break open channels that have long been closed.

Conflict can expose the need to create or clarify church vision. It will show the need to explain the purpose of proposed changes more clearly.

Conflict Resolution Strategies

There are several conflict resolution strategies that can be effective when used appropriately.

1. Withdrawing or Avoiding

The goal of the *withdrawing/avoiding* strategy is to avoid the conflict as much as possible or to "avoid being identified with either side" in the conflict.[4] The avoider may physically withdraw or stay away from the conflict scene or from those involved in the conflict. The avoider may be present but uninvolved, quiet, emotionally distant, or preoccupied. Some avoiders talk incessantly in order to keep a conflict issue from being raised.

Strengths of this strategy: It can be used to keep a person out of conflicts that are unresolvable or endless.

Weaknesses or problems of this strategy: Avoidance often increases the anger of the other person because the avoider is unavailable for resolution. Consistent use of withdrawal will give the other person the feeling of being right and the avoider will feel passive and powerless.

Situations when withdrawing may be used effectively: (1) When you need more time before confrontation; (2) When confrontation could do more harm than good; or (3) when the issue is trivial or hopeless.

2. Yielding or Accommodating

The goal of the *yielding/accommodating* strategy is to "preserve the relationship at all costs."[5]

Strengths of this strategy: It brings a quick end to the conflict.

Weaknesses or problems of this strategy: The accommodating person ultimately denies his own interests in the desire to end the conflict. However, the ending of the conflict may be only on the surface; the conflict may simply go underground in the internal life of the one who yields. If this happens, the conflict will surface in other ways: coldness of relationship, internal turmoil, or physical problems. So yielding may produce only an appearance of agreement. The person who consistently yields will feel powerless and valueless.

Situations when yielding may be used effectively: (1) when the issue means more to others than to the yielder; (2) when the other person is very fragile; (3) when maintaining harmony is more important than resolution; or (4) when the yielder is convinced he is in the wrong.

3. Resolving or Collaborating

The goal of the *resolving/collaborating* strategy is to get everyone involved and come to mutually agreed results.

Strengths of this strategy: It involves all persons who are part of the conflict. Collaborating values both the relationships involved and the needs of the persons and the organization. Because of this, it has the best chance for a long-term resolution of the conflict and the building of trust between the persons involved in the conflict.

Weaknesses or problems of this strategy: Collaboration requires the cooperation of the other person(s). It requires a commitment to open, honest, nondefensive dealing with the issues. Because of this, it requires a higher level of maturity on the part of all persons involved.

Situations when resolving may be used effectively: (1) when the issues are so important that they cannot be overlooked or compromised. Actually, as the preferred strategy for conflict management, resolving ought to be used whenever possible; and (2) when all persons involved will be significantly affected by the decisions made. Keep in mind that sometimes, because of the intensity or the lack of readiness of the persons involved in the conflict, other strategies may need to be employed temporarily.

4. Compromising

The goal of the *compromising* strategy is to give a little to get a little and make the problem go away.

Strength of this strategy: Some kind of solution is achieved.

Weaknesses or problems of this strategy: There is a good chance that neither side will be truly satisfied with the solution. The result is better described as "we have just minimized our dissatisfaction."[6] Thus the relationship may experience distance, depending upon whether each person focuses on the part he won or the part he lost.

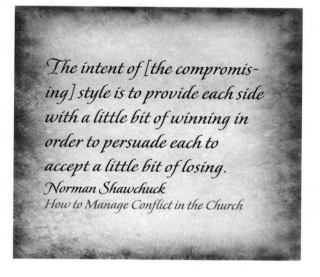

The intent of [the compromising] style is to provide each side with a little bit of winning in order to persuade each to accept a little bit of losing.
Norman Shawchuck
How to Manage Conflict in the Church

Situations when compromising may be used effectively: (1) when a temporary settlement of the issue is of greater benefit than no settlement. The issue cannot be too important if this solution is to work; (2) when time pressures requiring an immediate settlement make more productive solutions;[7] or (3) when both parties are strongly committed to mutually exclusive goals.[8]

5. Winning (i.e., Competing)

The goal of the *winning/competing* strategy is to win at any cost.

Strengths of this strategy: The winner's needs are met. In fact this is the winner's entire goal. His own needs are considered to be more important that those of the others involved.

Weaknesses or problems of this strategy: The winner's needs are met at the expense of the others involved. Winning destroys relationships, especially if winning is the person's characteristic strategy for solving conflict. Only in clear cases of emergencies is winning a truly productive strategy. The long-term results of this strategy may be "increasing covert hostility, halfhearted implementation of the solution,"[9] and withdrawal by the other persons.

There is only one *situation when winning may be used effectively*. Some emergency situations in which a difficult or controversial decision must be made are handled best by this style. For example, winning is the appropriate strategy when the treasurer of the church is discovered to be stealing funds.

Look back at page 84 (chapter 5: "The Leader's Temperament") and note the sentences you completed at the bottom of the page.

1. *What did you learn about your preferred strategy in resolving conflict from that exercise?*

_____

_____

_____

2. *Which of the five conflict resolution strategies listed above do you use most naturally? most often? Why?*

_____

_____

_____

All conflict resolution strategies are a mixture of your desire to maintain the relationship and to get what you want. The various conflict resolution strategies are depicted in the figure below.

Figure 12
STRATEGIES FOR CONFLICT RESOLUTION

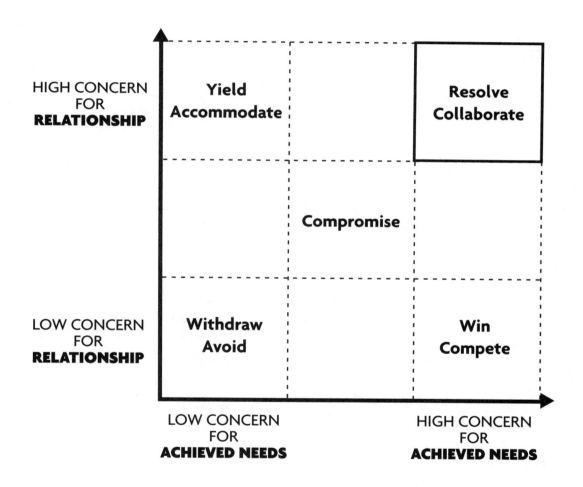

SOURCE: Adapted from Norman Shawchuck, *How to Manage Conflict in the Church* (Irvine, Calif.: Spiritual Growth Resources, 1983), 31.

PRINCIPLES OF CONFLICT RESOLUTION

The ultimate goal of handling conflict is resolution. Here are nine principles for dealing with the conflict and moving toward resolution.

1. Start with the right perspective on conflict.

Conflict is unavoidable, even among mature Christians. This is the natural result of being people not yet glorified, living in a fallen world. Remember, conflict can be used constructively, and a certain level of conflict is healthy.

The most critical element in bringing peace out of conflict is one's personal attitude. My attitude toward the other person(s) must be loving. In order for my attitude to be loving, I must be at peace with myself and aware of my own sinful ways of relating. Personal issues that have not been dealt with in my own life tend to show up powerfully in conflict situations.

When you feel you have been wronged by a fellow believer, always use the biblical process to seek a biblical solution (Matthew 18:15–17).

What are the steps in the process?

_____

_____

_____

_____

_____

A Christian perspective should control our approach. God is still sovereign, and the Holy Spirit can give insight and wisdom and strength. Christ has set us free from the domination of the flesh. We are still part of a body in which God desires unity and peace (Colossians 3:15). Our ultimate goal should remain that God is glorified by our actions and that others are encouraged and built up by involvement with us.

Do not ignore the fact that some conflicts are of a spiritual nature. Satan raised doubts in Peter's mind (Matthew 16:13–23). We are not to be ignorant of Satan's schemes (2 Corinthians 2:11).

2. Make prayer an integral part of the process.

Set a date to bring both parties together to resolve the conflict. Ask them to be diligent in prayer before the meeting. Encourage them to ask God to work in their lives and expose their part in the conflict and to give them understanding of those on the other side of the conflict.

When you get both sides together, spend time praying together before you discuss the issues. As appropriate, stop periodically during the process to pray about the specific issues you are dealing with at the time.

3. Deal with conflict at the lowest level of intensity possible.

As soon as tension is recognized, get together with the people involved to attempt to resolve the issues. The earlier this is done, the better. The further around the conflict cycle you allow things to go, the harder they will be to settle. The longer injustices are collected, the more issues there will be to resolve!

4. Generate valid and useful information about the issues in the conflict.

Ask hard questions of all parties to the conflict. Investigate allegations fully (Proverbs 18:17). There are two sides to every problem. Work to get a common definition of the problem. Until this is accomplished, the conflict cannot be resolved.

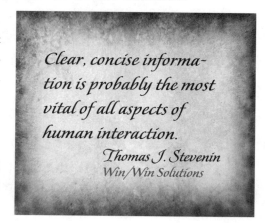

Clear, concise information is probably the most vital of all aspects of human interaction.

Thomas J. Stevenin
Win/Win Solutions

5. Keep everyone focused on the conflict issue.

When everyone meets, be sure the gathering focuses on the issue. Agree on the ground rules for the meeting. Four helpful rules are:

a. Give people permission to disagree.

b. Give people time to state their positions clearly. Do not let them be interrupted.

c. Protect people from being needlessly hurt. Do not allow personal attacks.

d. Keep the conversation civil, even when emotions are intense. Help people learn proper ways of expressing strong emotion.

6. Suggest options to give people paths to get out of conflict.

The deeper people get into conflict, the fewer options they see for how to get out. Conflict tends to escalate rapidly, especially in the emotional dimension. Before long, not only are our egos involved, but our very sense of personal survival may seem at stake. The more intense the emotional response, the more our focus is restricted to the idea we have to win. If we are not careful, our focus can lock onto winning and being "right" as the only viable option. Therefore the leader should offer options to help people find paths toward resolution.

7. Admit a mistake.

When you have been wrong, admit it and ask forgiveness. Attempting to hide a mistake or wrong will create a larger problem and will destroy people's trust in you. While it is hard for any of us to admit when we have sinned, or even failed, a forthright admission will gain more respect than a selfish attempt to preserve our invulnerability.

When you confess a sin, follow these five guidelines. First, *identify the sin clearly and take personal responsibility for it*. Acknowledge that what you did was wrong. There is no true confession without this acknowledgment (Psalm 51:3–4).

Second, *make your confession to everyone affected by your action*. The circle of people affected is probably wider than you think. It certainly includes the wife or husband of the person you sinned against. Pain is normally shared with those closest to us. The circle may include others as well.

Third, *avoid the following tempting confessional pitfalls*:

   a. *The Artful Dodge:* "If I have offended you . . ." and other similar words. This commonly used approach:

      ✦ assumes little or no personal responsibility.

      ✦ does not indicate that you believe what you did was wrong; rather it implies that the problem is with the other person for being easily offended.

      ✦ does not acknowledge the sinfulness of what was done.

      ✦ places all of the responsibility on the other person to forgive . . . without acknowledging anything specific that needs to be forgiven.

      ✦ makes the other person appear to be vindictive and unforgiving if he or she does not grant forgiveness, even though nothing has been admitted that needs to be forgiven!

   b. *The Angry Attack:* "I may have . . . but you . . . !" or "Well, you're just as wrong!!!"

   c. *The Creative Memory:* "I never said that. I would never say such a thing. What I said was . . . !"

   d. *The Political Deflection:* "I'm sorry you thought . . . , but I never meant. . . ."

   e. *The Defensive Rationalization:* "What I did wasn't so bad. Other people do a lot worse!"

Fourth, *express sorrow and regret for the wrong* and its impact on the other person(s).

Fifth, *be willing to accept the consequences*. All sin has consequences. At the least, it will take some time to rebuild the trust lost by the sin. In some cases restitution is appropriate. A good question to ask here is, "What can I do to make this right between us?" Then, be willing to do it.

8. Use your leadership capital wisely.

The greatest influence you have comes from the level of trust people have in you. Take care to maintain that trust by not acting selfishly or rashly.

Don't use your authority as a leader to coerce people into compromising their position. It is better to "agree to disagree" than to force an agreement that requires the other person to compromise his/her beliefs. You may gain your point, but you will lose the respect of the person you coerce. You will probably also lose his or her future cooperation.

Guard your own emotions and be careful what you say during a disagreement. In the end, whatever you do, do not make the problem worse.

9. Realize that not all conflict will be resolved—at least not right away.

Sometimes people have too much invested in the conflict to let go of it and resolve it. Some people use the opportunity to remain angry at others so that they will not have to confront their own personal issues. Others use bitterness toward others to justify their own failures. In such cases, do what you can to maintain the relationship so that if the other person has a change of heart and is ready to reconcile and resolve the conflict, there will not be an extra load of grievances to deal with.

Evidently Paul and Barnabas split without resolving the difference between them. Though the Scripture does not give the details, the dispute was later resolved. Sometimes it takes us a while to open ourselves up enough to allow the Holy Spirit to work in us.

DESTRUCTIVE PEOPLE IN THE CHURCH

AGGRESSORS Aggressors are always on the march for their own ideas. They push their viewpoint incessantly, regardless of merit. Often they win just by wearing others down.

Their battle cry is, "The best defense is a good offense!"

SELF-INFLICTED WOUNDED These people seem to be against everything. They attack other's ideas with ferocity. Sometimes they attack other people directly. When they are around, you know you are always in for a fight.

Their battle cry is, "They may win, but we'll make 'em pay!"

COMMANDERS

Commanders are those who need to be in control, to call the shots. They are also known individually as the "church boss." Commanders feel that without their control, the church will falter and die. They are therefore indispensable and must be consulted on all decisions. Each commander is the power broker in the church.

Their battle cry is, "I'm in charge here at the church!"

SNIPERS

Snipers operate from hiding places. They hide behind others, or they talk secretly behind your back, sending deadly bullets to destroy your credibility, damage your reputation, and undermine your influence. Because they camouflage their efforts so skillfully, you seldom know where the shot came from. Nor do you know when or from what angle the next one is coming.

Their battle cry is whispered as they tighten the trigger, "Watch your back, Jack!"

SMART BOMBS

These are the perfectionists, the people who are always right. On whatever issue, theirs is the only correct approach. No other approach is rational or biblical or spiritual. Those who do not agree are seen as obstacles. Since, to the Smart Bombs, these are issues of right and wrong (they are right; others are wrong), there is almost a moral obligation to remove the obstacles, and any means of doing so is justified. They often employ snipers. Smart Bombs must win. In the end, they blow up the ministry.

Their battle cry is, "I'm right! You'll see!"

STEALTH BOMBERS

These are the people who simply try to destroy you because they disagree with you. When you least expect it, they will roll a hand grenade under your door and feel relieved to have you out of the way. They also like letter bombs. "Dear Elder Bob, I don't like to say this, but I feel that I must tell you that . . ."

Their battle cry is, "Yea, though I walk through the valley, I will fear no evil, for I'm the meanest man in the valley!"

PSY-WARRIORS Psy-warriors win by spreading misinformation. They are experts at "spin" and know how to make a lie sound believable. They rewrite history with such bold artistry that eyewitnesses to the same events are left scratching their heads in bewilderment. They are experts at making you feel like you were in the wrong.

Their battle cry is, "And there are lots of others who feel this way!"

STRATEGISTS Strategists are the power players who are skilled at getting what they want. They are adept at finding and exploiting weaknesses that open the way to achieve their goals. They are the manipulators who devise clever strategies to build their power base or get the votes they need. They skillfully use the other types of problem people to further their own strategies.

Their battle cry is, "My ends justify any means!"

SELF-INFLICTED WOUNDED The SIWs are always wounded. In fact, they find it so convenient to be wounded that they look for things to be wounded or offended about. Being wounded is a way to control others while exempting themselves from responsibility for constructive involvement with them. Besides that, it gets them lots of attention.

Their battle cry is, "No pain, no gain!"

Notes

1. Edgar Schein, *Organizational Culture and Leadership* (San Francisco: Jossey-Bass, 1987), 270.
2. Calvin Miller, *The Empowered Leader: 10 Keys to Servant Leadership* (Nashville: Broadman & Holman, 1995), 130.
3. E. K. Morrison, *Leadership Skills* (Tuscon, Ariz.: Fisher, 1983), 149.
4. Norman Shawchuck, *How to Manage Conflict in the Church* (Irvine, Calif.: Spiritual Growth Resources, 1983), 23.
5. Ibid., 24.
6. Glenn M. Parker, *Team Players and Teamwork* (San Francisco: Jossey-Bass, 1990), 42.
7. Shawchuck, *How to Manage Conflict in the Church*, 26.
8. Morrison, *Leadership Skills*, 157.
9. Shawchuck, *How to Manage Conflict in the Church*, 27.

T W E N T Y

TIME MANAGEMENT FOR CHURCH LEADERS

FEW ACTIVITIES HOLD THE PROMISE OF GREATER personal satisfaction than church ministry. But few activities in life are as demanding of our time as church ministry. Church ministry focuses on serving people's needs, and the needs are always greater than our resources of time and energy.

Time is our most precious resource—and a nonrenewable one. Once it is spent, it is gone. That is why God in His Word warns us to "number our days" (Psalm 90:12). The entire Psalm 90 relates to our use of time and puts the time management question in a broader context.

> *Nothing else, perhaps, distinguishes effective executives as much as their tender loving care of time.*
>
> *Peter Drucker*

Read the entire psalm and summarize the thought in the three sections, using the questions below:

Section 1: The shortness of life (vv. 1–6)

What does Moses realize about God?

_____

_____

_____

_____

What is true of man?

_____

_____

_____

Section 2: The effect of our choices (vv. 7–12)

How did Moses' generation get in the situation they were in?

_____

_____

_____

Make a note of the emotionally powerful phrases used to describe life lived apart from God's blessing (cf. vv. 7, 9–10, also 5–6 in the previous section).

_____

_____

_____

_____

What does Moses mean when he says, "Teach us to number our days" (v. 12)?

_____

_____

_____

The purpose of numbering our days is to present to God a "heart of wisdom" (v. 13). Describe what you think a heart of wisdom would be like.

_____

_____

_____

Section 3: The desire for significance (vv. 13–17)

What is it that brings joy and satisfaction to life?

_____

_____

Notice at the end of the psalm the parallel between God's work and our work and the repetition of the phrase "confirm the work of our hands." The term "confirm" has the idea of giving a sense of permanence. What is Moses asking for here?

_____

_____

_____

How do you experience this same longing? What forms does it take in your life?

_____

_____

_____

What work of your hands do you want God to "confirm"? Another way of saying this is, "What do you want the ultimate impact of your life to be?"

_____

_____

_____

THE KEY TO TIME MANAGEMENT

All of the techniques will be useless if the desire to make better use of your time is not there. Thus . . . the determining thing is what you value most. Many people will complain about their lack of time to do the things they "really want to do." But if you observe them, it becomes apparent that they are, in fact, living according to their values. We all have some level of disparity between our "proclaimed values," those values we say are important to us, and our "practiced values," those values we actually live by.

Sometimes those who find their time has slipped away will discover, upon honest reflection, that very high on their list of practiced values are things like:

+ freedom to do whatever they feel like doing at the time
+ not having to be bound by a plan or schedule
+ freedom from having to make difficult choices between alternatives

Proper management of time requires that we be (1) effective and (2) efficient in our use of time, and that we (3) delegate whenever possible. In the following discussion of these three time management principles, you will evaluate your methods and approaches.

PRINCIPLE ONE: BE *EFFECTIVE* IN SPENDING YOUR TIME

Be as effective as possible in the way you spend your time. Effectiveness comes from choosing to spend your time in ways that are in harmony with your values and that contribute to the fulfillment of your life vision. This is a good time to review your answers to the questions about your personal values (chapter 7: "The Leader's Values and Goals") and your personal life vision (chapter 13: "Developing Vision for Your Life"). Use the chart on the next page to update your values and vision.

	MY VALUES What is most important to me in . . .	MY VISION What I dream of seeing happen in . . .
My relationship with God		
My personal life		
My relationship with my spouse		
My relationship with my children		
My professional life and relationships		
My ministry		

Once you have completed the chart "My Values, My Vision," it's time for an evaluation. Complete the chart "How I Did . . ." on the next page to determine your choices that day.

You cannot be a good steward of controlling this precious resource of time if you do not know where it goes. Periodically review your day and ask yourself, "Did my values and vision affect my schedule today? Is what I am currently doing important enough to exchange a day of my life for it?"

The bottom line on effectiveness is: **Focus** *on doing the will of God.* The apostle Paul exhorts Christians, "Therefore be careful how you walk, not as unwise men but as wise, making the most of your time, because the days are evil. So then do not be foolish, but understand what the will of the Lord is" (Ephesians 5:15–17).

This is the most basic principle for effective time management. As you choose how to spend your time, ask yourself, "Does this activity help me do what I know to be the will of God in the most important areas of my life?" This passage is an encouragement to spend time on the things that are eternally important, given the fact that the whole direction of society is in the other direction.

PRINCIPLE TWO: BE AS *EFFICIENT* AS POSSIBLE IN THE WAY YOU SPEND YOUR TIME

If effectiveness has to do with spending your time on the right things, efficiency has to do with gaining more time to spend effectively. Often, even when we are trying to be effective in our use of time, we allow time to get away from us because of poor habits or inattention. We all have the same amount of time; some use theirs more efficiently than others.

We recommend six practices to make your use of time more efficient. They are: (1) plug time leaks, (2) eliminate time wasters, (3) plan and set your priorities, (4) establish measurable goals and workable plans, (5) develop systems to do repetitive tasks, and (6) evaluate regularly your level of "drivenness."

How I Did

Evaluate the way you spent your time yesterday, consulting the chart "My Values, My Vision." Think through the day and ask yourself:

1. Was my choice of the way I spent my time determined by my values, and did it contribute to fulfilling my vision?
2. How can I improve my choices so they may be more in harmony with my values and better fulfill my vision?

	HOW I DID . . .	HOW I CAN IMPROVE . . .
6:00 A.M.		
7:00		
8:00		
9:00		
10:00		
11:00		
12:00 P.M.		
1:00		
2:00		
3:00		
4:00		
5:00		
6:00		
7:00		
8:00		
9:00		
10:00		
11:00		

Practice One: Plug your time leaks.

The telephone can be a major time waster. Get "caller ID" or find some other way to screen your calls. The television can eat up great amounts of time if you are not careful. Turn it off; get rid of it. Or look through the week's TV schedule on Sunday and mark (choose) those programs that fit your values and vision. (Note: a certain amount of relaxation is a legitimate value. Just sitting in front of the television, however, is a colossal waste of time.) Then, when the program you have chosen to watch is finished, turn it off.

Low-priority tasks, which "won't take long" and you find pleasurable, can eat up lots of your time. Somehow they always seem to expand into hours, partly because they are enjoyable, so you take just a little longer. . . .

Interruptions take up more time than just that of the interruption itself. The time needed to refocus your thought and get back into your subject is the hidden cost of the interruption. Everyone in ministry must learn to balance the importance of being able to meet people's needs when they occur (the interruption) and the requirement of having the time to accomplish the tasks that must be done.

> *Most time is wasted, not in hours, but in minutes. A bucket with a small hole in the bottom gets just as empty as a bucket that is deliberately emptied.*
>
> Paul J. Meyer
> *Spirit of Leadership*

What are the primary holes through which your time drains away?

_____

_____

_____

What can you do about them?

_____

_____

_____

_____

Practice Two: Eliminate time wasters.

Do you know those activities that waste your time? Some of the big ones are:

+ daydreaming

+ finding something interesting on your desk while you are supposed to be working
+ handling papers or letters four or five times
+ allowing meetings to last too long
+ inefficient use of your computer
+ allowing certain people to take too much of your time

The first step in eliminating time wasters is to identify them. What are the biggest time wasters in your life?

_____

_____

_____

What can you do about them?

_____

_____

_____

_____

Practice Three: Take time to plan and set your priorities.

Having reviewed and sharpened your set of values, you are in a position to plan and prioritize your time. Your value system will actually control how you spend your time. People spend their time differently because they value different things.

Your plan will include time set aside for the things that are most important to you. Include time for

+ *spiritual disciplines,* which deepen your relationship with God,
+ *physical disciplines,* which maintain your health and fitness,
+ *relational times,* which enrich your relationships with your spouse and children and the other relationships which are important in your life, and
+ *personal growth* opportunities, which enable you to develop greater personal capacities to serve.

Choose a scheduling scheme that fits your personality and activities. There is a wide assortment of planners and calendars on the market. Every size and style of notebook and paper planner imaginable is readily available. Electronic planners and calendars are now small enough to fit easily in your pocket. Choose one, use it, and stick with it. When you schedule:

1. Set aside time for the indispensable disciplines. Schedule these first, preferably at the same time each day.

2. Budget time for primary relationships. Work at relationships by scheduling time for them. Make use of "double-booking" when possible. For example, make supper a sacred time for the family. You all have to eat, so why not make it a regular relationship-building time too?

3. Know the rhythms of your life. Distinguish between slack time and prime time.

Are you a morning person or a night person?

_____

When do you do your best mental work which requires concentration?

_____

When do you most easily relate personally to other people?

_____

As much as you have opportunity, schedule your time accordingly.

4. Group similar activities you have planned: telephone calls, errands, etc.

5. Spend your time doing what you do well. Spend most of your time doing those things for which you are most gifted.

6. Decide *before* you must make a decision what is "better" and what is "best" for you. This is where a clear set of values and vision is very helpful.

7. Also, a well-thought-through biblical philosophy of ministry will greatly assist in planning how you spend your ministry time.

8. Learn to say no with anticipation and freedom. (You are not the Messiah. And even He did not do everything.) You have proper priorities and they are being implemented.

9. Delegate. You do not have all of the gifts. God has equipped others to do some things better than you. (See the final section of this chapter for a further discussion of delegation.)

Practice Four: Establish measurable goals and workable plans.

Use the process you worked with in chapter 17 (under "Strategic Planning") to set measurable goals in each primary area of your life. Include your spouse and family in the process.

Here is an exercise that will act as an example. You will establish goals for your ministry:

Think about your ministry responsibility in your church. What is the purpose of your ministry?

_____

_____

_____

What are the few really important things that need to be done? What three things, if done well, will result in the greatest amount of progress toward fulfilling the purpose of your ministry?

1. _____

2. _____

3. _____

Now, write two or three clear goals in each area:

1. _____

Goal # 1 _____

Goal # 2 _____

Goal # 3 _____

2. _____

Goal # 1 _____

Goal # 2 _____

Goal # 3 _____

3. _____

Goal # 1 _____

Goal # 2 _____

Goal # 3 _____

Practice Five: Develop systems to do repetitive tasks.

Develop a system to pay your monthly bills, to handle your mail, to clean your pool, to mow your yard, etc. A system will save you lots of time. You will have the tools at hand, the processes won't require reinvention every week, and you can think about other things while accomplishing many of your repetitive tasks.

Practice Six: Conduct a regular, honest evaluation of your level of "drivenness."

Drivenness is a condition in which you feel you "must" do things. It is a feeling that you have no choice in certain decisions. Pastors often think they "must" go and see that person or they "must" agree to serve in that position or they "must" attend that meeting, etc. If you have this feeling often, you should carefully evaluate the reasons why you feel this way.

Drivenness comes from our independent attempts to satisfy our deepest personal needs, such as the need for acceptance, self-esteem, or significance. However, an ongoing sense of drivenness typically is caused by one or more of the following: (1) wanting to please others, not God; (2) being strongly influenced by others' expectations; (3) placing higher values on doing rather than being; (4) having wrong priorities and a disordered life; and/or (5) having no clear goals—actually false goals.

> *No leader sets out to be a leader per se, but rather to express himself freely and fully. That is, leaders have no interest in proving themselves, but an abiding interest in expressing themselves. The difference is crucial, for it's the difference between being driven, as too many people are today, and leading, as too few people do.*
> *Warren Bennis*
> *On Becoming a Leader*

While drivenness manifests itself in both socially acceptable and unacceptable ways, pastors and other Christian leaders most often express drivenness in ways that are socially acceptable but personally destructive.

We normally express our drivenness in one of two ways:

1. *Rebellion.* This is generally not socially acceptable. The rebellious person is self-

absorbed, totally focused on meeting his own needs.

2. *Performance.* This is socially acceptable and often honored. The performance-driven person is also self-absorbed, seeking to meet his own needs through performing.

Pastors and church leaders or workers are much more likely to express drivenness through a high performance standard which requires them to always perform for others.

Figure 13

COMMON WAYS OF EXPRESSING OUR DRIVENNESS

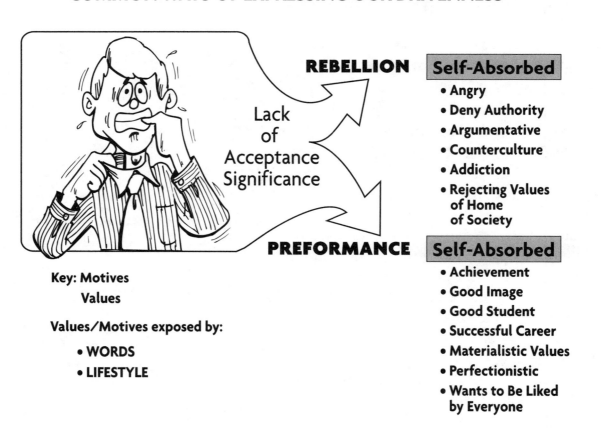

Drivenness, whether expressed as rebellion or performance, means yielding to self-absorbed attitudes and actions (see figure 13). Ultimately it is a spiritual problem, which can only be solved by repentance of our selfish attempts to gain acceptance and significance by our own efforts apart from God.

Repentance in this case involves an admission that some of our behavior (even that which outwardly seemed good) is sinfully motivated. Repentance also leads to a growing willingness to trust God to meet our deepest needs. Until this is done, we will still be driven to do things because of a compelling feeling of necessity. What is involved in that necessity is our own feeling of significance or acceptance, not a concern for the person ministered to or the job done. Until this issue is handled, time management is impossible because the hidden values of striving for significance and acceptance apart from trusting God will cause us to violate whatever time management structure we set up. The driven person cannot say no.

PRINCIPLE THREE: DELEGATE WHENEVER POSSIBLE

The practice of delegating is a matter of both being effective and efficient. Delegation reduces your own workload. It frees up time for you to do the things that only you can do, especially to give leadership to the church. Delegation allows you time to work in your own area of strength or spiritual gifts, and at the same time, it gives other people the opportunity to work in the area of their spiritual gifts. Indeed, it's as pragmatic and effective today as it was in Moses' time, as the following exercise will show.

Moses' Story

Read the story of Moses and Jethro in Exodus 18:17–27. Discuss and answer the following questions:

1. *What caused Jethro's concern for his son-in-law, Moses?*

   _____

   _____

2. *What were the dangers in the way Moses was working?*
   a. For the people? _____

   _____

   b. For Moses himself? _____

   _____

3. *What was Jethro's proposed solution to the problem he observed?*

   _____

   _____

   _____

4. *What benefits would be experienced if Jethro's advice was implemented?*

   _____

   _____

5. *In what ways are you operating similarly to Moses?*

_____

_____

_____

_____

6. *How often do you feel like you are "worn out?" Frustrated? To what extent has a feeling of drudgery replaced a feeling of excitement about your ministry? How high is your level of motivation? How often do you feel like you are "alone" in the work of the ministry?*

_____

_____

_____

_____

The Meaning of Delegation

Delegating is the process of entrusting the accomplishment of certain tasks to others. Delegation is not abdication. While some responsibility is given to the person to whom the task is delegated, the leader still retains overall responsibility to see that the task is done. Abdication describes the leader who does not follow through by checking periodically or providing assistance needed; he simply hopes the task will get done without any further involvement from him.

The Benefits of Delegation

The benefits of delegation are many. Motivation is higher when a person is contributing. People care more about the outcome when they are responsible for the outcome. Meaningful involvement creates a stronger sense of commitment to the group and its goals.

"Delegation is central to participation and growth, to working and being accountable," Max DePree noted. "Through delegation, leaders give their witness in the active practice of beliefs. Delegation is one kind of legitimate participation. Delegation is both an essential organizational function and an important gift to followers."[1]

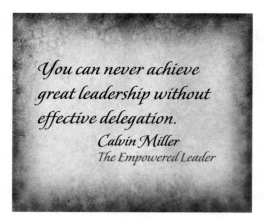

You can never achieve great leadership without effective delegation.
Calvin Miller
The Empowered Leader

Being entrusted with a worthwhile task stimulates creativity and initiative and gives others an opportunity for growth and development. In addition, delegation is one of the essential steps in developing future leaders. Note that pastors or church leaders who do not delegate will not develop the other leaders needed for the church to grow and extend its ministry.

If delegation is so good, why don't leaders delegate more? There are many reasons; some of them relate simply to poor planning. Other reasons are more dangerous. For example, sometimes leaders fail to plan far enough ahead. This makes it too late to delegate. Then they feel guilty asking someone else to do the job.

Sometimes they fear that the job delegated will not be done properly and therefore do it themselves. These reasons for not delegating are fairly simple to fix, the first by proper planning, the second by proper supervision.

The more dangerous reasons include a lack of commitment to develop others through delegation, coaching, and accountability. This may be simply a lack of foresight, or it can be the result of insecurity manifested in fear that someone else will be recognized and appreciated for the job done. This is far more serious, because this is a character issue in the life of the leader. Another character issue is unfounded egotism that makes the leader feel that he can do it better than anyone else.

The Dangers of Not Delegating

If you don't delegate tasks, you face several dangers:

+ You get so overcome with work that you do not do anything well.
+ You begin to feel discouraged.
+ You feel an extraordinarily heavy burden of responsibility.
+ You deprive the people you lead. You deprive them of your own best efforts, because you are overburdened. You deprive them of the gifts and skills of others who are not given the opportunity to serve because you are doing it all.
+ You will create or reinforce the view that "the pastor does it all."
+ People will become discouraged and disinterested.

SIX ELEMENTS OF EFFECTIVE DELEGATION

Many already know the benefits of delegating and the dangers of not delegating tasks and responsibilities. How can you delegate effectively? Here are six elements of effective delegation:

1. Choose the task.

Make a list of the tasks that you do regularly. Then ask yourself these questions:

+ Which of these tasks must I do? Which are so foundational to my responsibilities as a pastor or leader that normally only I can do them?

+ Even if there are some tasks which I must do, would the ministry of the church be strengthened by allowing others to participate in this task also?

+ Which of the tasks can be given to others to do?

+ Which of the tasks are causing me the most difficulty?

+ Which tasks am I gifted to accomplish? Can I focus on those for which I am gifted and allow other believers to do the others?

+ Which tasks are not in my area of giftedness? Are there others in the church who are gifted in ways which would allow them to do this task more easily?

Then evaluate carefully your use of time on tasks that you do not do regularly. Ask yourself, *Which of these tasks could someone else have done*? Then ask, *What would have happened if I had not done the task*? Be honest. Would the ministry of the church have been hindered? If the task really was important enough to be done, would someone else have done it?

Finally, make a list of tasks which could be delegated to others.

2. Assign responsibility.

Select the best person to accomplish this task. The person should be capable of accomplishing the task successfully and take the responsibility willingly. Ideally the person will feel a commitment to accomplish the task.

Once the person is selected, be sure to clearly define the task to be accomplished, and clearly express your expectations. Those expectations should include the completion date and standards of quality.

Note carefully: Delegation gives you another chance to reaffirm the vision to that person. Do not miss the opportunity to connect the task the person will do with the accomplishment of the church or ministry vision.

3. Give authority.

The person must be given whatever authority is required to accomplish the task. If the leader retains the authority, then the person must always come to the leader for permission to act. The leader should do the coordination necessary for others to know the person has authority to act.

4. Structure accountability.

The leader should provide clear lines of accountability so the person knows to whom he is responsible. Clear accountability frees the person from confusing relationships with those who might hinder the accomplishment of the task.

5. Provide support.

The leader must provide the resources needed to complete the task. This may include providing the training necessary to accomplish the task. Encouragement and assistance will also be needed.

6. Give credit.

When the task is completed, be sure to give credit to the person responsible through both personal and public acknowledgement.

Note

1. Max DePree, *Leadership Jazz* (New York: Dell Publishing, 1992), 154.

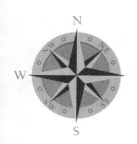

PREPARING YOUR LIFE STORY

PREPARING YOUR LIFE STORY IS A GREAT WAY to see your pilgrimage of faith and character development to the present. It should also provide confirmation of how God has gifted and developed you for leadership. As noted in chapter 3, we can uncover our life story by creating a Life Story Chart and then transferring its information to a Life Story Worksheet. Finally, we present our Life Story to others in a number of creative ways, including a Life Story Diagram. Samples of a chart, worksheet, and diagram follow to show how these may be completed.

SAMPLE LIFE STORY CHART

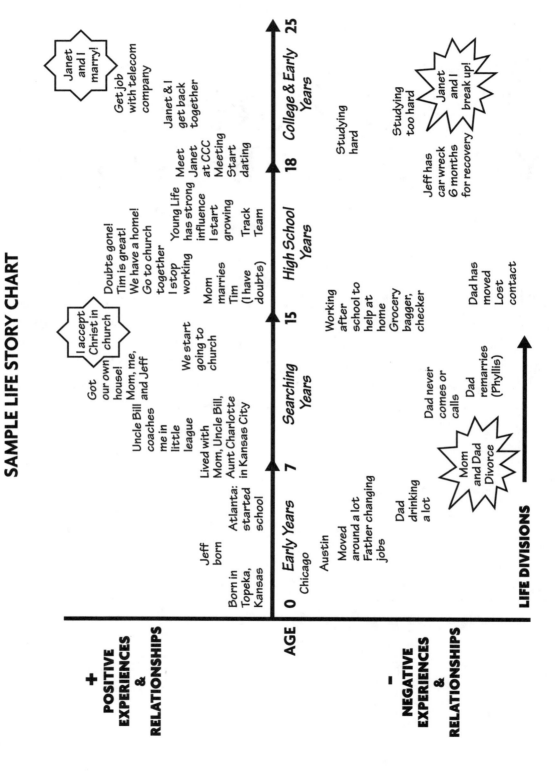

A SAMPLE LIFE STORY WORKSHEET

LIFE DIVISIONS	Early Years 0	Searching Years 7	High School Years 15	College and First Job Years 18 25
CHAPTER TITLES	Living with Instability	Searching for Stability	Finding a Sure Foundation	Launching Out
BRAIN-STORMING Formative Events, Hard Times, Good Times, Impacting Family Experiences, etc.	• I was born in Topeka, Kansas, April 17, 1975 (first child) Father was in grad school • We moved around a lot, Chicago, Austin, Atlanta Father was changing jobs • Jeff born February 6, 1978 • Dad started drinking . . . a LOT; he argued with Mom • I started school in Atlanta, teacher's pet	• MOM AND DAD DIVORCE! • We moved in with Uncle Bill and Aunt Charlotte in Kansas City • Uncle Bill was my best friend, he coached my Little League team, taught me to hit! • We started going to church • Mom got good job, we got our own house! She works a lot • Dad NEVER calls or visits	• Dad remarries (Phyllis) • I ACCEPT CHRIST at church • I work at grocery store to help • Mom starts dating Tim, I have doubts about him. They marry; I discover he is a great guy; we go to church as a family! • I can stop working; join track team at school • In Young Life I begin to grow	• At KU I met Janet at a Campus Crusade meeting, we started dating, break up, then get back together • Lost track of Dad, no address • Jeff has bad car wreck, takes 6 months to recover • I make top grades but study too hard, too important to me • JANET AND I MARRY • Good job with telecom, Dallas
GOD'S AUTHORSHIP What was God doing in these situations? How did He use them in your life?	It seemed like we were always moving so I never had any friends. I looked for ways to be accepted. I loved school, was the teacher's pet because I tried to do everything right. God was letting me experience the instability so that later I could appreciate stability in Him, not in anything else.	Dad's drinking, arguments with Mom and divorce were very painful. My Uncle Bill and Aunt Charlotte showed real love to us. God used this to show me what love can be like. Going to church for the first time, I began to hear about God's love and had an example to understand it. I saw the consequences of my dad's bad choice.	Through church ministry I accept Christ and find a sense of stability in His love and faithfulness. Young Life helps me grow. Time turns out to be another example of God's love to me. God's blessing allows me to stop working and enjoy school. I joined the track team and brought some guys to Young Life, one later accepted Christ.	Janet is God's gift to me. I almost "blow it" because I am too into getting max grades. I still struggle with getting my significance through my performance rather than from Christ. I am growing in this, but it shows up too often. God is so faithful to give me Janet. We grow together. I am asking God to help me be a stable, growing husband, and some day, father.

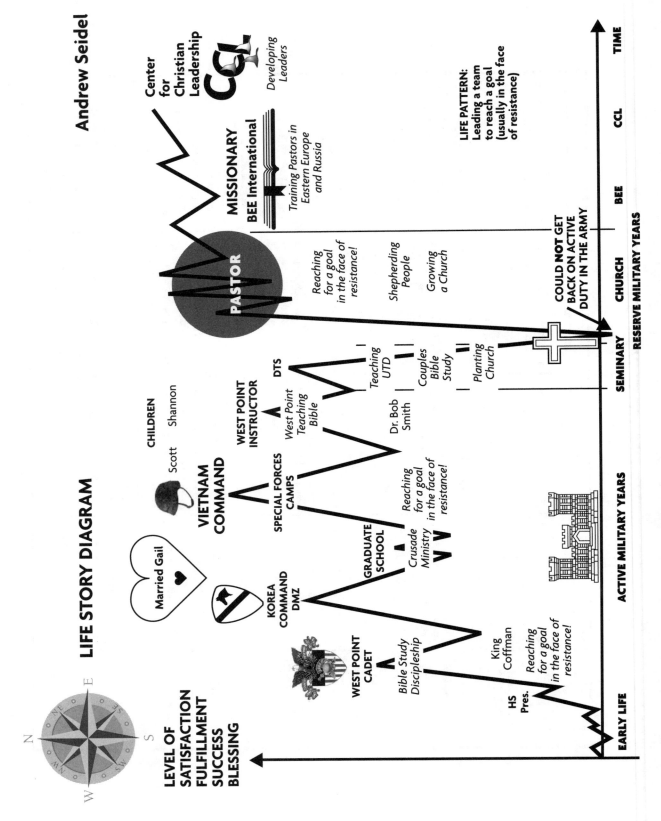

292

SELECTED
LEADERSHIP BIBLIOGRAPHY

Leadership—General

Bennis, Warren G. *On Becoming a Leader.* Reading, Mass.: Addison-Wesley, 1989.

*Bennis, Warren G., and Robert J. Thomas. *Geeks & Geezers: How Era, Values, and Defining Moments Shape Leaders.* Boston: Harvard Business School Press, 2002.

Blanchard, Ken. *The Heart of a Leader.* Tulsa, Okla.: Honor Books, 1999.

Collins, Jim. *Good to Great.* New York: HarperCollins, 2001.

DePree, Max. *Leadership Is an Art.* New York: Dell, 1989.

Goleman, Daniel, Richard Boyatzis, and Annie McKee. *Primal Leadership.* Boston: Harvard Business School Press, 2002.

Hesselbein, Frances, and Paul M. Cohen. *Leader to Leader.* San Francisco: Jossey-Bass, 1999.

*Kouzes, James M., and Barry Z. Posner. *The Leadership Challenge.* 2nd ed. San Francisco: Jossey-Bass, 1987.

Quinn, Robert E. *Deep Change.* San Francisco: Jossey-Bass, 1996.

Spears, Larry C. *Insights on Leadership.* New York: John Wiley & Sons, 1998.

Leadership—Christian

Anderson, Leith. *Leadership That Works.* Minneapolis: Bethany, 1999.

Barna, George. *Leaders on Leadership.* Ventura, Calif.: Regal, 1997.

Finzel, Hans. *Empowered Leaders.* Nashville: Word, 1998.

Lewis, Phillip V. *Transformational Leadership.* Nashville: Broadman & Holman, 1996.

*MacMillan, Pat. *The Performance Factor.* Nashville: Broadman & Holman, 2001.

*Marshall, Tom. *Understanding Leadership.* Kent, England: Sovereign World, 1991.

Means, James E. *Leadership in Christian Ministry.* Grand Rapids: Baker, 1989.

Miller, Calvin. *The Empowered Leader: 10 Keys to Servant Leadership.* Nashville: Broadman & Holman, 1995.

Osborne, Larry W. *The Unity Factor: Getting Your Church Leaders to Work Together.* Dallas: Word, 1989.

*Sanders, J. Oswald. *Robust in Faith.* Chicago: Moody, 1965.

*Weems, Lovett H. *Church Leadership: Vision, Team, Culture, Integrity.* Nashville: Abingdon, 1993.

Leadership—Character/Internal Issues

Carter, Les, and Jim Underwood. *The Significance Principle.* Nashville: Broadman & Holman, 1998.

Cashman, Kevin. *Leadership from the Inside Out*. Provo, Utah: Executive Excellence, 1998.

Dyer, Charles. *The Power of Personal Integrity*. Wheaton, Ill.: Tyndale, 1997.

Guinness, Os. *Character Counts*. Grand Rapids: Baker, 1999.

*McIntosh, Gary L., and Samuel D. Rima Sr. *Overcoming the Dark Side of Leadership*. Grand Rapids: Baker, 1997.

*McNeal, Reggie. *A Work of Heart*. San Francisco: Jossey-Bass, 2000.

Milco, Michael R. *Ethical Dilemmas in Church Leadership*. Grand Rapids: Kregel, 1997.

The Arbinger Institute. *Leadership and Self-Deception*. San Francisco: Berrett-Koehler, 2000.

Leadership—Development

Clinton, J. Robert. *The Making of a Leader*. Colorado Springs: Navpress, 1988.

Conger, Jay A., and Beth Benjamin. *Building Leaders: How Successful Companies Develop the Next Generation*. San Francisco: Jossey-Bass, 1999.

Garvin, David A. *Learning in Action*. Boston: Harvard Business School Press, 2000.

Longenecker, Harold L. *Growing Leaders by Design*. Grand Rapids: Kregel, 1995.

Maxwell, John C. *Developing the Leader Within You*. Nashville: Nelson, 1993.

*McCauley, Cynthia D., ed. *The Center for Creative Leadership Handbook of Leadership Development*. San Francisco: Jossey-Bass, 1998.

Leadership—Organizational Issues

Morrison, E. K. *Leadership Skills: Developing Volunteers for Organizational Success*. Tuscon, Ariz.: Fisher, 1983.

*Schein, Edgar H. *Organizational Culture and Leadership*. San Francisco: Jossey-Bass, 1991.

Leadership—Pastoral

Dale, Robert D. *Pastoral Leadership*. Nashville: Abingdon, 1986.

Hull, Bill. *The Disciplemaking Pastor*. Old Tappan, N. J.: Revell, 1973.

*Lawrence, Bill. *Effective Pastoring*. Nashville: Word, 1999.

Perry, Lloyd M., and Norman Shawchuck. *Revitalizing the 20th Century Church*. Chicago: Moody, 1982.

Change

Anderson, Leith. *Dying for Change*. Minneapolis: Bethany, 1990.

*Conger, Jay A., Gretchen M. Spreitzer, and Edward E. Lawler. *The Leader's Change Handbook*. San Francisco, CA: Jossey-Bass, 1999.

Herrington, Jim, Mike Bonem, and James H. Furr. *Leading Congregational Change: A Practical Guide for the Transformational Journey.* San Francisco: Jossey-Bass, 2000.

Johnson, Spencer. *Who Moved My Cheese?* New York: G.P. Putnam's Sons, 1998.

*Kotter, John P. *Leading Change.* Boston: Harvard Business School Press, 1996.

O'Toole, James. *Leading Change.* New York: Ballantine, 1995.

Southerland, Dan. *Transitioning: Leading Your Church Through Change.* Grand Rapids: Zondervan, 1999.

Conflict Management

Gangel, Kenneth O., and Samuel Canine. *Communication and Conflict Management.* Nashville: Broadman, 1992.

*Sande, Ken. *The Peacemaker.* Grand Rapids: Baker, 1997.

Stevenin, Thomas J. *Win/Win Solutions.* Chicago: Northfield, 1997.

*Susek, Ron. *Firestorm: Preventing and Overcoming Church Conflicts.* Grand Rapids: Baker, 1999.

Mentoring/Coaching

Gangel, Kenn. *Coaching Ministry Teams.* Nashville: Word, 2000.

Hendricks, Howard G., and William D. Hendricks. *As Iron Sharpens Iron.* Chicago: Moody, 1995.

Time Management/Delegating

Cook, M. *Streetwise Time Management.* Holbrook, Mass.: Adams Media, 1999.

*Covey, Stephen R., A. Roger Merrill, and Rebecca R. Merrill. *First Things First.* New York: Simon & Schuster, 1994.

Mackenzie, R. Alec. *The Time Trap.* New York: American Management Association, 1997.

Vision

*Barna, George. *Without a Vision, the People Perish.* Glendale, Calif.: Barna Research Group, Ltd., 1991.

*———. *Turning Vision Into Action.* Ventura, Calif.: Regal, 1996.

Collins, James C., and Jerry I. Porras. *Built to Last.* New York: Harper Collins, 1997.

Malphurs, Aubrey. *Developing a Vision for Ministry in the 21st Century.* Grand Rapids: Baker, 1999.

Nanus, Burt. *Visionary Leadership.* San Francisco: Jossey-Bass, 1992.

Stanley, Andy. *Visioneering.* Sisters, Ore.: Multnomah, 1999.

* Indicates the preferred books in each section.

CHARTING A BOLD COURSE TEAM

ACQUIRING EDITOR:
Mark Tobey

COPY EDITOR:
Jim Vincent

BACK COVER COPY:
Julie-Allyson Ieron, Joy Media

COVER DESIGN:
Ragont Design

INTERIOR DESIGN:
Ragont Design

PRINTING AND BINDING:
Sheridan Books, Inc.

The typeface for the text of this book is
Berkeley

253
54581

108062